Middle English
Marian Lyrics

Middle English Texts

General Editor

Russell A. Peck
University of Rochester

Associate Editor

Alan Lupack
University of Rochester

Advisory Board

Rita Copeland
University of Texas

Thomas G. Hahn
University of Rochester

Lisa Kiser
Ohio State University

Thomas Seiler
Western Michigan University

R. A. Shoaf
University of Florida

Bonnie Wheeler
Southern Methodist University

The Middle English Texts Series is designed for classroom use. Its goal is to make available to teachers and students texts which occupy an important place in the literary and cultural canon but which have not been readily available in student editions. The series does not include those authors such as Chaucer, Langland, or Malory, whose English works are normally in print in good student editions. The focus is, instead, upon Middle English literature adjacent to those authors that teachers need in compiling the syllabuses they wish to teach. The editions maintain the linguistic integrity of the original work but within the parameters of modern reading conventions. The texts are printed in the modern alphabet and follow the practices of modern capitalization and punctuation. Manuscript abbreviations are expanded, and *u/v* and *j/i* spellings are regularized according to modern orthography. Hard words, difficult phrases, and unusual idioms are glossed on the page, either in the right margin or at the foot of the page. Textual notes appear at the end of the text, along with a glossary. The editions include short introductions on the history of the work, its merits and points of topical interest, and also include briefly annotated bibliographies.

Middle English
Marian Lyrics

Edited by
Karen Saupe

Published for TEAMS

(The Consortium for the Teaching of the Middle Ages)

in Association with the University of Rochester

by

Medieval Institute Publications

WESTERN MICHIGAN UNIVERSITY

Kalamazoo, Michigan — 1998

Library of Congress Cataloging-in-Publication Data

Middle English Marian lyrics / edited by Karen Saupe.
     p.   cm. -- (Middle English texts)
  Includes bibliographical references and index.
  ISBN 1-58044-006-1 (pbk. : alk. paper)
  1. Mary, Blessed Virgin, Saint--History of doctrines--Middle Ages,
600-1500--Poetry. 2. Mary, Blessed Virgin, Saint--Legends--Poetry.
3. Christian women saints--Palestine--Poetry. 4. Christian poetry,
English (Middle) I. Saupe, Karen. II. Series: Middle English
text (Kalamazoo, Mich.)
PR2061.M38M34 1998
821'.1080351--dc21

                                               98-40417
                                             CIP

ISBN 1-58044-006-1

Contents

Mary at the Foot of the Cross

The Assumption and Mary as Queen of Heaven

Poems in Celebration of Mary

List of Plates

Abbreviations

Archiv = Archiv für das Studium der Neueren Sprachen und Litteraturen

B13 = Carleton Brown, *English Lyrics of the Thirteenth Century*

B14 = Brown, *Religious Lyrics of the Fourteenth Century*

B15 = Brown, *Religious Lyrics of the Fifteenth Century*

BL = British Library

CA = Catena Aurea

CS = Chambers and Sidgwick, *Early English Lyrics*

CT = Canterbury Tales

DBT = A Dictionary of Biblical Tradition in English Literature

DH = Dobson and Harrison, *Medieval English Songs*

EEC = Greene, *Early English Carols,* second ed.

EETS = Early English Text Society

Index = Brown and Robbins, *The Index of Middle English Verse*

LH = Luria and Hoffman, *Middle English Lyrics*

MED = *Middle English Dictionary*

OED = *Oxford English Dictionary*

PL = *Patrologia Latina*, ed. Migne

STS = Scottish Text Society

Acknowledgments

I am grateful to the British Library for permission to reproduce *The Nativity*, Biblia Pauperum leaf b (plate A); to the Pierpont Morgan Library for permission to reproduce *The Assumption* from MS M.945, fol. 42a (plate B); to the Musée national du moyen âge — Thermes et hôtel de Cluny for permission to reproduce *Vierge Ouvrante* (plate C); and to the Houghton Mifflin Company for permission to reprint Chaucer's "ABC" from *The Riverside Chaucer*, third edition. I also wish to thank the British Library; the Bodleian Library; the Master and Fellows of Balliol College, Oxford; the President and Fellows of Corpus Christi College, Oxford; the Master and Fellows of Jesus College, Oxford; the Warden and Fellows of Merton College, Oxford; the Bursar of New College, Oxford; the Librarian of Magdalen College, Oxford; the Master and Fellows of Trinity College, Cambridge; the Master and Fellows of Gonville and Caius College, Cambridge; the Master and Fellows of St. John's College, Cambridge; the Syndics of the Cambridge University Library; the Director and University Librarian of the John Rylands University Library of Manchester, the Dean and Chapter of Worcester; the Stanbrook Abbey; the Trustees of the National Library of Scotland; the Göttingen University Library; and the Huntington Library for the use of materials in their manuscripts. I am grateful to the National Endowment for the Humanities for its generous support of the Middle English Text Series.

I owe thanks to many individuals as well. Without Russell and Ruth Peck, this book would not exist. At the University of Rochester, Alan Lupack provided assistance at every stage of this project, from acquiring research materials to editing final drafts. Melissa Bernstein assisted in checking manuscripts and preparing final copy. Mara Amster and Dana Symons gave the manuscript thorough proofreadings, and Jennifer Church produced the camera-ready copy. At Calvin College, Gary Schmidt carefully read portions of the volume and suggested revisions, and Mark Williams assisted with Latin translations. At Medieval Institute Publications, Thomas Seiler and Juleen Eichinger have provided invaluable support in the production of the Middle English Texts Series and this volume. Elsewhere, Carol Suddath read early drafts, and all my family provided encouragement and many diversions.

Middle English Marian Lyrics

Introduction

> Almighty and al merciable queene,
> To whom that al this world fleeth for socour,
> To have relees of sinne, of sorwe, and teene,
> Glorious virgine, of alle floures flour,
> To thee I flee, confounded in errour.
> Help and releeve, thou mighti debonayre,
> Have mercy on my perilous langour.
> Venquisshed me hath my cruel adversaire.[1]

So begins a late-fourteenth-century poem composed at the request of Blanche, Duchess of Lancaster, in circumstances which reflect a scene characteristic of Marian devotion at the apex of its flourishing. The influential Blanche, a woman known for her piety, seeks devotional material in the vernacular for her personal use, and perhaps also for instructional use within her great household. She makes her request of a courtier in the service of her husband, John of Gaunt. The courtier, Geoffrey Chaucer, turns to an ABC prayer in one of the most popular works of the day among French and English aristocracy, Guillaume de Deguilleville's *La pèlerinage de vie humaine*.[2] Chaucer's adaptation is an eloquent manifestation of the enthusiastic religious sensibility of its audience. The poem demonstrates the centrality of the Virgin Mary to devotional literature among the highly sophisticated Christians of the age. In many ways, their devotion to Mary is the key to their refinement; she is the model of courtesy and of faith. In condensing Guillaume's twelve-line stanzas into eight-line stanzas, Chaucer relies masterfully on the full range of Marian epithets which resonate throughout his culture's uses of Mary as muse, mediator, intercessor, comforter, instructor and gracious model for

---

[1] Chaucer, Geoffrey, "An ABC," ed. R. T. Lenaghan in Larry D. Benson, ed., *The Riverside Chaucer*, third ed. (Boston: Houghton Mifflin, 1987), pp. 637–40. See Appendix A for full text.

[2] Guillaume composed this poem in 1331 and completed a revision in 1355. John Lydgate translated the entire *La pèlerinage* into English in the fifteenth century, incorporating Chaucer's translation of the ABC poem into his own.

feeling, piety, and discipline. In the "A.B.C. called La priere de Nostre Dame"[3] (see Appendix A), the first word of each stanza fixes an image that evokes what Donald Howard calls a "centrifugal" thought pattern[4]; the meditator's focus on each image, often on Mary as the embodiment of some quality ("Almight[iness]," "Bounty," "Comfort," and so on), triggers a host of associations which focus the reader's heart on these qualities.

Chaucer uses common Marian typology here: she is the burning bush, the flower of flowers, the queen of mercy, the vicar and mistress of the world, and the governess of heaven. The legalistic imagery is noteworthy and typical: the guilty speaker, fearful of the "grete assyse / Whan we shule come bifore the hye justyse" (lines 36–37), appeals to the compassionate and generous Mary as an advocate who will surely plead on his behalf at the bar of heaven. And Mary, "largesse of pleyn felicitee" (line 13), will not refuse the penitent supplicant.

In choosing a French source, Chaucer mines a rich vein, the continental vernacular tradition. His works echo other Marian poems, some well known, some obscure. The prologue to The Prioresse Tale (see Appendix B) emphasizes Mary's virtue in lines of pure praise, evocative of the Psalms.[5] The prologue to The Second Nun's Tale likewise contains an *Invocatio ad mariam* which employs a number of epithets and images common to the English Marian lyrics (see Appendix C). Chaucer's verses reflect widespread sensibilities; the Second Nun's and the Prioress' words would have sounded familiar to medieval audiences whose devotion to Mary found expression in lyrics, hymns, carols, plays, and well-known legends.

Mary's prominence in medieval literature led G. G. Coulton to remark that "it is difficult to see how the ordinary medieval worshipper can have avoided the conclusion that, for practical purposes, Mary mattered more to him than Christ."[6] This may be an exaggeration, but the mother of Jesus was indeed a beloved and central figure in the hearts and minds of medieval Christians. As a non-judgmental figure of graciousness and kindness, she served well as an ever-available mediator and model for believers who sought to reconcile guilt and hope. The poems selected for this volume provide a sampling of the rich tradition of Marian devotion expressed in Middle English lyrics.

----

[3] The title is that given by Thomas Speght in his 1602 edition of Chaucer's *Works*, who writes that the poem was made "at the request of Blanche Duchess of Lancaster, as praier for her privat use, being a woman in her religion very devout" (fol. 347r). If Speght is accurate, the poem is one of Chaucer's earliest surviving poems, from the 1360s.

[4] *Chaucer: His Life, His Works, His World* (New York: Dutton, 1987), p. 90.

[5] In form and subject matter, The Prioress' Tale itself is typical of the miracles genre rather than the lyric tradition.

[6] *Five Centuries of Religion*, vol. 1 (Cambridge: Cambridge University Press, 1929), p. 151.

Introduction

Background: Mary and Church History

As the primary source of historical information about the mother of Jesus, the Bible provides few details. Luke offers accounts of the Annunciation (1:26–38), Mary's visit to her cousin Elizabeth (1:39–56), the birth of Jesus (2:1–7), and her conversation with the twelve-year-old Jesus upon finding him in the temple (2:41–51). Mary figures in Matthew's briefer account of the Nativity, the visit of the Magi, the flight into Egypt, and the return to Nazareth (1:18–2:23). John describes Jesus' first miracle (2:1–12), performed at his mother's request, when he changes water into wine at a wedding feast. Matthew, Mark, and Luke describe an incident in which Jesus' mother and brethren[7] come to speak with him (Matthew 12:46–50; Mark 3:31–35; Luke 8:19–21). John reports Mary's presence at Jesus' Crucifixion (19:25–27). Matthew (27:55) and Mark (15:40–41) identify Mary the mother of James and Joseph, apparently brothers or cousins of Jesus, as being present at the Crucifixion. On Easter morning, Mary the Mother of James is at the empty tomb (Mark 16:1; Luke 24:10); Matthew identifies only "the other Mary" (i.e., not Mary Magdalene) there (28:1). Finally, the Book of Acts reports that Mary was present with the disciples at Christ's ascension into heaven (1:14).

But as Christianity spread, questions about Jesus' origins led to speculation; legends and apocryphal accounts began to fill the gaps in Mary's story. It was a primarily Christological interest in Mary that prompted such writings as the second-century *Protevangelium,*[8] attributed to Jesus' brother James.[9] This book and the sixth-century *Pseudo-Matthew*, which is derived from it, describe the details of Mary's remarkable life from her conception and birth to the Annunciation and birth of Jesus and the flight into Egypt. The story of her long-childless parents, Anna and Joachim, and the miraculous conception is patterned after the Old Testament stories of Anna, mother of Samuel, and of Sarah, mother of Isaac, as well as the Gospel accounts of Elizabeth, mother of John the Baptist, and of the conception of Jesus. Accounts of Mary's death and bodily assumption into heaven began to appear in the fifth century.[10] These stories, transmitted in such works as the thirteenth-century *Golden Legend*

---

[7] Because belief in Mary's perpetual virginity was widespread among early Christians, the translation of this word (the Greek *adelphoi* may mean either "brothers" or "kinsmen") had important implications. Some commentators assumed these brothers were sons of Joseph by a previous marriage; St. Jerome believed they were simply cousins of Jesus.

[8] This title was given in the sixteenth century to a work known earlier as *The Book of James*; though the name is not medieval, I use the designation *Protevangelium* throughout this volume to avoid confusion with the Book of James in the New Testament.

[9] See Wilhelm Schneemelcher, p. 423.

[10] The late-fifth-century *Transitus Mariae* is the oldest known written example. Jaroslav Pelikan summarizes the development of legends of Mary's dormition and assumption in *Mary Through the Centuries*, ch. 15. See also note to §77, lines 50–51, below.

and the fourteenth-century *Cursor Mundi*, were well known in the Middle Ages. But although minor details from these accounts figure into the general body of Marian legends, extant Middle English lyrics — unlike the cycle plays or saints' legends — owe relatively little to these apocryphal sources. Instead, they tend to focus on her roles as maiden, mother, queen, and mediator. Theologian Wolfhart Pannenberg argues that while Christology endeavors to understand the theological significance of historical events, Mariology attempts to symbolize or personify that significance, to embody the meaning of the events (pp. 144–50). So it is, perhaps, that Marian lyrics focus on a figure who is herself less important as a historical figure than as a symbol of faith and obedience to God.

In fact, it was a typological code of symbols which shaped Mary's identity for later Christians. Various Old Testament characters and images prefigured her. In the second century, St. Irenaeus of Lyons called Mary the New Eve, following Paul's identification of Christ as the New Adam;[11] he also associated her with the woman clothed with the sun in Apocalypse (Revelation). In the fourth century, St. Ambrose made extensive use of typology to describe Mary, and such imagery was absorbed into the liturgy. Medieval poets assembled catalogues of typological readings that allow readers to meditate on the various attributes of Mary: in §88, "Marye, mayde mylde and fre," Mary is equated with Sarah, Judith, Esther, the burning bush, the sling by which David slew Goliath, and the dew on Gideon's fleece. Gregory I and subsequent commentators equated Mary with the *sponsa* of Canticles (Song of Solomon).[12] In such figurings, Mary stood for the Church (the Bride of Christ) as well. The Marian feast masses, particularly for the Assumption, emphasize this bridal imagery. Pannenberg describes Mary as "the symbol of humanity receiving the grace of God in faith in contrast to the old humanity symbolized by Eve, and thus also the symbol of the church in its relation to God" (p. 145). This equation took shape early in the development of Christian thought.

Pre-Christian myths also helped to shape the legends of Mary. As Christianity spread, the art and traditions of old and new cultures blended, and the Blessed Virgin assumed some of the mythic and iconographic roles of Isis and Ceres (mother goddesses); Minerva and Diana (virgin goddesses); and Rhea (a virgin who conceived by the god Mars). In Apuleius' second-century work *The Golden Ass*, the narrator recounts meeting a goddess who identifies herself as Minerva, Venus, Diana, Proserpine, and Isis; the goddesses are seen as interchangeable figures. Such fluid identities were easily absorbed into the figure of Mary.[13] But while some

---

[11] On the importance of this image, see Pelikan, ch. 3.

[12] See E. Ann Matter, *The Voice of My Beloved: The Song of Songs in Western Medieval Christianity* (Philadelphia: University of Pennsylvania Press, 1990), ch. 6.

[13] The influence of such associations is uncertain. Michael P. Carroll cautions that Mary's comparison with Isis is limited, as early Christians would not have associated their heavenly queen with promiscuity;

similarities to pagan goddess figures were inevitable as Marian iconography took shape, biblical typology dominated the development of imagery and Mariology.

Until the late fourth century, when Christianity was experiencing a surge of growth and expansion to become the primary religion of the Roman Empire, Marian devotion focused mainly on Mary the Virgin. But in the early fifth century, Nestorius, Patriarch of Constantinople, challenged Mary's commonly-accepted title *Theotokos* (god-bearer or mother of God),[14] prompting lively and widespread debate before the issue was settled at the Council of Ephesus in the year 431.[15] The attention drawn by this controversy led to increased devotion to Mary as Mother of God, a focus that may also, Geoffrey Ashe suggests, reflect "the Catholic world's spiritual response to the barbarians" as Christians sought comfort in their faith (p. 193). The fifth century, then, marks the beginnings of steady growth in Marian devotion.[16]

Such growth was reflected in Christian liturgical practices. Hilda Graef remarks that litanies to the saints became so unbalanced with petitions to Mary that separate litanies to her were introduced (p. 232); these litanies gave way to feast days. In the seventh century, Rome recognized four Marian feasts: the Purification, Annunciation, the Assumption, and the Nativity of Mary. After some early inconsistencies in practice, the English church adopted these feasts by the late eighth century (Clayton, pp. 30–38). By the end of the Anglo-Saxon era, England was full of Marian shrines, chapels, and relics (many of which were later destroyed during the Reformation). The number of Marian feasts and masses had increased substantially, and Mary Clayton argues that Anglo-Saxon Marian devotion was sufficiently strong to provide inspiration for the rest of Europe.

The twelfth century saw the beginnings of a trend toward emphasis on the human, emotional aspects of faith, and Mary provided both a focus and a model for affective devotion. Through his widely circulated prayers and such works as the *Cur Deus Homo*, St. Anselm of Canterbury advanced the belief that redemption depended upon Christ's humanity. Among the twelfth-century Cistercians, Mary's most influential champion was St. Bernard of Clairvaux. Rejecting the controversial doctrine of the Immaculate Conception (that is, the idea that Mary was herself

---

he cites Lewis Farnell in arguing, moreover, that Mary was the first to be imagined as a virgin mother. See Carroll, pp. 8–10.

[14] Nestorius objected to the term because to him it implied that Mary had engendered her own Eternal Creator, that God had originated in Mary's womb. He preferred *Anthropotokos*, mother of man, or *Christotokos*, mother of Christ. But *Theotokos* was already in widespread use, and since those opposed to Nestorius interpreted his objections as a denial of Jesus' godhead, Nestorius was labeled a heretic and Mary's designation as *Theotokos* was officially adopted as dogma at Ephesus.

[15] For details, see Pelikan, ch. 4, and Hilda Graef, pp. 101 ff.

[16] Mary Clayton provides a useful overview of pre-Anglo-Saxon devotion to Mary in *The Cult of the Virgin Mary in Anglo-Saxon England*, pp. 1–24.

free of original sin), he argued that what made her union with God significant was not her extraordinary virtue, but her simple humanity. This idea, of course, made it possible to regard Mary with empathy as well as awe, and such empathy inspired renewed devotion. Bernard's influence was widely felt, and his Marian meditations provided the models for many later works.

By the early Middle Ages, the Church had prescribed that Saturdays and several feast days be devoted to Mary. The Lateran Council of 1215 made the *Ave Maria* compulsory learning for every layman. Among the oldest English Marian lyrics are rhymed translations of that prayer which appear alongside the Pater Noster (the Lord's Prayer) and the Creed as basic learning materials. But as this volume attests, the *Ave Maria* was soon augmented with hundreds of other verses devoted to Mary. Throughout the Middle Ages, English pilgrims visited Marian shrines and Lady chapels at Winchester, Ely, Walsingham, and elsewhere. Artistic depictions of religious scenes were everywhere during the Middle Ages: in paintings, statues, windows, rood-screens, and books — illuminated manuscripts for the literate and block books like the *Biblia Pauperum* (see Plate A) for those who preferred or depended upon pictures. Mary was a key figure in such art; again, Pannenberg's characterization of Mariology as the attempt to embody the theological significance of historical events suggests that Mary is primarily important *as* a symbol. The visual iconography (owing much to Jacobus de Voragine and his scriptural and apocryphal sources) carried over into the literature, where a shorthand symbolism of images often conveys a host of associations. The figure of Mary signified many things to many people; her position in the culture was complex, which helps to explain the wealth of art created in her honor. But three roles dominate devotional and artistic depictions of Mary: she is recognized primarily as Maiden, Mother, and Queen.

To focus on Mary as *Maiden* is to celebrate her purity, her beauty (internal and external), her pristine worthiness to participate in God's redemptive plan. Mary was identified as Virgin through Matthew's account of the Nativity of Jesus (1:23). In order to explain the significance of the birth, Matthew invokes Isaiah's prophecy: "Behold a virgin shall conceive, and bear a son, and his name shall be called Emmanuel" (Isaias 7:14). Since Matthew's source was the Septuagint rather than its Hebrew source, he used the Greek translation of the Hebrew *'almah* (young woman), which was *parthenos* (virgin).[17] Luke also identifies Mary as a virgin (*parthenon*, 1:27). The point was no doubt initially made in order to emphasize her son's divinity. But it had further implications for Mary herself; it was perhaps a recognition of the virgin birth as a symbol of her union with the Holy Spirit that led later Christians to ponder the possibility of her perpetual virginity. In the apocryphal *Protevangelium*, the midwife who

---

[17] The Revised Standard Version translates "young woman" from the Hebrew, rather than "virgin" from the Vulgate. But Pohle argues that the Hebrew *'almah* does, in fact, connote "virgin" elsewhere, specifically in Genesis 24:43, Exodus 2:8, and Psalm 67:27 (RSV 68:25) (pp. 84 ff.). For further discussion of the issue, see Marina Warner, pp. 19–21.

delivers Jesus announces that Mary is a virgin; when the doubting midwife Salome checks, her hand withers (20:1 ff.). In the later *Pseudo-Matthew*, the midwife Zelomi declares, "as there is no defilement of blood on the child, there is no pain in the mother. A virgin hath conceived, a virgin hath borne, and a virgin she hath continued."[18] Mary's perpetual virginity was proclaimed dogma at the Second Council of Constantinople in 381.[19] Church Fathers Ambrose of Milan (d. 397), Jerome (d. 420), and Augustine (d. 430) wrote extensively on Mary's virginity, setting forth the definitive arguments that came to inform medieval theology.[20]

The lyrics which celebrate Mary's virginity emphasize her beauty and goodness, often comparing her to a lily, a burning bush, the enclosed garden, or a spotless mirror. They often focus on the wonder she must have felt, and so there is a combination of veneration and empathy in the songs that celebrate the Annunciation. The Virgin Mary is not simply the paragon of human goodness; she is the embodiment of the union of God and humankind.

Ambrose identified six virtues in Mary: "The secret of modesty, the banner of faith, the secret of devotion, the Virgin within the house, the companion for the ministry [of Christ], the Mother at the temple."[21] Jaroslav Pelikan observes that the second triad of virtues allows Ambrose to go beyond Jerome's emphasis on virginity to focus on the complex image of Mary as *Mother* (p. 120).

In the earliest biblical reference to Mary, Mark identifies Jesus as the son of Mary (6:3). Matthew twice names her as Jesus' mother (1:16 and 13:55). That Mary was the mother of Jesus was never questioned. That she was *theotokos*, mother of God, was a debated point which drew particular attention in the fifth century (see above). Once so designated, she was sometimes figured as well as "chamber of the Trinity" (as in §88, line 2, or in Plate C), the earthly dwelling place of Father, Son, and Holy Spirit.[22]

---

[18] *Pseudo-Matthew*, ch. 13, in B. Harris Cowper, pp. 51–52.

[19] Joseph Pohle outlines the doctrine and theology of this dogma in *Mariology*, pp. 83–104. See also Pelikan, ch. 8.

[20] Graef describes each figure's contribution to Mariology in *Mary: A History of Doctrine and Devotion*, vol. 1, pp. 77–100.

[21] *Concerning Virgins* 2.2.15, qtd. in Pelikan, p. 120.

[22] According to Father Johann G. Roten of the Marian Library and International Marian Research Institute at the University of Dayton, the epithet appears to have originated with Pseudo-Isidore of Seville (*Liber de ortu et obitu patrum*, PL 83, col. 1285) and came to be associated with "Shrine Madonnas" erected during the late Middle Ages in Europe. Such statues could be opened to display additional religious scenes; the Trinity image was called "the throne of God" or *le chez de dieu*. He writes: "The motif disappeared after the Council of Trent [1546–63], probably to avoid controversy over mixing a marian and a trinitarian motif" (private correspondence, 16 February 1996).

She was also a human mother, and the natural affections between mother and child, Ashe argues, were the roots of Marian devotion. Yet she was not simply the prototypical maternal goddess through which motherhood is venerated. As mother of God, she was the human mother through which God *was* human, through whom Christ received his "coat" of flesh (see §60, line 18: "My robe he haveth opon"),[23] to be treasured as the means through which Christ understands humanity. And thus she is the one through whom everyone who has known a mother/child relationship might come to understand the events of Christ's life.

In the humble circumstances of the Nativity — the poor travelers forced to seek shelter in a cave or barn — the emphasis in medieval artistic depictions of the Nativity is nevertheless celebratory; the event is commemorated as the birth of the savior, and his mother is portrayed as joyful. Only a very few lyrics deviate from this tone. The notion of her painless childbirth (see note to §15, line 3) is frequently alluded to in the lyrics. But Mary came to know the pain of motherhood at the Crucifixion, and so she participates fully in the human maternal experience. Lyrics which focus on Mary's motherhood often juxtapose the Nativity and the Crucifixion to reflect the full range of the maternal experience, both joy and pain.

Mary's designation as *Queen of Heaven* depends primarily on belief in Christ's resurrection and ascension, through which he claims the throne of heaven. In Luke's account of the Annunciation, Gabriel promises that Mary will give birth to one who is to be "king over the house of Jacob forever" (Luke 1:32). As mother of the king, then, Mary is elevated to royal status. Metaphorically, moreover, Mary reigns in the sense of being preeminent in Christian virtue. Medieval theologians argue that as a perfect follower of Christ, Mary has won the "crown of righteousness" (2 Timothy 4:8), the "crown of life" (James 1:12, Apocalypse 12:10) and the "crown of glory" (1 Peter 5:4). Typological readings of Psalm 44:10, 3 Kings 2:19, and Esther 2:17 and 5:3 reinforce the image of Mary as queen as well. Thus, though Mary's queenship was not proclaimed doctrine until 1954,[24] images of Mary wearing a crown begin to appear in Christian art as early as the sixth century. In the seventh century the writings of St. Martin and St. Agatho refer to Mary as queen; in the next century liturgies employ the title, and Gregory II calls her "ruler of all Christians" (Schmidt, pp. 502–03). Clayton argues that in Anglo-Saxon England, the regal imagery coincides with societal rise of queenship and "enhances the position" of Anglo-Saxon queens (p. 165). It is a particularly important image in the feudal Middle Ages; Marina Warner writes that "the image of the Virgin as queen is

---

[23] See, for example Anselm, *Oratio 52 ad S. Virginem Mariam* (PL 158, col. 957).

[24] Firmin M. Schmidt outlines the Church's position on Mary's queenship in "The Universal Queenship of Mary" (*Mariology*, ed. Juniper B. Carol, vol. 2, 493–549). The body of that essay predates the 1954 *Ad caeli reginam*, a papal proclamation establishing the feast of Our Blessed Lady as Queen, but an appendix describing that encyclical completes the chapter.

scored so deep in western imagination that many Catholics still think of her as a medieval monarch" (p. 115).[25] Certainly the image receives unparalleled attention in the Middle Ages.

Mary and Medieval Christians

Popular medieval religious beliefs were often understood through secular analogies. Individuals sought sympathetic mediators to defend them to judges. To the medieval Christian, Christ was both human and divine; he was Mediator, but also Judge, and therefore to be feared. As virtuous virgin, queen of heaven, and loving human mother, Mary was perceived as a powerful and accessible intercessor.

In the *Fasciculus morum*, a typical fourteenth-century preaching handbook, the sinner is counseled to appeal to Christ through his mother: "We can be assured of [Christ's] grace and forgiveness if we will go confidently to [Mary] while he is with her." One who is afraid to pray to Christ is compared to one who has angered his king; he "goes secretly to the queen and sends her some gift so that she may pray and intercede with the king her lord for him." So the sinner should

> go to the Mother of Mercy, the Queen of Heaven and Earth, and send her as a gift something special, such as waking, fasting, prayer, or almsgiving. At this she will certainly, like a loving mother, hasten to come between you and Christ your father who wants to chastise you for your failing, and she will stretch her mantle between you and his rod. And he will surely relinquish all punishment or at least soften it to a large extent, so that we will go free without grief.[26]

This is a rather pragmatic description of the relationship between Mary and the sinner. Though St. Bernard of Clairvaux was also aware of her function as mediatrix, his words give a fuller description of the relationship evident in Marian lyrics:

> Let us therefore venerate Mary in the very marrow of our hearts, with all the feelings in our breasts, and with all our devotion; for this is the will of Him who has ordained that we should have all through Mary. . . . In all things and in all ways she provides for us in our wretchedness: she soothes our agitation, she stirs our faith, she strengthens our hope, she

---

[25] Warner has argued that this distorts the ideals of the Sermon on the Mount. But the vision of Mary as queen symbolizes a realization of the heavenly reward promised to the faithful. To exalt the one most faithful in service is, in fact, to fulfill Jesus' words in the beatitudes (Matthew 5:3–12).

[26] *Fasciculus morum: A Fourteenth-Century Preacher's Handbook*, ed. and trans. Siegfried Wenzel, p. 73.

dispels our mistrust, and gives strength to us in our faint-heartedness. . . . The Son hears the prayer of His mother, and the Father hears the prayer of His son. My little children, this is the sinners' ladder, this is the firm ground of my confidence, this is the whole reason of my hope.[27]

For Bernard, Mary provides comfort and inspiration; she serves as a model for his own devotional life.

Three centuries later, Margery Kempe shows a similar — if more intense — emotional orientation. When she falls into despair, near the beginning of *The Book of Margery Kempe*, Jesus appears in her mind and says, "Dowtyr, thynke on my modyr, for sche is cause of alle the grace that thou hast."[28] Margery immediately begins to meditate upon the life of Mary, first through a vision of St. Anne, then of Mary's birth, her childhood until she is twelve, her dress, the Annunciation, the visitation, the Nativity, and the flight into Egypt. To all these glimpses Dame Margery responds from the perspective of the Passion, weepingly. Subsequently, Mary appears again and again to Margery as her comforter and intercessor. Her understanding of Mary, clarified through meditation, has little to do with politics, far more to do with affective concerns and personal relationships. For her, identification with the physical, sensory details of Mary's life enriches her appreciation of Christ's life and God's love. Her meditative methods illustrate a key principle in medieval religious art: meditation, a right heart, is inspired by sensory stimuli. The visual or verbal image provides a catalyst for inward contemplation. For Margery, Mary mediates by providing her with the very language of meditation.

Mary in the Middle English Lyrics

Mary's prominence in the medieval mind is evident from her prominence in Middle English literature. When the first collections of miracle stories (the *Golden Legend* and the *South English Legendary*, for example) were compiled in England in the twelfth century, Mary figured in numerous legends. She is a central figure in the mystery cycles, particularly the N-Town plays. The Pearl poet was particularly fond of Mary: in *Cleanness* (lines 1069 ff.), Mary is presented as an example of purity; in *Pearl* the title character is herself a lesser Mary; Sir Gawain too is devoted to Mary and stops to observe her feast before discovering Bercilak's castle. Countless romances and secular poems begin or end with invocations to Mary. And of

---

[27] *Nativitate B. V. Mariae*, PL 183, col. 441; trans. Rosemary Woolf in *The English Religious Lyric in the Middle Ages*, p. 118.

[28] *The Book of Margery Kempe*, ed. Lynn Staley (Kalamazoo: Medieval Institute Publications, 1996), p. 32.

course she is the subject of hundreds of medieval poems, songs, carols, and prayers which survive today.[29]

The characteristics of these religious lyrics range widely in form, tone, and aesthetic quality. Some of the poems survive in commonplace books, on flyleaves, or as incidental pieces in longer works. Many appear in liturgical manuscripts, hymnals, and sermon notebooks. Others are preserved in private devotional materials — "closet hymnals," books of hours, and fifteenth-century presentation books. Still more occur in portable collections.[30] Most of the poems printed in this anthology survive in single manuscripts, but a few appear in dozens of sources. In some cases, as with Lydgate's use of Chaucer's ABC, early poems are revised and adapted to reflect new purposes. The thirteenth-century Nativity poem "Nu this fules" (§16) is transformed into a fifteenth-century courtly allegory of the Annunciation (§13). Taken together, these diverse expressions of Marian devotion reflect the intertwined development of poetic techniques and devotional practices.

The Franciscans played a significant role in the making of early lyrics of and to Mary. St. Francis had called his disciples *joculatores Dei* or "God's minstrels." Rossell Hope Robbins and David L. Jeffrey believe that they were the principal authors of religious lyrics until the Black Death, Robbins suggests, broke their spirit. Their contributions are among the earliest; in fact, Jeffrey points out that "what appeared to be the seven earliest religious carols were from Franciscan manuscripts of preaching materials" (p. 7). Though others give more credit to the influence of the Dominicans[31] (Robbins attributes only forty percent of the early lyrics to the Franciscans [p. 44]), Jeffrey goes so far as to claim that before 1350 "the existence of the popular short-verse genre in England" is a "particular phenomenon of Franciscan spirituality" (p. 261).

The Franciscan order, which first reached England in the thirteenth century, was committed to evangelism and the revitalization of Christianity. Franciscan preachers relied on appeals to the heart as well as the intellect, and the religious lyric — hymn, prayer, or sermon tag — was a particularly effective tool for reaching the sensibilities of popular audiences. The Franciscans

---

[29] It is impossible to know what has been lost, but Carleton Brown theorized that because good religious poetry was preserved and circulated for its inspirational and instructive value, we still have most of the best (and therefore most frequently anthologized) poetry produced during the Middle Ages (B13, p. 132). Rossell Hope Robbins felt this was an exaggeration, but argued that we have at least a representative sampling of the lyrics composed during that century (*On the Mediaeval English Religious Lyric*, p. 44).

[30] Robbins prefers this term for such pocket-sized collections of such verses as MS Sloane 2593 or Eng. Poet 3.1; sometimes called minstrel books, the origins and uses of these books are uncertain. See Andrew Taylor, "The Myth of the Minstrel Manuscript," *Speculum* 66 (1991), 43–73.

[31] The Dominicans were known for their devotion to Mary; they celebrated the Little Office of the Virgin Mary each day and are credited with introducing the Rosary prayer. So it is likely that they also composed poetry about Mary.

focused on awakening the individual believer rather than promoting the institution or the fine points of doctrine. They emphasized meditation on the human, physical details of the Nativity and the Crucifixion, and they stressed emotional rather than logical engagement. Mary, through whom "the Word became flesh," was a natural and favorite point of focus for such devotion, for she provided human access to the divine.

The Franciscans wrote for two kinds of audiences: the educated religious and the illiterate lay folk. Some lyrics were used for private devotion among members of the order. Franciscans and others also prepared materials for lay catechism and inspiration. Among the earliest lyrics are verse translations of the basic teachings of the Church, including the *Ave Maria*. Preaching tags, often short verses, appeared in preaching handbooks like the *Fasciculus morum* or John Grimestone's commonplace book and were used as illustrations to reinforce sermon themes.[32] These verses might be translations, parodies, adaptations of hymn lyrics, or original verses. Carols and vernacular hymns offered further opportunities for instruction or meditation and for celebration. The lyrics incorporated themes and materials from various sources — the Bible, patristic writings, and the liturgy — as well as earlier songs, prayers, poetry, and meditations.

Until the fifteenth century, medieval vernacular religious lyrics were composed primarily for functional, not aesthetic, purposes. In general, the intent of the lyrics is usually either homiletic or reflective (Jeffrey, p. 260); the purposes are related and often overlap. In both cases, the poetry tends to be unselfconscious and honest, and the lines are simple and straightforward. Jeffrey characterizes the verse as

> more often physical than metaphysical, immediate than reflective, roughly simple than elaborately careful. It is usually characterized by emotion rather than thought, by force of style rather than by elaboration of argument, and by a dramatic movement toward radical identification of the "subject" with the object of the poem. (p. 2)

Of the authors (usually anonymous), Douglas Gray comments: "They are not primarily concerned with the construction of an enduring object for other people to admire, but rather for other people to *use*" (*Themes*, p. 60). Art is intended as a means rather than an end. The value of the reflective lyric is that it "directs the reader's mind to the *memoria* of an event in the divine scheme, to the understanding of it, and urges his will to action" (Gray, *Themes*, p. 60).

Contrition, the first act of penance, is essentially a change of heart, a spiritual sorrow growing out of love for God and hatred for one's sin. The Franciscans strove to effect this change of heart through the experience of emotional identification with the speaker in a lyric.

---

[32] Wenzel discusses the use of such verses in *Preachers, Poets, and the Early English Lyric*; see especially pp. 80–81.

Thus the poet often begins by locating the speaker (and the reader) in a familiar setting, perhaps with some reference to the weather, the season ("Nou skrinketh rose ant lylie flour"), or the time of day ("Als I lay upon a nith"). Such a setting could evoke a predictable mood from which the speaker might turn to contemplation of spiritual concerns. Because affective devotion depends upon the ability to "understand" or internalize religious beliefs through association with personal experience and emotion, Mary is a favorite and familiar focus. By meditating on Mary's experience at her son's birth or death, the reader finds human access to divine events, moving from the concrete reality of the immediate world toward the abstract and transcendent significance of events. Though it is less true of fifteenth-century lyrics, the earlier Marian lyrics tend to celebrate her earthly experiences and concerns, those with which the believer could most easily empathize.

Yet while the lyrics of the period speak convincingly to the individual, they maintain a universal quality:

> The medieval poet speaks not only for himself, but in the name of the many; if he uses the poetic "I" it will be in a way which may be shared by his readers. It is a poetic stance which cannot be accurately described either as "personal" or as "impersonal." (Gray, *Themes*, p. 60)

Perhaps this is due to the fact that writers were not, as Rosemary Woolf puts it, concerned with their own particular moods, but "only with what kind of response their subject should properly arouse in Everyman" (p. 6). Contrition was held to be essential to conversion and penance (reunion with God), and many theologians held that a contrite sinner was justified even without the full sacrament of penance (i.e., confession and satisfaction). Thus the authors had a definite focus in mind for the audience's meditation: "they concern themselves more with eliciting emotional response [to produce an appropriate spiritual response of contrition] than with describing or analyzing emotional experience on the assumption that the experience is valuable in and of itself" (Woolf, p. viii).

Mary, for her humanity, her virtue, and her unique role as point of connection of human and divine, was a natural focus for meditation and petition. In English literature of the thirteenth century, Woolf observes, "there are no poems which consist solely of praise, nor are there any which, like many French poems to the Virgin, reserve the prayer until the last stanza" (p. 124). Mary is valued primarily as intercessor, and even poems like §8, "Edi beo thu, hevene quene," are essentially petitions for mercy. But in the fourteenth-century mood of affective piety, lyrics like *Ave maris stella* (§58) appear which place more focus on the contemplation of Mary's life and the praising of her virtues. Mary is valued as a model for Christian living.

The earliest English Marian lyrics are often simple translations from Latin — basic Christian teachings or hymns. Woolf seeks to establish Latin and French roots for the English religious lyric tradition, though others place less emphasis on such influences. G. L. Brook explains that sometimes "religious lyrics were written to amplify single lines from the liturgy, and the Latin line which suggested the lyric was often incorporated into the poem either as a refrain or as an integral part of each stanza" (p. 15). He suggests that Latin hymns may have served as models for stanza form — yet secular lyrics, he adds, offer similar models. He notes instances where the phraseology of a religious lyric closely imitates that of a secular one and probably used the same tune (p. 16). In discussing the English carol's ties to Latin poetry, Richard Leighton Greene comments that "behind them [both] is the song of the unlettered people"; he finds the ultimate roots of the English carol in popular dance-song (*EEC*, p. cxvii). And Jeffrey explicitly disagrees with Woolf on the importance of Latin sources. Because affective devotion emphasizes and affirms the human, it is essentially popular and therefore, Jeffrey argues, most readily expressed in the vernacular. Greene discusses the influence of Latin hymns in macaronic carols, but notes that even when an English lyric borrows several lines from the same Latin piece,

> This is not necessarily a sign that the carol is in any sense a partial translation or even an imitation of that hymn, although often it celebrates the same occasion. It may merely indicate that the lines of the particular hymn were fresher or firmer in the memory of the carol-writer than were others. (*EEC*, p. lxxxviii)

Jeffrey finds the native connections to secular poetry far more significant than Latin influences, arguing that to write in English at all during the Anglo-Norman period had strong implications (p. 1). Ultimately, both sources — the English secular tradition and the Latin — are evident as important influences: direct translations and macaronic lyrics are intermingled with echoes of popular ballads and folk songs.

Though the authors borrowed freely from a variety of literary traditions (the *chanson d'aventure*, complaint, debate, hymn, carol, or the *ballade*), the language and style of popular, rather than courtly, literature seemed most appropriate for their intentions in pre-fifteenth century lyrics. Woolf notes that the relative absence of "technical or imaginative flourish" prevents disruption of the reader's meditation (p. 8). Gray also comments:

> Simplicity and unaffectedness are the characteristic features of the style. Paradox and word-play are not avoided, and verbal decoration is by no means totally absent. . . . The majority, however, either avoid self-conscious or complex figurative expressions altogether, or are content with traditional metaphors and images. (*Selection*, p. ix)

To describe the relative plainness of the early lyrics is not, however, to imply either a general lack of skill or a lack of concern with aesthetics. Artistic awareness was well-developed among some authors and audiences. St. Thomas Aquinas defended the use of poetic technique by preachers (Wenzel, p. 65); many medieval artists were well aware that, as St. Bonaventure had realized, art might provide the "mystical possibility of comprehending the harmony of Creation" (Jeffrey, p. 99). Through art one might realize the *Imago Dei*, and, in the subject of

Mary, one might best recognize and celebrate the perfection of human potential to reflect God's image. Thus even the most pragmatic composer of Marian verse would make use of some art. The function of imagery evolved from the simple, usually visual uses during the early period — Gray mentions how frequently the reader is invited to "look" or "see" (*Themes*, p. 41) — into more artistically self-conscious, even aureate, approaches in the fifteenth century. Since the medieval poet associated imagery with the intellect, with the imagination, its primary use in devotional poetry was to stimulate the reader to imagine himself part of the scene so that he might experience personally the appropriate emotions. Unusual visual images might engage attention and aid the memory. The imagery of the early lyric is often characterized as "vivid." Brook adds "homely" and "picturesque," noting the freedom and "lively imagination" apparent in the coining of new words (p. 21).

The fifteenth century would bring more aesthetic sophistication, "some new awareness of the potentialities of imagery" (Woolf, p. 13). Yet the earlier lyrics seem to benefit from the absence of what would appear in the late Middle Ages. Brook writes:

> Their excellence is largely due to the fitness of Middle English to be a lyrical language. It is more sonorous than modern English, which is clogged with unstressed words and with long words of Latin origin, valuable for the expression of abstract ideas but of little use to a lyric poet. The Middle English vocabulary is rich in words for the common things of life, and most of these words are short and expressive. (p. 21)

Brook also comments that much of the strength of these lyrics comes from the vitality of a vocabulary free of predictable associations.

However secondary aesthetic considerations may have been, some of the lyrics achieve remarkable poetic effectiveness. Gray characterizes them as maintaining an admirable balance of tone:

> Many of the English lyrics have the intimate tenderness and pathos which are characteristic of the best works produced by this [affective] tradition. A tough realism, a sense of man's inadequacy, a precise and delicate use of language save them from the emotionalism and cloying sweetness into which affective devotion may degenerate. The best of them avoid the dangers, on the one hand of an arid formalism, and on the other of an unrestrained popular enthusiasm, to achieve a remarkable dignity, moderation, and clarity. (*Selection*, p. xi)

In her examination of the lyrics which focus on Mary, Woolf makes similar observations, characterizing the tone as a "direct and dignified intimacy" suggested by the balance of formal descriptions "which make the Virgin noble and remote" and the "simple pleas in English, which suggest a direct and dignified intimacy" (p. 127). Siegfried Wenzel compares the early lyrics with their Latin counterparts and finds that "much of the intellectual vigor and verbal sophistication of medieval Latin sequences and hymns" are lost but are "compensated by gains in simplicity and the creation of a more intimate tone with the help of an everyday vocabulary and the dialogue form" (pp. 59–60).

The preservation of a medieval religious lyric is, of course, no guarantee of poetic merit. What we have represents a wide range of literary abilities. Gray reminds us that

> The devotional lyric was one of the many expressions of medieval religious experience. It . . . was an integral part of the religious life of contemporary society. This can give an immediacy and an emotional urgency which is not found in some forms of medieval literature, but it also means that it was sometimes fatally easy to write verses which were ephemeral, with devotional or didactic material not transformed into poetry. (*Themes*, p. 37)

As interest in religious poetry (good and bad) grew beyond the early influence of the Franciscans, the religious "professionals" continued to use devotional lyrics for private meditation, but now pious educated laypeople might also learn hymns for devotional use with the mass. Gray writes, "It is important to remember the extent and the variety of the audience of late medieval devotional literature — it was in fact virtually the whole of contemporary literate society, from the high nobility to the humblest who could read (and even those who could be read to)" (*Themes*, p. 33). Such diversity in audience led, of course, to greater diversity in styles, forms, and attitudes toward subject matter.

Some fifteenth-century writers took a path away from the simplicity of the earlier lyric. Woolf comments on this shift:

> There can, perhaps, never have been a poetry which was more exclusively written in the language of the common people — at least until the fifteenth century, when the religious lyric was caught by the fashion for aureate diction. At that period a different criterion of stylistic propriety was used, and the style sought for became one sufficiently dignified to suggest the magnitude of the subject. (p. 8)

Though the aureate style and its "artifices of diction and metre" (Woolf, p. 274) appealed to the noble, educated audiences of the fifteenth century, some modern readers express a real distaste for the trend. Those who, like Woolf, praise the "unstudied freshness" of earlier works tend to dislike the results of increased artistic consciousness. Carleton Brown comments that while hymns and songs grow in volume, they "show a certain loss of fervour and tend to become formal exercises" (B15, p. xx). Though the style associated with the fifteenth-century Lydgate group must be at least partially an attempt to give new life to an old tradition, Woolf finds in it an "artificiality and straining for effect that may be called stylistic insincerity" (p. 8) and remarks that some of the poems convey "an impression of aridity" (p. 239). Only Audelay, she believes, "encouraged by the theme [of the five joys], is able to break through ornateness and formality to the affective meditation of the earlier poetry" (p. 297).

There does seem to be a general shift in orientation, well-illustrated by the poems on the

Joys of the Virgin. Writers like Chaucer and Lydgate engender a linguistic self-consciousness in vernacular writers, an unprecedented awareness of stylistic possibilities. As Brown notes:

> Whereas in the fourteenth century these, with their recital of the Annunciation, Nativity, and Resurrection, concerned themselves with the terrestrial joys, the scene in almost all the fifteenth-century pieces is transferred to heaven, and the praises of the Virgin are sung by cherubim and celestial choirs. One misses the touch of human reality also in the Songs of the Assumption and the Coronation of the Virgin, in which the sense of artificiality is increased by the pomposity of the aureate style. (B15, p. xx)

While the scene moves from an earthly, familiar setting to heaven, stylistic and tonal concerns seem to shift in focus from the reader to the subject matter itself — and sometimes to the author's artistic abilities. Both ways, the later lyrics often seem less geared to the reader's experience and emotional engagement.

But it is unfair to judge fifteenth-century poetry in terms of thirteenth- or fourteenth-century expectations. "Affective meditation" was perhaps no longer the purpose of much religious poetry; in the case of Mary, appeals to her humanity gave way to celebrations of her glory as Queen of Heaven. The religious art lyric, best represented by John Lydgate's work, is generally, in Derek Pearsall's words, "expository and celebratory; there is comparatively little penitential or devotional writing."[33] Pearsall describes the aureate style as "florid Latinate diction, with the Latin barely digested into English" (*Lydgate*, p. 262); it is frequently employed in poems about Mary, especially in poems of the five (or seven, or fifteen) joys because such lyrics "rely for their structure on the accumulation of recondite allusions and images" (p. 262). The intended effect is, unlike that of the typical fourteenth-century lyric, more one of intellectual than emotional engagement.[34] Pearsall says of Lydgate's Mary poems:

---

[33] *John Lydgate* (Charlottesville: University of Virginia Press, 1970), p. 256.

[34] By contrast, some have noted in the fifteenth-century lyric an increase in dramatic lyrics such as the Marian laments and those modeled after courtly love poems. Brown mentions that "the fifteenth century was marked by a rapid growth of interest in the religious drama" (B15, p. xxi), apparently reflected in the lyrics. Again, Woolf dislikes the trends. In some cases, she writes, "the effect suggests that the author felt that unless every emotion was heightened to the point of hysteria, and every gesture or action made melodramatically compelling, the reader might remain unmoved" (p. 8). Yet the dramatic influence was not all bad, Woolf feels: she speculates that the fifteenth-century growth of lyrics on the Nativity "was stimulated by the mystery plays, in which the Nativity became detached from its liturgical season, and in which the relevant human sentiments were thoroughly explored" (p. 148). Of course, the majority of Nativity lyrics of the period are carols, products of a different path from that taken by Lydgate and his followers.

> They are totally lacking in the tenderness, intimacy, fervour, and pseudo-eroticism of the Bernardine and Franciscan traditions, and concentrate on the celebration of the mystery and splendour of the Virgin. The heaping-up of invocation, epithet, image, and allusion is meant to overwhelm with excess, hardly to be comprehended. The aim is not to stir to devotion, but to make an act of worship out of the elaboration of the artefact. The extraordinary vocabulary, the strained imagery, the alliteration, and the hypnotic repetition of invocatory sentence-patterns have much the same effect of assault on the sensibilities as the flamboyant decoration of late Gothic. (p. 268)

The imagery of Lydgate's poetry, he continues, "means more than it says, and means it in a special way — not in terms of a sensuous association which is apparent to all, but in terms of intellectual and conceptual associations which have to be learnt" (p. 271). Such an orientation must have appealed to an audience of educated nobility by encouraging a very different kind of meditative process than that suggested by older lyrics. But the Franciscans' affective influence did continue during the fifteenth century, most notably in the carol.

Richard Leighton Greene claims the carol form originated in a well-known ring-dance tradition.[35] The carol — sung and danced — was performed at feasts and celebrations (hence its association today with Christmas). By the fifteenth century, the word was associated simply with the song form consisting of a burden before the first stanza, repeated after each stanza. Greene calls the genre "popular, that is, one degree removed from traditional folk-song, and yet lower in the scale of education and refinement than the courtly lyric or scholarly Latin poem" (*EEC*, p. cxxxiii). The Franciscans were "probably the most active group of carol-writers and carol-singers, the 'professional class' whose interest and activity propagated and preserved the texts of the carols" (Greene, *EEC,* p. clvii). James Ryman alone contributed 163 carols to a single manuscript.

Again, Mary is a popular focus: the subject is most often either the Nativity or the five joys. Macaronic lyrics are common, appearing more in carols (where the repetitive stanza form encourages the alternation of elegant or solemn foreign phrases with their translations) than in any other English form (Gray, *Themes*, p. xxxi). Woolf cautions, "It is difficult to judge the carols as literature, for the discrepancy between style and content appears a radical defect when they are read, but largely disappears when they are sung" (p. 294). The familiarity of the form, like the cliché phrases and familiar images, must have allowed even the most derivative carol to evoke worshipful responses.

The purpose of this volume is to present the full range of medieval culture's effort to voice itself — its joys and its anxieties — through Mary. The English lyricists wrote of Mary in

---

[35] *EEC*, p. xlvii. Most scholars share this view; however, Robbins argued that the form originated with Latin processional hymns.

devotion and celebration; they addressed her in prayer and in praise; they allowed her to speak in lullabies and dialogues with Jesus at the cross; they envisioned Mary in a stable or on a heavenly throne. In the medieval lyrics of Mary we hear many voices, the scholarly and the popular, the solemn and the jubilant. We respond to a range of emotions: admiration, wonder, joy, sorrow, fear, compassion, penitence, reverence, and gratitude. In the Marian canon we find most of the styles and forms of medieval religious lyric and many traces of the secular tradition.

The tradition represented by the lyrics suggests that what was most important about Mary was her unique identity as the point of connection between the divine and the human, the intersection of spirit and flesh. Through her Christians might learn to comprehend the mysteries of God become human. Through her they might experience the emotional magnitude of Christ's life, death, and resurrection. In her they might find the ultimate model of faithfulness and hope, along with a precious means of seeing their way feelingly to sanctity.

The early poems in this volume are arranged according to the events of Mary's life; they are followed by poems which address Mary in prayer and praise. There is, however, a great deal of overlap in the subjects treated in individual poems. What follows is a general introduction to each section.

The Annunciation

> Hail Mary, full of grace,
> The Lord is with thee.
> Blessed art thou among women,
> And blessed is the fruit of thy womb.[36]

Louis Althusser has described the phenomenon of interpellation, or "hailing," as the means by which ideology "recruits" or "transforms" the individual into a subject.[37] Certainly the Annunciation is an epitome of this gesture. In Luke 1:26–38, the angel Gabriel greets Mary by name and delivers the news which defines her role: she will conceive the son of God. Her response signifies Mary's recognition of her place in the world, her part in God's plan for the redemption of humankind, her "always-already" defined role. In echoing Gabriel's greeting, *Ave Maria* (Hail Mary), the poets reaffirm the Christian ideology of reception.

The story of the Annunciation does not appear in the earliest accounts of Jesus' life; it seems

---

[36] The *Ave Maria* is a liturgical prayer based on Gabriel's and Elizabeth's greetings to Mary (Luke 1:28 and 42).

[37] "Ideology and Ideological State Apparatuses," *Lenin and Philosophy and Other Essays*, trans. Ben Brewster (London: Verso, 1971), pp. 160 ff.

to have been recorded later in response to curiosity about his background. Medieval Christians knew the story of the Annunciation from Luke (written c. A.D. 85) and from the apocryphal *Protevangelium* of James (c. A.D.150). It became a fundamental part of medieval Christianity, an event dramatized in every cycle of the Corpus Christi plays and celebrated during every Saturday mass. The Annunciation provides the foundation for all Marian devotion; the frequency with which the lyrics repeat Gabriel's greeting testify to its importance. Traditionally the first of the Five Joys, the Annunciation is mentioned in nearly all of the extant medieval Marian lyrics. Commentators such as Jacobus de Voragine, after Irenaus and Jerome, saw in Gabriel's visit to Mary a reversal of the Fall: *Eva* (Eve), who was visited by a serpent and cast out by the Archangel Michael, is redeemed (reversed) through Gabriel's *Ave* as Mary, visited by her angel, is filled with the grace Eva lost (see note to §9, line 8). This emissarial visit promises that the tree of Jesse, long blighted by the Fall, will again bear fruit; the Fall associated with the tree of Eden is redeemed through the Christ-bearing tree, the cross.

The poets know Mary to be worthy of praise because Gabriel has proclaimed her status and purpose in the world — good news, indeed. Mary's response, "Behold the handmaid of the Lord; be it done to me according to thy word" (Luke 1:38), affirms her ideological compliance and worthiness. She is the means by which the culture reinscribes its truth. Bernard of Clairvaux composed a series of four homilies on Mary;[38] in his estimation, her obedience is a crucial factor in the redemption plan. He insists that Mary's "virginity is a praiseworthy virtue, but humility is by far the more necessary" (Homily 1, p. 9; see also Homily 4, pp. 54–55). She sets the pattern for even God himself to become humble and obedient in taking on himself human form. Mary's submissiveness to God is, then, a quality to be desired not only in women, but in all individuals.

The liturgy adopts the passage from Luke as the Gospel reading for the first Mass in Advent and for the Feast of the Annunciation (March 25). In the Sarum Missal, it also appears as a sequence for the Mass of the Blessed Virgin Mary (Warren, *Sarum*, Part 2, p. 78). One of the earliest Marian feasts, "Lady Day," was widely celebrated in the western Church from the seventh century on.

In Luke and the *Protevangelium*, the Annunciation is followed with an account of Mary's visit to her cousin Elizabeth, who is pregnant with John the Baptist; when John leaps in her womb at the recognition of Mary's greeting, Elizabeth proclaims Mary blessed, and Mary responds with the *Magnificat* (Luke 1:46–55), a canticle based on Hannah's song (I Samuel 2:1–10). I have included James Ryman's translation of the *Magnificat* (§6) in this section because the Visitation and Mary's song echo and reflect upon the importance of the

---

[38] *Homilies in Praise of the Blessed Virgin Mary by Bernard of Clairvaux and Amadeus of Lausanne,* trans. Marie-Bernard Saïd and Grace Perigo, Cistercian Fathers Series No. 18-A (Kalamazoo: Cistercian Publications, 1993).

Annunciation by dramatizing Mary's joyful and faithful response.

The visual iconography of the Annunciation comes primarily from the *Protevangelium*. In this account (reminiscent of the story of Isaac and Rebekah), Gabriel meets Mary at a well where she has gone to draw a pitcher of water, and then follows her to her room, where she has been spinning purple and scarlet wool for a veil for the Temple. Artists often depict the conception with a dove (symbolizing the Holy Spirit) entering or speaking into Mary's ear; the trope illustrates conception by the word of God. Illustrations incorporate other traditional symbols as well, e.g., a lily, a rose, or some other flower symbolizing Mary's purity, or a psalter (recalling David and the tree of Jesse, of which Mary is the flower).

The section begins with a fourteenth-century verse translation of the Annunciation Gospel, followed by three poems which incorporate retellings of the event into prayers and longer narratives. In "Mary moder, meke and mylde" (§5), we imagine ourselves addressing Mary as she wonders about the future; it is an unusual, but not incongruous, situation in that the speaker forgoes the usual petitions for Mary's blessing in favor of offering assurance to Mary that all will be well. Ryman's version of the *Magnificat* (§6) translates expansively the passage from Luke; §7 takes us beyond the Gospel passage to imagine in *chanson d'aventure* form Mary's thoughts as she waits for the birth of her son. "Edi beo thu" [Blessed art thou] (§8) and the lyrics which follow echo Gabriel's greeting and introduce many of the standard images of Mary and the immaculate conception. "Edi beo thu" mixes lines from various Latin hymns with courtly love conventions and provides an introduction to one facet of the courtly cult of Marian devotion. The *Ave maris stella* poems (§s 9 and 10; see also §58) are more general poems of praise, yet in recalling the Annunciation they remind us that this event is the beginning of all devotion to Mary. "I syng of a myden" (§13) and "At a spryng wel" (§14) represent more consciously artistic and more abstract responses to the event; the latter sets the story in the context of a romance, perhaps reflecting the popularity of the chivalric cult of Mary, homage to which recurs in so many fourteenth- and fifteenth-century chivalric romances.

The news of the Annunciation invites joyful anticipation of Jesus' birth, and many of the lyrics in this section were composed as celebratory carols or songs.

The Nativity

With the Nativity comes the wonder of the incarnation of God in human form, through which Mary becomes mother, daughter, and sister of God. Here lies a paradox: Mary shows herself to be most human, as a mother, yet most divine, as mother of God. Most of the Nativity poems mention Mary; the poems selected for this volume emphasize her place in the event. These prominently echo the songs of the Annunciation in defining Mary's place in human salvation as mediatrix and supplicator, her blessedness, and her purity. Some poems simply narrate events from the Nativity to the Epiphany, relying on information from the Gospels and the apocryphal *Protevangelium* and *Gospel of Pseudo-Matthew* for crucial detail. Others focus on the significance of those events. The occasion offers opportunities for affective speculation: some imagine the thoughts of Mary and Joseph at the birth of Jesus. There are several lullabies, some of them prophetic dialogues between Mary and the infant Jesus. In §29, "Als I lay upon a nith," a dreamer meets Joseph, who describes the mystery of the Nativity from his unique perspective: he may more easily believe that a virgin would give birth to a child than that Mary would be unfaithful. Many of the Nativity poems are carols, an appropriate form for the celebratory nature of the event.

Judging by the lyrics which survive today, interest in the Nativity as a specific focus for meditation developed relatively late in the Middle Ages. Before the late fourteenth century, with the exception of "Nu this fules" (which Woolf classifies as an Annunciation lyric), the Nativity is treated only in poems of the five joys, and there formally (see, for example, §76). John Grimestone's commonplace book, dated 1372, provides seven of the earliest extant Nativity lyrics, and in that collection, as Rosemary Woolf notes, "The newness of the subject is perhaps there indicated in the fact that, although this is an alphabetical preaching-book, the poems are not copied under a heading of the Nativity, but are included in some preliminary material or under the heading of the Passion" (p. 143). But beginning in the late fourteenth century, the story of Jesus' birth is addressed in a variety of ways. Woolf attributes this new interest to the phenomenon of the cycle plays, "in which the Nativity became detached from its liturgical season, and in which the relevant human sentiments were thoroughly explored" (p. 148).[39] Carols like §26 and §27 reflect what became a particularly English tradition, an emphasis on the mother/child relationship that is treated less formally than in other traditions. In Latin and European poetry of the age, as Woolf points out, "the subject of the second joy was usually taken as an opportunity to reiterate the doctrine of the perpetual virginity of Mary rather than for meditation on the Mother and Child" (p. 147). But in England, the event is explored from a variety of angles. §15 tells the story of the Nativity with, as it were, a closeup lens focused on Mary's place in the story. Every stanza is anchored by this focus. In §18, on the other hand, the poet chooses a wide-angle lens, using the occasion as the center of the story of humankind's redemption.

The lullaby is an important form here. Woolf comments:

> The lullaby is in fact the predominant form of the Nativity poem, and it is able to draw directly on the homely and familiar, for both the form and the words, 'lull', 'lullay', 'lullaby', lowly and onomatopoeic in origin, seem only to have entered literature and the written language with the Nativity poems. There is, however, a difficulty here in that the

---

[39] See, for example, the York Tille Thekers play of the Nativity and the Wakefield Second Shepherd's Play.

medieval conception of a lullaby cannot be defined from outside the Nativity poems themselves, as traditional homely lullabies survive only from many centuries later. (p. 151)

In these expressions of mother/child intimacy, the poet often imagines a dialogue between Mary and the infant Jesus. Such dialogues often foreshadow the events to follow, the events of the Crucifixion.

Mary at the Foot of the Cross

John's gospel reports that Mary was present at her son's Crucifixion and that Jesus bequeathed her to John's care. The circumstance of Mary's presence at the foot of the cross has captured the imagination of countless artists and meditators.[40] But the situation raises several basic theological questions. If Mary is the mother of Christ and shares his knowledge of the divine plan, why does she sorrow at his suffering? In the *Liber de Passione Christi et Doloribus et Planctibus Matris Eius* (the Book of the Passion of Christ and the Sorrows and Laments of his Mother), commonly attributed to Bernard of Clairvaux,[41] the author imagines a dialogue with Mary in which she explains that she prayed to take on some of her son's pain — perhaps simply a mother's willingness to make a sacrifice for her child. The explanation that best justifies the outpouring of meditational lyrics on Mary's sorrows is that she participated voluntarily in her son's fully human suffering in order to empathize with his experience and the experience of *all humanity.*[42] Some theologians held that Mary gave birth to Jesus without pain (see note to §15, line 3). If so, then, as a witness to his Crucifixion, she shares the motherly suffering she was spared earlier: "Nu thu fondest, moder milde, / Wat wyman drith [suffer] with hir childe, / Thei thu clene maiden be" (§32, lines 37–39). Having come to undestand this pain, Mary is able to guide others into a fuller appreciation of the Crucifixion; in §39, she advises the observer: "Who cannot wepe come lerne at me" (line 11).

In Bernard's dialogue, the speaker asks Mary to tell the story of her experience at the foot

---

[40] The *Planctus Mariae* form grew popular in the twelfth century. On its development, see G. C. Taylor, "The English Planctus Mariae," *Modern Philology* 4 (1906), 605–37.

[41] See *PL* vol. 182, cols. 1134–42; Migne notes that it is not known whether the piece is by Bernard of Clairvaux or Bernard Clarae-Vallensis. A Middle English metrical version of that work appears in the Vernon MS at fol. 287a; it is printed, with the Latin text and the Cambridge University MS Dd.1 English version, in G. Kribel, "Studien zur Richard Rolle de Hampole," *Englische Studieren* 8 (1885), 84–114.

[42] In "The Virgin's Gaze: Spectacle and Transgression in Middle English Lyrics of the Passion" (*PMLA* 106 [October 1991], 1083–93), Sarah Stanbury explores the ways Mary's gaze on her son's body provides meditational focus in several Passion lyrics; "visual empathy" connects the reader to Mary's experience and, through her, to Christ's.

of the cross so that he can share her sorrow. She describes the pain she felt watching her son suffer and recounts her plea to die with him. Jesus says that her sorrow wounds him most of all, but Mary cannot help grieving. Jesus explains the purpose of his suffering, commends her to the care of John, and dies. Mary mourns as her son is placed in the tomb. The dialogue is punctuated by Bernard's interruptions and Mary's exclamations of sorrow, details frequently rehearsed in the lyrics.

But Mary's motherly suffering takes on an added dimension in the lyrics that call attention to her son's identity as God: what she fears is both the universal experience of human loss *and* the loss of God himself. And in this awareness lies the full impact of the lyrics. Sarah Appleton Weber comments on such mother/son dialogues as §25:

> The poet uses Mary's limited human view as the source of drama in the poems on the compassion of Mary. In these poems, the poet will focus on the pains of Christ and exclude the implications of the future joyful outcome of the crucifixion, until the suffering portrayed reaches a great degree of intensity. In this way his poem can reflect the immensity of the consequences of sin which cause such pain, and through this knowledge it can turn man's heart toward Christ. (pp. 71–72)

Christians meditate on the dark hours of the Crucifixion in order to apprehend the magnitude of Christ's sacrifice; the more deeply the sorrow is felt, the more joyfully the Resurrection may be celebrated.

The lyrics in this section augment the gospel accounts of the Crucifixion with material from Bernard's dialogue; Anselm's *Beatae Mariae et Anselmi de passione Domini* provides a similar model in which Anselm asks Mary to narrate the events of the Passion, and she does so, using the words of the Gospels and the Psalms. From such models, the poets develop a variety of approaches. The Latin sequence *Stabat juxta Christi crucem* is paraphrased in §32 and is used as the basis for a dialogue between mother and son in §33. In variations on this theme, poets imagine dialogues between Mary and Jesus, his tormenters, the poet, and even the Cross. In still others, the speaker meditates on Mary's sorrows, sometimes speaking to her; the best known example is §38, "Nou goth sonne under wod." In §31, a narrator recounts the events of the Passion, emphasizing visual images of Mary's presence at each moment; thus the hearer's attention is focused *through* Mary on her son's suffering. As in other poems on the Passion in which we are prompted to contemplate Christ's wounds, visual iconography provides imaginative stimuli for meditation.

A particularly effective strategy in evoking contemplation is to juxtapose scenes from the Crucifixion with Nativity scenes, drawing on the contrast of moods to emphasize the intensity of Mary's sorrow. §35, for example, while not, strictly speaking, a lyric, introduces §36 with a series of ironic reversals rich in imagery. Dialogues at the foot of the cross recall lullabies and dialogues with the infant Jesus; as those dialogues hinted at the sorrows to come, so do these remind us of the somber joy that follows this dark time.

Context shapes these lyrics: those in which Mary seems mired in despair are often found in sermons. These lyrics evoke an intense moment of reflection, of affection, but they function in a greater context, as moments in salvation history. The lyrics which appear in meditational collections inevitably end in joy, for the Christian commemoration of Mary's sorrowing makes sense only insofar as the sorrowing finally gives way to the Easter celebration.

And in fact Mary's maternal pain at the Crucifixion is doubly significant in light of Jesus' words to his disciples at the Last Supper:

> Amen, amen, I say to you, that you will weep and lament, but the world shall rejoice; and you shall be sorrowful, but your sorrow shall be turned into joy. A woman about to give birth has sorrow, because her hour has come. But when she has brought forth the child, she no longer remembers the anguish for her joy that a man is born into the world. And you therefore have sorrow now; but I will see you again, and your heart shall rejoice, and your joy no one shall take from you. (John 16:2–22)

In this group of Crucifixion lyrics we find Mary sorrowful, angry, even bitter — moods rarely associated elsewhere with the Mary of the Immaculate Conception. In §43, a long dialogue between Mary and the Cross, Mary's progress from anger to understanding is designed to guide the meditator through a psychological process of healing and spiritual growth. Here she is most fully identifiable as one of the human race; identification with her emotional trauma becomes a means through which the reader/meditator may grow from despair or anger into an understanding of the fuller significance of the Crucifixion and its place in the redemption story.

The Assumption and Mary as Queen of Heaven

Though only one of the poems here deals directly with Mary's Assumption into heaven, the story has a direct bearing on poems which address Mary as Queen of Heaven. The story, recorded in the apocryphal book of John the Evangelist and in Dionysius' *Book of the Names of God,* is an attempt to solve the mystery surrounding Mary's later days. Since there was no account of her death and no known burial place, some Christians reasoned that she must not have died (see Clayton, pp. 8–9). According to the creation accounts in Genesis, death is a consequence of sin; according to medieval doctrine, Mary was sinless. Another line of argument reasoned that if Mary *had* died, Jesus would not have allowed the blessed womb to decay in obscurity. Jacobus de Voragine treats the matter in detail, first relating an account of the Assumption from John the Evangelist, then reporting the writings of St. Jerome and St. Augustine on the matter (*Golden Legend*, vol. 2, pp. 77–97). St. Augustine argues that "putrescence and the worm are the shame of the human condition. Since Jesus has no part in that shame, Mary's nature, which Jesus, as we know, took from her, is exempt from it" (*Golden Legend,* p. 83); furthermore, "the throne of God, the bridal chamber of the Lord, the tabernacle of Christ is worthy to be kept in heaven rather than on earth" (p. 84). Finally, he reasons, since "God has willed to preserve incorrupt the modesty of his mother's virginity, why would he not wish to save his mother from the foulness of putrefaction?" (p. 96).

Though it was not proclaimed dogma by the Roman Catholic Church until 1950, belief in the Assumption of Mary was widespread in the Middle Ages (see note to §77, lines 50–51), and the feast of the Assumption was celebrated on August 15 beginning in the seventh century.[43] At this feast, Mary is recognized as Queen of Heaven. The liturgy suggests several sources for the iconography of this poetry. The introit comes from Apocalypse (Revelation) 12:1, which describes the woman clothed with the sun; the gradual, Psalm 44:11–12, 14, describes the king's daughter with golden robes and the woman who will, with her son, defeat the serpent. The epistle (Judith 13:22–25, 15:10) invokes praise originally addressed to Judith: "Thou art the glory of Jerusalem, thou art the joy of Israel, thou art the honor of our people" (15:10). The readings also commemorate the fulfillment of Mary's prophecy in the Magnificat — "all generations shall call me blessed" (Gospel: Luke 1:41–50, or Communion: Luke 1:48). The imagery in these poems is glorious and apocalyptic. Macaronic and aureate language seem created for the purpose, as attempts to make a new language suitable for praising the heavenly queen. In §50 the poet imagines Mary's coronation, finally asking her intercessory blessings. The writer of §51 protests his inadequacy — "The aureat beames do nat in me shyne" (line 7) — but of course they do, and the poet proceeds to recall the Queen's past mercies. §52, "Lefdy blisful, of muchel might," offers pure praise without petition; it is unusual in that regard, as the next section demonstrates.

Mary Mediatrix and Penitential Poems

Many medieval English penitential prayers are addressed to Mary rather than to Christ. Woolf comments: "An appeal to Mary was a sign of sincere remorse, for, once the idea of a hierarchy of appeal had been accepted, a direct and immediate invocation of Christ might suggest a presumptuous unawareness of one's own sinfulness rather than a theologically correct recourse to the only and ultimate source of forgiveness" (p. 113). As Mary first mediated between God and humankind when she bore Christ, medieval Christians perceived

---

[43] For further discussion of the tradition, see Warner, ch. 6; on its theological significance, see Pelikan, ch. 15.

her as a natural intercessor. Graef summarizes the argument of the fourteenth-century theologian Theophanes of Nicaea:

> She is likened to the earth, because Christ's flesh was taken from her, therefore she is the source of benediction for all men, and she herself is the centre that unites all creatures with one another and with God. For she has borne her Son and God in her motherly womb; therefore she is the receptacle of the divine fullness, from which God's gifts and graces flow out to all rational creatures. She alone has access to all these treasures, because Christ can be approached only through her. (p. 335)

The poems in this section address Mary as compassionate queen. The purpose is specific: to ask for Mary's help. In all these selections, the speaker begs Mary to intercede, to "pray for us." The process of penance (discussed fully in Chaucer's The Parson's Tale) involves three stages: contrition, confession, and satisfaction. The penitential poems observe this pattern, emphasizing the speaker's sinful condition and desire to repent, in order to guide the reader through a similar process.

Meditations on the Joys of Mary

Organized meditation — on the rosary, for example — guided Christians in structured spiritual exercises. Meditation on Mary's "joys" recalls the events of Mary's life in terms of their spiritual significance; her experiences symbolize the story of all humankind's redemption, from faithfulness on earth to heavenly reward. The desire to structure such meditations in fives (recalling the five letters in the name "Maria" and the stigmata, the five wounds Christ received on the cross — also a popular focus for meditation) produced variations. The Franciscan tradition of the five joys included the Annunciation, the Nativity, the Resurrection of Christ, the Ascension of Christ into heaven, and the Assumption of Mary into heaven. §75 and §76 demonstrate this tradition. But sometimes the Epiphany (the visit of the Magi) is included and the Ascension omitted, as in §74 and §77. The poet who composed §73 combined both traditions to describe six joys; Crowne notes that the number five was "neither peculiar to England nor absolute there" (p. 308). A related tradition of describing the *heavenly* joys — often seven (as in §72) or even fifteen (as with Lydgate) — is represented by §72. While the poems in this section tend toward formality rather than personal engagement, they reflect, perhaps, a complete sense of Mary's significance in the world.

Chansons d'Aventure and Love Quests

E. K. Chambers proposed the term *chansons d'aventure* (*CS*, p. 266) to describe those poems which imitate a variety of secular, chivalric French songs known in England as early as 1300.[44] The form reached its peak in England in the late fourteenth and early fifteenth centuries. In its secular, amorous manifestation, the song tells of a despondent dreamer/speaker who goes out into the country, where he meets a woman and speaks with her. In the religious adaptations of the form, the distressed dreamer usually discovers Mary (though there are also poems in which the dreamer meets Christ), and by speaking with her or observing her, comes to a fuller understanding of his own circumstance. In §77, the speaker thinks upon Mary's five joys as he rides, and his mind turns from his own immediate pleasures to eternal bliss. The rider in §78 ponders his own "folie" (line 13) as he rides, falling into despair until he recalls Mary's "medicine" (line 30) and prays for mercy. In the well-known *Quia amore langueo*, §79, the dreamer sees a vision of Mary, who laments humankind's sinful state and implores the dreamer to be mindful of her love for him and for all. This is a love poem; so too is §80, in which the speaker extols the virtues of his lady, whose identity is concealed until the final stanza. The poet combines a love poem with a prayer for intercession in §83. The overlap of religious and amorous secular conventions — language, imagery, and forms — leads to the possibility of multiple interpretations. Poems §81 ("Maiden in the mor lay") and §82 ("Lulley, lulley, lully, lulley, / The fawcon hath born my mak away") have stimulated debate: though their origins are probably secular, they may be read as Marian allegories (see notes to these poems). And perhaps they were intended to convey such double meanings. The sense of play is evident throughout this section, as poets venture beyond simple didactic verse to ponder paradoxes and wonders. The dreamer/speaker and the reader share in patterns of adventure and discovery.

Poems in Celebration of Mary

The final poems in this volume, with the exception of §87 and §88, come from the fifteenth century, and as such represent a shift (as discussed above) from the style and emphases of earlier Marian lyrics. Aureate language and highly formalized descriptions produce a kind of poetry very different from the verses composed by the Franciscans and their contemporaries. Walter F. Schirmer's comments on Lydgate's Marian poetry apply as well to the works of his followers:

---

[44] On the characteristics and traditions of this form, see Helen Estabrook Sandison, *The "Chanson d'aventure" in Middle English,* Bryn Mawr College Monographs, vol. 12 (Bryn Mawr: Bryn Mawr College, 1913).

We no longer sit with the Holy Family at a common table; we are far below them. Christ is no longer "sweet" or "dear", but "mighty" and "heavenly". Mary is no longer the consoling lover or the mother playing with her child; nor is she the courtly lady, Chaucer's "lady brighte". Instead she is the queen of heaven, the image radiating mercy, enshrined in mystical ornamentation. Hence his revelling in her brightness and splendour (where courtly lyrics would have emphasized her beauty); hence his abstraction, his representation of the spiritual or moral essence of images which he no longer visualizes in the flesh. (p. 197)

But while this distanced, formalized conception of Mary occurs frequently, the full picture is something greater. Mary is *both* humble handmaiden and exalted queen of heaven, familiar mother and noble intercessor, and the lyrics included here demonstrate the full range of that recognition.

Sources

The authors of most of the lyrics in this collection are anonymous. John Lydgate (c. 1370–c. 1451) is credited with authorship of §12 and §51, and possibly §19. William Dunbar (c. 1456–c. 1513) is responsible for §91 and possibly §86 and §89. Other identified authors include John Audelay (fifteenth century) for §4, Thomas Hoccleve (c. 1369–1426) for §68, William Huchen (fifteenth century) for §85, and John Hawghton (fifteenth century) for §28. Marian poems by Chaucer make up the appendices. Three other individuals who figure prominently in the present volume, but who are not widely known, warrant further introduction.

Friar William Herebert (d. 1333) was a lecturer at the Franciscan Convent in Oxford. His commonplace book, MS BL Addit. 46919, contains twenty-three English poems, mostly translations and paraphrases of Latin hymns, liturgical pieces, and scripture. Four Marian poems in the collection appear to be Herebert's own compositions and show authorial revisions. Three of these are included in the present volume; the fourth is a paraphrase of Luke 1:26–38 (printed by Reimer, pp. 135–36). There has been some debate about the purpose for which his lyrics were intended. Brown speculates that they were meant as sermon tags to be used by Franciscan preachers, while others believe they were meant to be sung.[45]

The name of James Ryman, a Franciscan friar in Canterbury, appears in a manuscript dated 1492, in which 163 pieces, mostly carols, are recorded. Greene notes that Ryman is thus "responsible for a quarter of all the extant English carols of date earlier than 1550" (*EEC*, p. clv). Greene speculates that Ryman observed the popularity of the carol form and wrote his poems to be sung by "his preaching brothers and their audiences" (*EEC*, p. clv). Mary is the

---

[45] On the debate, see Stephen R. Reimer, p. 21.

subject of about one-fourth of Ryman's compositions. Several of his carols concern the Annunciation and the events preceding the Nativity (see Greene, *EEC*, nos. 143–55). His work is represented here by §6, §18, §30, §55, and §56.

Friar John Grimestone's commonplace book (MS Advocates 18.7.21), dated 1372, is a compilation of alphabetically-arranged sermon materials, including over 240 English poems. A few of the items in this collection may have been composed by Grimestone (about whom very little is known) himself. His book contributes seven items to the present volume: §24, §25, §29, §34, §37, §41, and §48.

The Texts

In many cases, these poems survive in unique versions. In instances offering multiple texts, I have generally chosen copy text based on three criteria: completeness, readability (e.g., dialects most accessible to inexperienced readers), and aesthetic quality (e.g., superior meter or imagery). Other things being equal, I have chosen the earliest version of a text, but this has not been a primary consideration. Preserving or reconstructing the "original" text was not, it seems, a particular concern for medieval scribes or audiences. Tim Machan suggests that our interpretation of some Middle English texts should depend upon a model of oral composition (p. 241). Vernacular poetry, as Machan demonstrates, shows characteristics of orality, and even when lyrics were not orally transmitted, cultural assumptions about the nature of vernacular texts were applied. The composers of medieval vernacular lyrics were not considered "authors," and the original sources were often unknown even to medieval scribes. The transmission of these texts was much like the oral transmission of folk songs today; scribes, as the evidence of multiple versions of lyrics shows, both worked from memory, producing unintentional variations, and consciously emended grammatical and stylistic forms, words and phrases, and the order of material. Derek Pearsall refers to the transmission of medieval texts as "recomposition" rather than "decomposition."[46] An extreme example occurs in §63 and §64, where two manuscripts offer substantially different versions of the same poem. Each surviving version of a Middle English lyric is in itself a valid social and literary artifact, and I have been more interested in offering a representative collection of pieces medieval audiences might hear and read than in attempting to reconstruct the oldest or "authorial" versions. I have recorded orthographical variants in the Notes only when they are likely to affect the text's meaning.

In keeping with the conventions of the Middle English Texts Series, I have modernized the

---

[46] See "Texts, Textual Criticism, and Fifteenth-Century Manuscript Production" in *Fifteenth-Century Studies*, ed. Robert F. Yeager (Hamden: Archon, 1984), pp. 126–27.

orthography of yoghs and thorns, regularized *j/i*, *u/v*, *ff/f*, *x/sh*, and employed modern punctuation and capitalization. I have made one significant deviation from the usual practice of the series. In other Middle English Text Series volumes, pronouns which refer to God are capitalized. That style seems inappropriate for the mother-child dialogues between Mary and Jesus, imposing overly formal overtones on familiar, intimate, and fundamentally human scenes. Since in these poems there is often no clear distinction between references to Jesus as man (Mary's son) and to Jesus as Son of God, this volume uses modern lower-case conventions instead of the series style.

Abbreviations are silently expanded. If final *e* in a multisyllabic word is a long vowel with syllabic value that is not orthographically distinguishable from *schwa*, I have added an accent (*é*). For the second person familiar pronoun, usually written *the* in the manuscript, I have transcribed *thee* to differentiate the pronoun from the definite article. Within individual lyrics and among those found in a common source such as MS Harley 2253, I have regularized forms of conjunctions and articles. Nevertheless, the lyrics in this volume display a variety of dialects, style, and quality as various as the emotions and ideas they express.

Citations from the liturgy refer to the Sarum rite, the predominant use in medieval England. For English translations of biblical passages I have relied on the Douai-Confraternity translation of the Vulgate. Where book, chapter, or verse citation differs from other translations, I have supplied the Revised Standard Version citation in parentheses.

Select Bibliography

The Poems: Editions and Criticism

Auden, W. H., and Norman Pearson, eds. *Poets of the English Language*. Vol. 1. New York: Viking, 1950.

Bennett, J. A. W., and G. V. Smithers, eds. *Early Middle English Verse and Prose*. Oxford: Clarendon Press, 1966.

Böddekker, Karl. *Altenglische Dichtungen des MS. Harl. 2253*. Berlin: Weidmannsche, 1878.

Brook, George L., ed. *The Harley Lyrics: The Middle English Lyrics of MS. Harley 2253*. Manchester: Manchester University Press, 1948.

Brown, Carleton, ed. *Religious Lyrics of the Fourteenth Century*. 1924. Second ed. Rev. G. V. Smithers. Oxford: Clarendon Press, 1952.

————, ed. *English Lyrics of the Thirteenth Century*. Oxford: Clarendon Press, 1932.

————, ed. *Religious Lyrics of the Fifteenth Century*. Oxford: Clarendon Press, 1939.

Bullett, G. *The English Galaxy of Shorter Poems*. London: J. M. Dent, 1933.

Burrow, John. *English Verse 1300–1500*. Longman Annotated Anthologies of English Verse. Vol. 1. London and New York: Longman, 1977.

Cecil, Lord David. *The Oxford Book of Christian Verse*. Oxford: Clarendon Press, 1940.

Chambers, E. K. *English Literature at the Close of the Middle Ages*. Oxford History of English Literature. Vol. 2, part 2. Oxford: Clarendon Press, 1945.

————, and F. Sidgwick. *Early English Lyrics, Amorous, Divine, Moral and Trivial*. London: A. H. Bullen, 1907. Rpt. New York: October House, 1966.

Cook, Albert Stanburrough, ed. *A Literary Middle English Reader*. Boston: Ginn and Company, 1915.

Coxe, H. O. *Catalogue of the Manuscripts in the Oxford Colleges*. 1852. Vol. 1. Republished Wakefield: EP Publishing and Menston: Scolar, 1972.

Craigie, W. A., ed. *The Asloan Manuscript: A Miscellany in Prose and Verse, Written by John Asloan in the Reign of James the Fifth*. Vol. 2. STS n.s. 16. Edinburgh: William Blackwood and Sons, 1925.

Davies, R. T., ed. *Medieval English Lyrics: A Critical Anthology*. London: Faber and Faber, 1963.

Dobson, E. J., and F. L. Harrison. *Medieval English Songs*. New York: Cambridge University Press, 1979.

Dronke, Peter. *The Medieval Lyric*. London: Hutchinson University Library, 1968.

Dunn, Charles W., and Edward T. Byrnes, eds. *Middle English Literature*. San Diego: Harcourt Brace, 1973. Rpt. New York: Garland, 1990.

Fehr, Bernhard. "Die Lieder der Hs. Add. 5665 (Ritson's Folio-Ms)." *Archiv* 106 (1901), 262–85.

―――. "Weitere Beiträge zur englischen Lyrik des 15. und 16. Jahrhunderts." *Archiv* 107 (1901), 48–61.

―――. "Die Lieder der Hs. Sloane 2593." *Archiv* 109 (1902), 33–72.

Furnivall, F. J., ed. *Political, Religious, and Love Poems*. EETS o.s. 15. 1866. Re-edited, London: Kegan Paul, 1903.

―――, ed. *Hymns to the Virgin and Christ*. EETS o.s. 24. London: N. Trübner, 1867.

―――, ed. *The Minor Poems of the Vernon MS*. Vol. 2. EETS o.s. 117. London: Kegan Paul, 1901.

Gray, Douglas, ed. *Themes and Images in the Medieval English Religious Lyric*. London and Boston: Routledge and Kegan Paul, 1972.

―――. *A Selection of Religious Lyrics*. Oxford: Clarendon Press, 1975. Rpt. as *English Medieval Religious Lyrics*. Exeter: University of Exeter Press, 1992.

Greene, Richard Leighton, ed. *A Selection of English Carols*. Oxford: Clarendon Press, 1962.

―――, ed. *The Early English Carols*. Second ed., revised and enlarged. Oxford: Clarendon Press, 1977.

Heuser, W. "Ave Maria." *Anglia* 27 (1904), 320–30.

―――. "Eine Vergessene Handschrift des Surteespsalters und die Dort Eingeschalteten Mittelenglischen Gedichte." *Anglia* 29 (1906), 385–412.

Hughes, Dom Anselm, and Gerald Abraham, eds. *Ars Nova and the Renaissance, 1300–1540*. New Oxford History of Music. Vol. 3. London: Oxford University Press, 1960.

Kaiser, Rolf. *Medieval English: An Old English and Middle English Anthology*. Third ed. Berlin: Rolf Kaiser, 1958.

Laing, David, ed. *The Poems of William Dunbar*. 2 vols. and Supplement. Edinburgh: Laing and Forbes, 1824, 1865 (Supplement).

Luria, Maxwell S., and Richard L. Hoffman, eds. *Middle English Lyrics*. New York: Norton, 1974.

MacCracken, Henry Noble, ed. *The Minor Poems of John Lydgate*. Part 1. EETS e.s. 107. London: Oxford University Press, 1911.

Mackenzie, W. Mackay. *The Poems of William Dunbar*. London: Faber and Faber, 1932.

Manning, Stephen. *Wisdom and Number: Toward a Critical Appraisal of the Middle English Religious Lyric*. Lincoln: University of Nebraska Press, 1962.

Mason, H. A. *Humanism and Poetry in the Early Tudor Period*. London: Routledge and Kegan Paul, 1959.

Mätzner, E. *Altenglische Sprachproben, Nebst Ein Wörterbuche*. Vol. 1. Berlin: Wiedmann, 1867.

The Myroure of Oure Ladye. Ed. John Henry Blunt. EETS e.s. 19. London: N. Trübner, 1873.

Morris, Richard, ed. *An Old English Miscellany*. EETS o.s. 49. London: Humphrey Milford, Oxford University Press, 1872.

Oliver, Raymond. *Poems Without Names: The English Lyric, 1200–1500*. Berkeley: University of California Press, 1970.

Owst, G. R. *Literature and Pulpit in Medieval England*. Cambridge: University Press, 1933.

Padelford, Frederick Morgan. "English Songs in Manuscript Selden B.26." *Anglia* 36 (1912), 79–115.

Patterson, Frank Allen. *The Middle English Penitential Lyrics: A Study and Collection of Early Religious Verse*. New York: Columbia University Press, 1911.

Peck, Russell A. "Public Dreams and Private Myths: Perspective in Middle English Literature." *PMLA* 90 (1975), 461–68.

Reimer, Stephen R., ed. *The Works of William Herebert, OFM.* Toronto: Pontifical Institute of Medieval Studies, 1987.

Reiss, Edmund. *The Art of the Middle English Lyric: Essays in Criticism.* Athens: University of Georgia Press, 1972.

Rickert, Edith, ed. *Ancient English Christmas Carols 1400 to 1700.* New York: Oxford University Press, 1928. [Modernized spelling.]

Robbins, Rossell Hope. "The Earliest Carols and the Franciscans." *Modern Language Notes* 53 (1938), 239–45.

———. "The Authors of the Middle English Religious Lyrics." *Journal of English and Germanic Philology* 39 (1940), 230–38.

———, ed. *Secular Lyrics of the XIVth and XVth Centuries.* Second ed. Oxford: Clarendon Press, 1955.

———, ed. *Early English Christmas Carols.* New York and London: Columbia University Press, 1961.

Sandys, William. *Christmas Carols, Ancient and Modern.* London: Richard Beckley, 1833.

Schipper, J. *The Poems of William Dunbar.* Vienna: Kaiserliche Akademie der Wissenschaften, 1891.

———. *Denkschriften der Kaiserlichen Academie der Wissenschaften in Wien* 42 (1894), 67–69.

Segar, Mary G. *A Mediaeval Anthology: Being Lyrics and Other Short Poems Chiefly Religious.* London: Longmans, Green and Co., 1915. [Modernized.]

Silverstein, Theodore. *Medieval English Lyrics.* London: Edward Arnold, 1971.

Sisam, Kenneth, ed. *Fourteenth Century Verse and Prose.* Oxford: Clarendon Press, 1921. Rpt. with corrections, 1955.

Sisam, Celia and Kenneth, eds. *The Oxford Book of Medieval English Verse.* Oxford: Clarendon Press, 1970.

Smith, G. Gregory, ed. *Specimens of Middle Scots.* Edinburgh: William Blackwood and Sons, 1902.

Speirs, John. *Medieval English Poetry: The Non-Chaucerian Tradition.* London: Faber and Faber, 1957.

Stainer, J. F. R., and C. Stainer, eds. *Early Bodleian Music: Sacred and Secular Songs, Together with other MS. Compositions in the Bodleian Library, Oxford.* 2 vols. London and New York: Novello, 1901. Rpt. Farnborough: Gregg Press, 1967.

Stevens, John, ed. *Mediaeval Carols.* Vol. 4 of *Musica Britannica: A National Collection of Music.* London: Stainer and Bell, 1952. [Modernized texts.]

Stevick, Robert D., ed. *One Hundred Middle English Lyrics.* Indianapolis: Bobbs-Merrill, 1964. Rpt. Urbana: University of Illinois Press, 1994.

Terry, Sir Richard R. *A Medieval Carol Book, The Melodies Chiefly from MSS. in the Bodleian Library, Oxford, and in the Library of Trinity College, Cambridge.* London: Burns Oates and Washbourne, n.d. [1931?].

Thérèse, Sister M. *I sing of a Maiden: The Mary Book of Verse.* New York: Macmillan, 1947. [Modernized texts, providing a good sense of international traditions of Marian verse, from Old Testament passages thought to prefigure her, to modern expressions of devotion.]

Weber, Sarah Appleton. *Theology and Poetry in the Middle English Lyric: A Study of Sacred History and Aesthetic Form.* Columbus: Ohio State University Press, 1969. [Discusses form and structure of several Marian lyrics in terms of theological implications.]

Wilhelm, James J., ed. *Lyrics of the Middle Ages: An Anthology.* New York and London: Garland, 1990.

Wright, Thomas. *Specimens of Old Christmas Carols, Selected from Manuscripts and Printed Books.* Percy Society, vol. 4. London: T. Richards, 1841.

————, and J. O. Halliwell, eds. *Reliquiae Antiquae, Scraps from Ancient Manuscripts.* London: J. R. Smith, 1841–43.

————. *Songs and Carols, Now First Printed, from a Manuscript of the Fifteenth Century.* Percy Society. Vol. 23. London: T. Richards, 1847. [Poems from Bodl. 29734 (English Poet e.1).]

————. *Songs and Carols from a Manuscript in the British Museum of the Fifteenth Century.* Warton Club no. 4. London: T. Richards, 1856. [Complete edition of Sloane 2593.]

————. "The Burden in Carols." *Modern Language Notes* 57 (1942), 16–22.

Wülcker, Richard P. *Altenglische Lesebuch.* 2 vols. Halle: M. Niemeyer, 1874–80.

Zupitza, J. "Die Gedichte des Franziskaners Jakob Ryman." *Archiv für das Studium der Neueren Sprachen und Litteraturen* 89 (1892), 167–338.

Reference and Background

Ashe, Geoffrey. *The Virgin.* London: Routledge and Kegan Paul, 1976.

Bernard of Clairvaux. *Homilies in Praise of the Blessed Virgin Mary.* Trans. Marie-Bernard Saïd. Cistercian Fathers Series no. 18-A. Kalamazoo: Cistercian Publications, 1993. Previously published in *Magnificat: Homilies in Praise of the Blessed Virgin Mary by Bernard of Clairvaux and Amadeus of Lausanne* (Kalamazoo: Cistercian Publications, 1979).

Brown, Carleton. *A Register of Middle English Religious and Didactic Verse.* 2 vols. Oxford: University Press, 1916.

Brown, Carleton, and Rossell Hope Robbins. *The Index of Middle English Verse.* New York: Columbia University Press, 1943.

Brown, Raymond E. *The Birth of the Messiah: A Commentary on the Infancy Narratives in Matthew and Luke.* Garden City: Image Books (Doubleday), 1979.

Carol, Juniper B., ed. *Mariology.* 2 vols. Milwaukee: Bruce Publishing Company, 1957.

Carroll, Michael P. *The Cult of the Virgin Mary: Psychological Origins.* Princeton: Princeton University Press, 1986.

Catena Aurea: Commentary on the Four Gospels, Collected out of the Works of the Fathers by S. Thomas Aquinas. 4 vols. Trans. J. H. N[ewman]. Oxford and London: John Henry and James Parker, 1841–45.

Clayton, Mary. *The Cult of the Virgin Mary in Anglo-Saxon England*. Cambridge: Cambridge University Press, 1990.

Connelly, Joseph. *Hymns of the Roman Liturgy*. Westminster, Maryland: The Newman Press, 1957.

Cowper, B. Harris, trans. and ed. *Apocryphal Gospels and Other Documents Relating to the History of Christ*. London: Williams and Norgate, 1870.

Crowne, J. Vincent. "Middle English Poems on the Joys and on the Compassion of the Blessed Virgin Mary." *Catholic University Bulletin* 8 (1902), 304–16.

Cunneen, Sally. *In Search of Mary: The Woman and The Symbol*. New York: Ballantine, 1996.

Daniel, Hermann Adalbert, ed. *Thesaurus Hymnologicus*. 2 vols. Leipzig: J. T. Loeschke, 1855–56.

A Dictionary of Biblical Tradition in English Literature. Ed. David Lyle Jeffrey. Grand Rapids: Eerdmans, 1992.

Dreves, Guido M., and Clemens Blume. *Analecta Hymnica Medii Aevi*. 55 vols. Leipzig: O. R. Reisland, 1886–1922.

Duffy, Eamon. *The Stripping of the Altars: Traditional Religion in England, c.1400–c.1580*. New Haven and London: Yale University Press, 1992.

Elliott, J. K. *The Apocryphal New Testament: A Collection of Apocryphal Christian Literature in an English Tradition*. Oxford: Clarendon Press, 1993.

Fasciculus morum: A Fourteenth-Century Preacher's Handbook. Ed. and trans. Siegfried Wenzel. University Park and London: Pennsylvania State University Press, 1989.

Ferguson, George. *Signs and Symbols in Christian Art*. London and New York: Oxford University Press, 1954.

Graef, Hilda. *Mary: A History of Doctrine and Devotion*. Vol. 1: *From the Beginnings to the Eve of the Reformation*. New York: Sheed and Ward, 1963.

Harrison, Frank L. *Music in Medieval Britain*. London: Routledge and Kegan Paul, 1958.

Hirn, Yrjö. *The Sacred Shrine: A Study of the Poetry and Art of the Catholic Church*. London: Faber and Faber, 1958.

Jacobus de Voragine. *The Golden Legend: Readings on the Saints*. Trans. William Granger Ryan. 2 vols. Princeton: Princeton University Press, 1993.

James, Montague Rhodes, ed. and trans. *The Apocryphal New Testament: Being the Apocryphal Gospels, Acts, Epistles, and Apocalypses*. Oxford: Clarendon Press, 1924. Rpt. with corrections, 1953.

Jeffrey, David L. *The Early English Lyric and Franciscan Spirituality*. Lincoln: University of Nebraska Press, 1975.

Julian, John. *A Dictionary of Hymnology*. Second ed. 2 vols. 1907. Rpt. New York: Dover, 1957.

Labriola, Albert C., and John W. Smeltz, trans. and eds. *The Bible of the Poor [Biblia Pauperum]: A Facsimile and Edition of the British Library Blockbook C.9. d.2*. Pittsburgh: Duquesne University Press, 1990.

Lauritis, Joseph A., Vernon F. Gallagher, and Ralph A. Klinefelter, eds. *A Critical Edition of John Lydgate's Life of Our Lady*. Pittsburgh: Duquesne University Press, 1961.

Legg, J. Wickham, ed. *The Sarum Missal, Edited from Three Early Manuscripts*. Oxford: Clarendon, 1916.

Levi D'Ancona, Mirella. *The Iconography of the Immaculate Conception in the Middle Ages and Early Renaissance*. New York: College Art Association of America, 1957.

Machan, Tim William. "Editing, Orality, and Late Middle English Texts." In *Vox Intexta: Orality and Textuality in the Middle Ages*. Ed. A. N. Doane and Carol Braun Pasternack. Madison: University of Wisconsin Press, 1991. Pp. 229–45.

Maskell, Rev. William, ed. *Monumenta Ritualia Ecclesiae Anglicanae, or Occasional Offices of the Church of England According to the Ancient Use of Salisbury the Prymer in English and Other Prayers and Forms with Dissertations and Notes*. 2 vols. London: William Pickering, 1846.

Meredith, Peter. *Mary Play from the N. Town Manuscript*. London: Longman, 1987.

Mone, Franz Joseph. *Lateinische Hymnen des Mittelalters*. Vol. 2: *Marienlieder*. Freiburg: Herder, 1854. Rpt. Aalen: Scientia, 1964.

The Oxford Dictionary of the Christian Church. Ed. F. L. Cross and E. A. Livingstone. Second ed. Oxford: Oxford University Press, 1974.

Pannenberg, Wolfhart. *Jesus — God and Man*. Trans. Lewis L. Wilkins and Duane A. Priebe. Philadelphia: Westminster Press, 1968.

Pelikan, Jaroslav. *Mary Through the Centuries: Her Place in the History of Culture*. New Haven and London: Yale University Press, 1996.

Pohle, Joseph. *Mariology: A Dogmatic Treatise on the Blessed Virgin Mary, Mother of God*. Adapted and ed. Arthur Preuss. St. Louis: Herder, 1953.

Power, Eileen. *Medieval Women*. Cambridge: Cambridge University Press, 1975.

Robbins, Rossell Hope. *On the Mediaeval English Religious Lyric; Volumes One and Three, Continuous Pagination; The Dissertation and Complete Notes*. Ph.D. diss., Emmanuel College, Cambridge, 1937.

————, and John L. Cutler. *Supplement to the Index of Middle English Verse*. Lexington: University of Kentucky Press, 1965.

Schirmer, Walter F. *John Lydgate: A Study in the Culture of the XVth Century*. Trans. Ann E. Keep. London: Methuen, 1961.

Schneemelcher, Wilhelm, ed. *New Testament Apocrypha*. Trans. R. McL. Wilson. Louisville: Westminster/John Knox Press; Cambridge: James Clarke, 1991.

Stevens, John. *Words and Music in the Middle Ages: Song, Narrative, Dance and Drama, 1050–1350*. Cambridge: Cambridge University Press, 1986.

Warner, Marina. *Alone of All Her Sex: The Myth and the Cult of the Virgin Mary*. New York: Alfred A. Knopf, 1976.

Warren, Frederick E., trans. *The Sarum Missal in English*. Parts 1 and 2. Library of Liturgiology and Ecclesiology for English Readers, ed. Vernon Staley, vols. 8 and 9. London: A. Moring, 1911.

Introduction

Wenzel, Siegfried. *Preachers, Poets, and the Early English Lyric.* Princeton: Princeton University Press, 1986.

Woolf, Rosemary. *The English Religious Lyric in the Middle Ages.* Oxford: Clarendon Press, 1968.

Woolridge, H. E. *Oxford History of Music.* Vol. 1: *The Polyphonic Period.* Part 1. Method of Musical Art 330–1400. Second ed. Rev. Percy C. Buck. London: Oxford University Press, 1929.

The Annunciation

1

	In that time, als was ful wel,	*as*
	Sende is the aungel Gabriel	*Sent*
	Fro God in til a cité,	*From; into a city*
	Hat Nazareth in Galilé,	*Called; Galilee*
5	Unto a maiden wedded riht	*properly*
	Til a man, whos name hight	*To; was called*
	Josep of the house of Davi;	*Joseph; David*
	And name of the maiden Mari.	*[was] Mary*
	And when the aungel was in gon,	*gone*
10	Unto hire he saide onon:	*her; at once*
	"Haile, ful of hape, God is with thee;	*full; grace (see note)*
	In wemmen blissed thou be!"	*Among women*
	When that sho hade herde thisse,	*she had heard this*
	In his sagh drofede sho isse,	*By his saying disturbed she is*
15	And sho soght for bi anni thing	*sought for any reason*
	What that migt be this hailsing.	*greeting*
	Then saide the angel witerli	*clearly*
	To hir that was so hali:	*holy*
	"Mari, drede thee nothing nou,	*fear you; now*
20	For hape at Gode funden has tou.	*grace from; found have you*
	Loke, in wombe onfong thou mon,	*Look; conceive you shall*
	And forthi salt tou bere a son,	*consequently shall you*
	And thou salt kalle his name Jesus,	*shall call*
	For God wil that it be thus.	*wills*
25	Swithe mekel sal he be,	*Very great shall*
	And Son of Heighest be kald sal he,	*Highest (God) be called*
	And Louerd sal give him ther with	*Lord*
	The sete of his fadir hous David,	*throne; father's*
	And in Jacob hous rike sal he,	*rule shall*
30	And of his rike no ende sal be."	*reign*
	Unto the aungel saide Mari:	

43

The Annunciation

<table>
<tr><td></td><td>"Hou mai this be? no man knaw I."</td><td>may; knew</td></tr>
<tr><td></td><td>And ansuerd the angel bright,</td><td></td></tr>
<tr><td></td><td>He saide to hire was ful of miht:</td><td>He who was full of might said to her</td></tr>
<tr><td>35</td><td>"The Hali Gaste sal come in thee al,</td><td>Holy Ghost; upon you</td></tr>
<tr><td></td><td>And miht and heighest inshadw thee sal,</td><td>power of the highest overshadow you shall</td></tr>
<tr><td></td><td>And forthi that heli born of thee,</td><td>consequently; holy [one]</td></tr>
<tr><td></td><td>Godes Sone be kalde sal he.</td><td></td></tr>
<tr><td></td><td>And loke, Elizabeth, thi nece unwelde,</td><td>kinswoman barren</td></tr>
<tr><td>40</td><td>Onfonges a son in hir elde,</td><td>Conceives; old age</td></tr>
<tr><td></td><td>And this moneth sext til hire is yhit,</td><td>this is the sixth month [of her pregnancy]</td></tr>
<tr><td></td><td>Gelde unberand that kald is it.</td><td>She who is called barren</td></tr>
<tr><td></td><td>For unimiht sal noght be</td><td>impossible shall nothing</td></tr>
<tr><td></td><td>At God, no worde I sai to thee."</td><td>With; no word I say</td></tr>
<tr><td>45</td><td>Then seide Mari with milde chier:</td><td>mild countenance</td></tr>
<tr><td></td><td>"Godes handemaiden lo me here!</td><td>behold</td></tr>
<tr><td></td><td>Als tou has saide, so mot it be</td><td>As you have said, so let it be</td></tr>
<tr><td></td><td>After thi worde unto me!"</td><td>According to</td></tr>
</table>

2

<table>
<tr><td></td><td>From heovene into eorthe, God gretynge he sende</td><td>God sent greeting</td></tr>
<tr><td></td><td>Bi on archaungle that to Marye wende.</td><td>By an; went</td></tr>
<tr><td></td><td>Milde wes that mayde, swete and swithe hende,</td><td>very courteous</td></tr>
<tr><td></td><td>And of fayre ibere. Gabriel hire grette, thus quethinde:[1]</td><td></td></tr>
<tr><td>5</td><td>"Edy beo thu, mayde, thus wunyinde;</td><td>Blessed be you; dwelling</td></tr>
<tr><td></td><td>Ther schal a child in thee kenyen and springe,</td><td>you quicken and spring forth</td></tr>
<tr><td></td><td>Ilef me Marie."</td><td>Believe</td></tr>
<tr><td></td><td>Marie him onswerede, myd stephne swithe mylde,</td><td>with voice very</td></tr>
<tr><td></td><td>"Hw myhte hit iwurthe that ich were myd childe?</td><td>How; happen; I; with</td></tr>
<tr><td>10</td><td>Monnes imone on me ne may nomon fynde."</td><td>Male company/intercourse; no one</td></tr>
<tr><td></td><td>Ofdred wes that mayde.</td><td>Afraid</td></tr>
<tr><td></td><td colspan="2">. . . . .</td></tr>
<tr><td></td><td>"Of thine swete wordes ich am swithe gled.</td><td></td></tr>
<tr><td></td><td>Ich am Godes wenche; ful wel ich habbe isped.</td><td>servant; fared</td></tr>
<tr><td></td><td>Al his wille beo ifuld, as thu havest iseyd."</td><td>be fulfilled; said</td></tr>
</table>

---

[1] *And of fair manner (bearing). Gabriel greeted her, saying thus:*

The Annunciation

15	Bidde we thilke Louerd, wende hwer we wende,	
	That to thee, swete mayde, Gabriel gon sende[1]	
	That for his swete moder luve, that feyr is and hende,	*mother's love; gentle*
	Bringe us to the blisse that lesteth buten ende. Amen.	*lasts without*

3

	Gabriel, fram evene kingh	*heaven's king*
	Sent to the maide swete,	
	Broute hire blisful tiding,	*her*
	And faire he gan hire greten:	*did he greet her*
5	"Heil be thu, ful of grace arith,	*Hail; truly*
	For Godes Sone, this evene lith,	*heavenly light*
	For mannes loven	
	Wile man bicomen	*Will (desires to) become man*
	And taken	*[desires to] take*
10	Fles of thee, maiden brith,	*Flesh; bright*
	Manken fre for to maken	*Mankind free to make*
	Of senne and devles mith."	*From sin; devil's might*
	Mildeliche im gan andsweren	
	The milde maiden thanne:[2]	
15	"Wichewise sold ichs beren	*How should I bear*
	Child withhuten manne?"	*without*
	Th'angle seide, "Ne dred te nout;	*The angel said, "Dread thee not*
	Thurw th'Oligast sal ben iwrout	*Through the Holy Ghost shall be accomplished*
	This ilche thing	*same*
20	Warof tiding	*Whereof news*
	Ichs bringe.	*I*
	Al manken wrth ibout	*mankind will be redeemed*
	Thur thi swete chiltinge,	*Through; child-bearing*
	And hut of pine ibrout."	*out of suffering [be] brought*

---

[1] Lines 15–16: *Let us ask that Lord, go where we go, / Whom to you, sweet maid, Gabriel did send*

[2] Lines 13–14: *Gently the mild maiden then began to answer him*

25	Wan the maiden understud	*When*
	And th'angles wordes herde,	*the angel's*
	Mildeliche with milde mud	*heart*
	To thangle hie andswerde:	*the angel she*
	"Hur Lordes theumaiden iwis	*Our Lord's handmaiden truly*
30	Ics am, that her aboven is.	*I; who is here above*
	Anenttis me	*Concerning me*
	Fulfurthed be	*Carried out be*
	Thi sawe,	*Your saying*
	That ics, sithen his wil is,	*So that I, since it is his will*
35	Maiden withhuten lawe	*A maiden outside the law [of nature]*
	Of moder have the blis."	*Enjoy the bliss of motherhood*
	Th'angle wente awei mid than	*The angel; with that*
	Al hut of hire sithte;	*out; her sight*
	Hire wombe arise gan	*womb grew*
40	Thurw th'Oligastes mithe.	*Through the Holy Ghost's power*
	In hire was Crist biloken anon:	*enclosed*
	Suth God, soth man ine fleas and bon,	*True; true; flesh; bone*
	And of hir fleas	*her flesh*
	Iboren was	*Born*
45	At time,	*At term*
	Warthurw us kam God won.	*Whereby God came to dwell with us*
	He bout us hut of pine	*bought (redeemed) us out of torment*
	And let im for us slon.	*himself for us be slain*
	Maiden moder makeles,	*mateless/matchless/immaculate*
50	Of milche ful ibunden,	*mercy; abounding*
	Bid for hus im that thee ches,	*Pray for us to him who chose you*
	At wam thu grace funde,	*With whom you found grace*
	That he forgive hus senne and wrake,	*our sin and injury*
	And clene of evri gelt us make;	*clean of every sin*
55	And evne blis	*heaven's bliss*
	Wan hure time is	*our*
	To sterven	*die*
	Hus give for thine sake	*Allow us*
	Him so her for to serven	*[Let us] serve him so here*
60	That he us to him take.	

The Annunciation

4

The angel to the vergyn said,
Entreng into here boure,   *Entering; her room*
Fore drede of quakyng of this mayd   *For fear of frightening*
He said, "Haile!" with gret honour;
5   "Haile be thou, quene of maidyns mo!   *numerous*
Lord of heven and erth also
Consayve thou schalt, and bere withale the Lord of myght,   *Conceive; thereby*
Hele of al monkyn.   *Salvation; mankind*
He wil make the thee gate of heven bryght,   *(see note)*
10   Medesyne of al our syn."   *Medicine for*

"How schuld I consayve and get?   *conceive and get with child*
No syn never I knew.   *sin (i.e., sexual intercourse)*
How schuld I breke that I have forehete   *break what I have promised*
Of thoght stedfast and trewe?"   *With*
15   "The grace al of the Holé Gost   *Holy*
Schal bryng ale forth, without boost;   *boast*
Ne dred thou tak, bot joy thou make, serten and sere.[1]
This message he send to thee
To dwel withyn thee ful pere   *full purely (see note)*
20   Throgh myght of his Fader fre."   *Father free*

The angel went thie lade fro;   *departed from the lady*
This womons wombe with wele,   *woman's; weal*
Hit wax gret as odur do.   *grew; others*
This blessid burthe of hele,   *birth; salvation*
25   He was in here wome, I wene,   *her womb; know*
The nombur ful of monethis nene;   *nine months*
Hent he out ged, batelis bede to al the flok,[2]
Beryng on his chulderis bloo   *shoulders bruised*
The holé cros that kene a knok   *holy cross; dealt a blow*
30   Unto oure dedly foo.   *foe*

---

[1] *Do not be afraid, but be joyful, certain and sure*

[2] *Until he went out, bidding all the flock to battle*

The Annunciation

Thys may bare chyelde with mylde chere;   *maiden bore [the] child*
This childe bede kepe hyer chaast.   *bid; herself chaste*
Goddus Sone heo broght us forthe and bere,   *God's Son she; bore*
Geffyng hym wombe and waast.   *Giving; belly and waist*
35 Then he blessud here sydus sere,   *sides both*
And so he did here pappus dere.   *breasts dear*
For thay ther that thay nyst nott hwat, in law as we fyende   *knew not what; find*
How these werkus wright arne   *works be wrought*
Hit was agaynes al monkynde,   *against all [laws of] nature*
40 A maydon to ber a barne.   *virgin; bear; child*

Make joy, modir of oure Lorde,   *mother*
That Cryst concevedust cleene;   *Who; conceived purely*
Angelus, men, and al this worlde,   *Angels*
God pes and rest us leane.   *Good peace; lend*
45 Mary, thy son thou for us pray,
As ye beth ful of mercy ay,   *you are; ever*
And sen us to, and soo to do away oure syn,   *see to us; sue*
And gef us helpe of thee,   *give us help from you*
Heven blys we may dwel in   *Heaven's bliss*
50 Afftur thys owtlary.   *After this outlawry*
        Explicitur.   *The end*

5

Nowel el el el el el el el el el el el:
Mary was gret with Gabriel.   *greeted by (see note)*

Mary moder, meke and mylde,   *meek*
Fro schame and synne that ye us schyllde,   *Shield us from shame and sin*
5 For gret on grownd ye gon with childe,   *great with child you walk on earth*
Gabriele nuncio.   *With Gabriel as messenger*

Mary moder, be not adred;   *afraid*
Jhesu is in your body bred,   *quickened*
And of your bryst he wil be fed,   *breast*
10 *Cum pudoris lilio.*   *With the lily of modesty*

The Annunciation

Mary moder, the frewt of thee   *fruit (Jesus)*
For us was naylid on a tre;   *tree (cross)*
In hevene is now his magesté,
Fulget resurrecio.   *The resurrection shines forth*

15   Mary moder, the thredde day   *third*
Up he ros, as I yow say;   *tell you*
To helle he tok the ryghte way,   *straight path*
Motu fertur proprio.   *Of his own volition*

Mary moder, after thin sone
20   Up thou steyist with hym to wone;   *ascend; dwell*
The aungele wern glad quan thou were come   *angels were; when*
In celi palacio.   *Into the palace of heaven*

6

Unto Marie he that love hath,
To here synge he *Magnificat.*   *her*

Thus seide Mary of grete honoure: *said*
"My soule my Lord dothe magnifie,
5   And in my God and savyoure
My spirite rejoyseth verily.

"For he the mekenes hath beholde   *meekness*
Of his handemayde, that Lorde so good;
That I am blessed manyfolde
10   Alle kynredes shall say, of myelde moode.   *generations; reverently*
"For he that is so full of myght
So grete thinges to me hath done;
Holy his name is ay of right,   *ever justly*
By whome our goostly helth is won.   *spiritual salvation*

15   "And in alle tho that hym doth drede   *those; fear*
(Truly thus seithe holy scripture)   *says*
His mercy dothe bothe spring and sprede,   *grow*
And of heven they be fulle sure.

"Thys myghty Lorde of grete renowne
20 By his swete Sonne the helthe hath wrought   *salvation*
Of meke people, and hath put downe
Prowde people onely with a thought.   *Proud; only*

"Tho that desireth that Lorde, oure helth,   *Those who*
That king of grace soo goode and swete,
25 Fro whome cometh alle goodenes and welth,   *From*
With alle vertue they be replete.   *will be filled*

"Of his grete mercy havyng myende,   *Remembering his great mercy*
He toke nature in Ysraell   *He became incarnate; Israel*
And became man to save mankynde,
30 To oure faders as he did telle."   *prophesy*

Joy be to God in Trinitie,
Fader and Sonne and Holi Goost,
That was and is and ay shall be
Both three and one, of myghtes most.

7

Nowel, nowel, nowel,
Syng we with myrth: *Sing; mirth*
Cryst is come wel
With us to dewell   *dwell*
5 By hys most noble byrth.

Under a tre
In sportyng me   *While entertaining myself*
Alone by a wod syd   *wood side*
I hard a mayd   *heard; maiden*
10 That swetly sayd,   *sweetly*
"I am with chyld this tyd.   *season*

"Gracyusly   *By God's grace*
Conceyvyd have I
The Son of God so swete;

50

15   Hys gracyous wyll

    I put me tyll   *submit to*

    As moder hym to kepe.   *keep*

    "Both nyght and day

    I wyl hym pray

20   And her hys lawes taught,   *hear his*

    And every dell   *every bit*

    Hys trewe gospell   *true*

    In hys apostles fraught.   *entrusted*

    "Thys goostly case   *spiritual condition*

25   Dooth me embrace   *Does embrace me*

    Withowt dyspyte or moke: *despite; mockery*

    With my derlyng   *darling*

    'Lullay' to syng   *'Lullaby'*

    And lovely hym to roke.   *lovingly; rock*

30   "Withowt dystresse

    In grete lyghtnesse   *lightheartedness*

    I am both nyght and day;

    This hevenly fod   *food/child (see note)*

    In hys chyldhod   *childhood*

35   Schal dayly with me play.   *daily*

    "Soone must I syng

    With rejoycyng

    For the tym is all ronne   *time; arrived*

    That I schal chyld   *give birth [to]*

40   All undefyld   *undefiled*

    The kyng of hevens sonne."   *heaven's*

8

    Edi beo thu, hevene quene,   *Blessed be you, heaven's queen*

    Folkes froure and engles blis,   *comfort; angels'*

    Moder unwemmed and maiden clene,   *immaculate (unblemished); pure*

    Swich in world non other nis.   *Such; no other is*

5   On thee hit is wel eth sene,   *In you it is easily seen*

The Annunciation

	Of all wimmen thu havest thet pris;	*you; prize (see note)*
	Mi swete levedi, her mi bene	*lady, hear my prayer*
	And reu of me yif thi wille is.	*have pity on me if*
	Thu asteghe so the daiy rewe	*You ascend like the ray of dawn*
10	The deleth from the deorke nicht;	*Which separates*
	Of thee sprong a leome newe	*From you sprang a new light*
	That al this world haveth ilight.	*That has lit all this world*
	Nis non maide of thine heowe	*There is no; complexion (demeanor)*
	Swo fair, so schene, so rudi, swo bricht;	*So; beautiful; fresh*
15	Swete levedi, of me thu reowe	*have compassion*
	And have merci of thin knicht.	*have pity on your knight*
	Spronge blostme of one rote,	*Blossom sprung from a single root [of Jesse]*
	The Holi Gost thee reste upon;	*rested upon you*
	Thet wes for monkunnes bote	*mankind's benefit*
20	And heore soule to alesen for on.	*their; redeem*
	Levedi milde, softe and swote,	*sweet*
	Ic crie thee merci, ic am thi mon,	*I; servant*
	Bothe to honde and to fote,	*Both hand and foot (i.e., completely)*
	On alle wise that ic kon.	*In all ways that I know*
25	Thu ert eorthe to gode sede;	*You are earth; good seed*
	On thee lighte the heovene deugh,	*On you alighted heavenly dew*
	Of thee sprong theo edi blede	*From you; the blessed fruit*
	The Holi Gost hire on thee seugh.	*here; sowed*
	Thu bring us ut of kare of drede	*out; care; fear*
30	That Eve bitterliche us breugh.	*bitterly [for] us brewed*
	Thu sschalt us into heovene lede;	*lead*
	Welle swete is the ilke deugh.	*this same dew*
	Moder, ful of thewes hende,	*noble virtues (ways)*
	Maide dreigh and wel itaucht,	*patient; instructed*
35	Ic em in thine love bende,	*I am; love bond*
	And to thee is al mi draucht.	*desire (see note)*
	Thu me sschildghe from the feonde,	*shield; fiend (devil)*
	Ase thu ert freo, and wilt and maucht;	*As you are noble, and will and may*
	Help me to mi lives ende,	*my life's end*
40	And make me with thin sone isaught.	*reconcile me with your son*

52

The Annunciation

Thu ert icumen of heghe kunne,   *high (great) lineage*
Of David the riche king;   *powerful*
Nis non maiden under sunne   *There is no*
The mei beo thin evening,   *Who may be your equal*
45   Ne that swo derne lovighe kunne   *Nor who so intimately can love*
Ne non swo swete of alle thing;   *so sweet in all things*
Thi love us brouchte eche wunne: *brought joy to each of us*
Ihered ibeo thu, swete thing.   *Praised be you*

Seolcudliche ure Louerd hit dighte   *Marvelously; Lord arranged it*
50   That thu, maide withute were,   *husband*
That al this world bicluppe ne mighte,   *[He] whom; confine*
Thu sscholdest of thin boseme bere.   *from your womb bear*
Thee ne stighte ne thee ne prighte   *You neither flinched nor felt pain*
In side, in lende, ne elles where: *loin*
55   That wes with ful muchel righte,   *completely right (appropriate)*
For thu bere thine helere.   *you bore your healer (savior)*

Tho Godes Sune alighte wolde   *When God's Son*
On eorthe al for ure sake,   *earth; our*
Herre teghen he him nolde   *Higher he would not tie himself*
60   Thene that maide to beon his make;   *Than to; be his mother/mate*
Betere ne mighte he thaigh he wolde,   *He might not have done better*
Ne swetture thing on eorthe take.
Levedi, bring us to thine bolde   *dwelling place (abode)*
And sschild us from helle wrake.   *shield; hell's vengeance*
                Amen.

9

Heyl, levedy, se-stoerre bryht,   *Lady, sea-star bright (see note)*
Godes moder, edy wyht,   *God's; blessed one*
Mayden ever vurst and late,   *first and last (i.e., always)*
Of heveneriche sely gate.   *kingdom of heaven [the] blessed gate*

5   Thylk *Ave* that thou vonge in spel   *That same; received; speech*
Of the aungeles mouhth kald Gabriel,   *From; mouth called*

The Annunciation

In gryht ous sette and shyld vrom shome, *security set us; shield from shame*
That turnst abakward Eve's nome. *name*

Gulty monnes bond unbynd, *mankind's bondage*
10 Bryng lyht tyl hoem that boeth blynd, *light to them who are*
Put vrom ous oure sunne *sin*
And ern ous alle wynne. *procure for us; joy*

Shou that thou art moder one, *Show; alone*
And he vor thee take oure bone *So that he for your sake receive our prayer*
15 That vor ous thy chyld bycom *[He] who for; became*
And of the oure kunde nom. *from you our [human] nature took*

Mayde one thou were myd chylde *alone; with child*
Among alle so mylde: *gentle*
Of sinne ous quite on haste *deliver us quickly*
20 And make ous meoke and chaste. *meek*

Lyf thou gyf ous clene, *give us fully*
Wey syker ous yarke and lene *Prepare and grant us a secure passage*
That we Jesus ysoe *So that; may see*
And ever blythe boe. *happy be*

25 To Vader, Cryst, and Holy Gost beo thonk and heryinge, *Father; be thanks; praise*
To threo persones and o God, o menske and worshypinge. *one; with honor*

10

Blessed Mary, moder virginall,
Integrate mayden, sterre of the see, *Perfect; star; sea*
Have remembraunce at the day fynall *final (Judgment Day)*
On thy poore servaunt now prayng to thee. *praying*

5 Myrroure without spot, rede rose of Jerico,
Close gardyn of grace, hope in disparage, *Enclosed garden (see note); disgrace*
Whan my soule the body parte fro *When my soul parts from the body*
Socoure it frome myn enmyes rage. *Shelter; enemy's*

The Annunciation

11

Ave
    Hayle mayden of maydyns, thorgth worde consaywyng,[1]
    Hayle mayden and moder, with thi mylke Cryst Jesu norescheng,   *nourishing*
    Hayle heven joye, thy blessednes that feddest heven kyng: *feeds heaven's*
    For hys love helpe thou me in peryle here leveyng.   *peril; living*

Maria
5   Mary, Cristes moder, thy body was hys boure,   *bower (chamber)*
    Mary, for that brythe offe wommen thou are floure,
    Mary, haven offe seker rest in stormys and eke in stowere:
    Have mynde of me in worldys wawys, that hope to thy sokour.[2]

Gratia
    Grace that was hyest was holy lyghth in thee,   *wholly settled/shining/alighted*
10   Grace that kyndest was made thee Jesus moder to be,   *most generous*
    Grace that was saddest in thee setteld, thou myghth noghth fle:[3]
    Now gracyus lady, of that grace sum qwhat graunte thou me.   *something*

Plena
    Fulle offe grace, madyn withouten pere,   *of; maiden; equal*
    Fulle offe alle worschepe, for heven kyng thou bere,   *worship; heaven's; bore*
15   Fulle that art offe alle peté, thou see sterre so clere;[4]
    When in synne I begynne to synken, here, lady, my prayere.   *sink, hear*

Dominus
    Lorde that in thee conseywyd was for savyng offe lesse and more,
    Lorde that wolde offe thee, mayden, so wonderly be bore,

---

[1] *Hail maiden of maidens, through the Word conceiving*

[2] Lines 6–8: *Mary, because of that birth you are the flower among women, / Mary, haven of sure rest in storms and also in strife: / Have mind of me in worldly woes, who trust to your protection*

[3] *Grace that was most solemn settled in you, you might not flee*

[4] *You who are full of all pity, sea star so clear*

The Annunciation

	Lorde that in thee wroghth that profycy seyde before:[1]	
20	For thi sake have mercy onne me, that I be noughth forlore.	*on; not lost*

Tecum

With thee the Trinité pyghth hys owen place,	*With you; chose; own*
With thee, when Christ wolde manne become to doe us alle grace,	*do*
With thee he ys and thou with hym, atwyn ye maye noughth pase:	
With hym to be, helpe thou me, ladye, that I maye see hys face.[2]	

Benedicta

25	Blyssyd madyn, pereles amonge wommen alle,	*peerless*
	Blessyd moder that was worthy oure Lorde to ley in stalle,	*lay; stall*
	Blessyd be thou in every tyme, ever blyssyd I wylle thee calle;	*will you call*
	Nowe blisful lady, blesse thou me, to dethe qwhen I schal falle.	*death when*

Tu

	Thou syttes, qwene icrownyd, an heye in heven blysse,	*sit; crowned; on high*
30	Thou reygnyst ever with thy sone, qhwere noe joye may mysse,	
	Thou hast powere in heven and erthe and in helle peyn to lysse:	
	That I come noughth to that place, good lady, thou me wysse.[3]	

In

	In heven thee worschepyn angels nyghth and daye,	
	In erthe thee honowereth alle cristenmens laye,	
35	In helle thee dredeth fendes alle that bethe offe fowle araye:[4]	
	Soe myghthtyfulle lady helpe, qhwere that I ne maye.	*where I may not*

---

[1] Lines 17–19: *Lord that was conceived in you for the salvation of less and more, / Lord that would of you, maiden, so wondrously be born, / Lord that through you wrought that [which] prophecy spoke before*

[2] Lines 23–24: *With you he is and you with him, between you may nothing interfere: / Help me, lady, to be with him, that I may see his face*

[3] Lines 30–32: *You reign forever with your son, where no joy may fail, / You have power in heaven and earth and in hell to relieve suffering: / So that I come not to that place (i.e., hell), good lady, guide me*

[4] Lines 33–35: *In heaven angels worship you night and day, / On earth the religion of Christians honors you, / In hell all foully arrayed fiends dread you*

The Annunciation

Mulieribus
>Wommen alle comforteth Mary, that bethe bothe good and wyse,
>Wommen alle in synne broghth helpe Mary that they may ryse,
>Wommen alle with woe begoe helpe Mary on thy gyse,
40   And me that daye, qwhen I schalle see thy sone, my justyse.[1]

Et
>And sethen, lady, howe grete thou art, yt mowe noughth be tolde,[2]
>And also howe mercyable bothe to yonge and olde,
>And howe thou savyst men with myghth oute offe the fendes holde —   *fiend's*
>Thy sokoure, lady, I prey also, that helpyth soe manyfolde.   *succor; helps so many*

Benedictus
45   Blessyd be that hey Fader that schope thee sweche a wyghth,
>Blessyd be hys owen Sone, in thee that wold alyghth,[3]
>Blessyd be that Holygost that made thee so bryghth.   *bright*
>That blessyd Trinyté, thee to serve, sende me grace and myghth.

Fructus
>Fruyt that offe thy wombe sprange that ys soe fayre and swote,   *of; is so fair; sweet*
50   Fruyt yt was that was byhote to come oute offe Jesses rote,
>Fruyt Jesus that blossimmyd offe thee for alle mannys kyndys bote,
>My sowle foode and lyf als soe ay thoughth thee be yt mote.[4]

Uteri
>Wombe, to thee was Cristus bowere, harbar offe alle clennes,
>Wombe, to thee als paradyse fulle offe alle swetnesse,

---

[1] Lines 37–40: *Mary comforts all women who are both good and wise, / Mary brought help to all women in sin that they may rise, / Help all woebegone women, in your manner, / And [help] me that day when I shall see your son, my judge*

[2] *And since, lady, your greatness cannot be told*

[3] Lines 45–46: *Blessed be that high father that created you such a one, / Blessed be his own son, who would alight in you*

[4] Lines 50–52: *Fruit it was that was promised to come from Jesse's root, / Jesus, the fruit that blossomed from you for all mankind's salvation, / Be always my soul's food and life and thought*

55 Wombe, offe thee was prinsys palyce that most ys offe prowes,[1]
   For the byrghth of that wombe helpe, Mary, in dysstres.   *birth; distress*

 Tui
   Thyn ys alle heven court, redy at thyn heste,   *Thine; heaven's; command*
   Thyn ys here alle holycherche, bothe by west and este,   *in west*
   Thyn ys every crysten man in erthe, bothe mest and leste,
60 For thyn I am, thou schylde me frome Satan, that fowle beste.[2]

 Jesus
   Jesus ys oure blyssed Lorde that made alle thynge offe noughth, *things from nothing*
   Jesus ys oure sawyour that with hys blode ous boughth, *savior; blood; us bought*
   Jesus ys kyng offe all peté that soe with man hathe wrowgghth —
   Nowe Jesus, Mary moder sone, ay be ye in my thowghth.[3]

 Amen.
65 Amen nowe seythe alle lerned men with here letturure,   *say; their letters*
   Amen seythe nowe lewede men dewotely thee to honoure, *now ignorant; devoutly*
   Amen to thee with alle here myghth say every creature, *with all their might*
   Amen, worchep ever be to thee, qwyle any thynge schalle dure. *while; last*
    Amen.

12

   Hayle, glorious lady and hevenly quene,
   Crownyd and regnyng in thy blysfull cage,   *Crowned; cloister*
   Helpe us pylgryms in erthely tene,   *misery*
   In worshyp of all thy pylgremage.   *pilgrimages*
5 Thy holy concepcion was thy furst pylgremage,

---

[1] Lines 53–55: *Womb, in you was Christ's bower, harbor of all purity, / Womb, in you as paradise full of sweetness, / Womb, in you was the palace of the prince of most prowess, / For the birth of that womb, help, Mary, in [my] distress*

[2] Lines 59–60: *Thine is every Christian man on earth both most and least, / Because I am yours, you shield me from Satan, that foul beast*

[3] Lines 63–64: *Jesus is king of all pity who has dealt so with man (see note) — / Now Jesus, Mary mother's son, be always in my thought*

The Annunciation

Cuius honore tu nobis fave;	*By which honor, protect us (see note)*
And here we knelyng before thyne image	*kneeling*
Tibi concepte dicimus "Ave."	*To you, who has conceived, we cry "Hail"*
Hayle, glemeryng sterre now in thy byrthe,	*glimmering; birth*
10 To all this world thow spredyst thy lyght;	
Thy joyfull name yeveth us myrthe.	*gives; joy*
Now blessyd be he that Mary thee hyght,	*who called you Mary*
For thorow all the worlde thow yevest thy lyght,	*throughout; give*
O maris stella, domina pia.	*O pious lady, star of sea*
15 With all oure hert and all oure might	*hearts; might*
Tibi clamamus "Ave Maria."	*To you we cry "Hail Mary"*
Hayle, gloryous lady, as Gabriell seyde	
When he came doune on hys message;	*down with his message*
God was made man, hys modyr a mayde:	*his mother a virgin*
20 Lo, lady, thys was thy swete mariage.	*marriage*
So full of grace, unbynde oure bondage,	*unbind our bonds*
Mater divina, virgo serena,	*Mother of God, serene virgin*
And thus shall we sey for oure homage,	*our*
Ave Maria, gracia plena.	*Hail Mary, full of grace*
25 Hayle, joyfull lady in the byrthe of Cryste,	
God is with thee, kyng in thy lappe;	*lap (womb)*
With ox and asse in a crybbe thou lyest,	*manger*
With Joseph, and Jesu sokyng thy pappe.	*sucking at your breast*
Well ys thee, lady, that dydyst hym wrappe,	*who did clothe him*
30 *Ipsum exora que manes secum*	*Beseech him, you who remain with him*
That he wold yeve oure enemy a knappe:	*blow*
Gracia plena, dominus tecum.	*Full of grace, the Lord is with you*
Hayle, floure of clennes without corrupcion,	*flower of cleanness*
Thow beryst the frute of all chastité,	*bear; fruit; chastity*
35 And yet thow madyst thy purificacion,	
To puryfy oure sowles for thy charyté.	
Have mynde, good lady, of oure freelté,	*Remember; frailty*
Et vita nostra plena reatu;	*And our life full of guilt*
Now pray thy son of hys benignité,	*mercy*
40 *Dominus tecum, benedicta tu.*	*The Lord is with you, blessed are you*

The Annunciation

Hayle, wofull lady in hys swete passion,   *woeful*
Scorgyd and naylyd, dying on the roode;   *Scourged and nailed; cross*
Sende us thy comfort in oure tribulacion,
For thy sonnys love that shed hys bloode.   *son's; who; his*
45 But joyfull gladnes dyd change thy moode,   *did*
Cum surrexit sanis vulneribus,   *When he arose with wounds healed*
And ever in the feth, full trew thou stoode,   *faith; true*
Benedicta tu in mulieribus.   *Blessed are you among women*

Hayle, blessyd lady in Crystes assension,   *Christ's ascension*
50 Bothe glad and hevy when he dyd sty;   *heavy; did rise*
Make in thy prayers for us som mencion,   *some mention*
That we may folow when we shall dy.   *die*
Aftyr thy socoure we call and cry   *For your protection*
Ut mereamur luce frui,   *That we may deserve to enjoy the light*
55 That we may deserve the blessyd lyght to sty,   *to the blessed light to rise*
Et benedictus fructus ventris tui.   *And blessed is the fruit of your womb*

Hayle, blessyd lady in thyn assumpcion,   *assumption*
Next to the Trinitie syttyng in trone,   *on throne*
And holde excusyd our gret presumpcion   *excuse our great presumption*
60 To whom we make oure carefull mone.   *[You] to whom; plea*
Oure hertys ar dry and hard as a stone: *hearts*
Funde lacrimarum nobis consolamen,   *Pour out for us the consolation of tears*
And he be oure comfort hens when we gone,   *when we go hence*
Fructus ventris tui Jesus Christus. Amen.   *The fruit of your womb, Jesus Christ*

65 Now farewell, lady, and pray for us,
For thy fyve festes and thy joyes fyve,   *feasts*
That thy son swete, oure Lord Jesus,
Wyll save us all, bothe dede and alyve.
For thyse fyve joyes on thee woll we clyve,   *to you will we cleave*
70 And above all angeles now joyes has thou sevyn;   *now you have seven joys*
Helpe us, fayre lady, thys lyfe whyle we dryve,   *while we endure this life*
And after our endyng God send us hevyn.
    Amen.

60

The Annunciation

13

I syng of a myden   *maiden*
  That is makeles: *matchless/mateless/immaculate (see note)*
Kyng of alle kynges
  To here sone che ches.   *For her son she chose*

5   He cam also stylle   *as peacefully (see note)*
      Ther his moder was   *Where*
    As dew in Aprylle
      That fallyt on the gras.   *falls*

    He cam also stylle
10   To his moderes bowr   *bower (chamber)*
    As dew in Aprille
      That fallyt on the flour.   *flower*

    He cam also stylle
      Ther his moder lay
15 As dew in Aprille
      That fallyt on the spray.   *foliage (branch)*

    Moder and mayden
      Was never non but che;   *she*
    Wel may swych a lady   *such*
20   Godes moder be.

14

At a spryng wel under a thorn   *well spring; thorn bush*
Ther was bote of bale a lytel here aforn; *help for suffering; before*
Ther bysyde stant a mayde   *stands*
Fulle of love ybounde.   *bound*
5   Ho so wol seche trwe love   *Whoever would*
Yn hyr hyt schal be founde.   *her it*

61

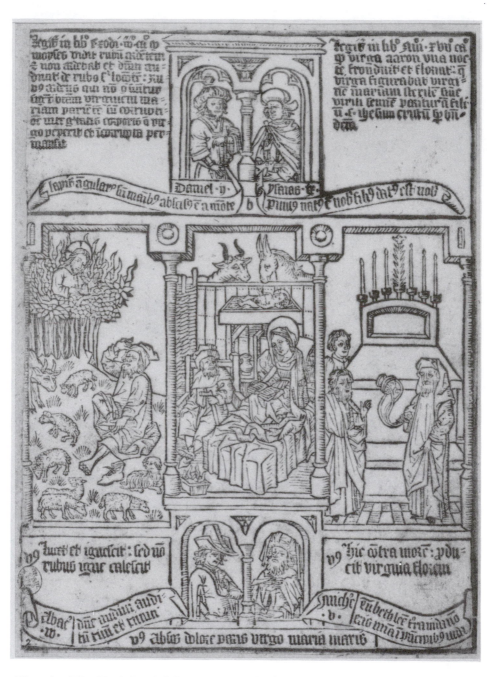

Plate A: **The Nativity**. Biblia Pauperum, leaf b (c. 1470) British Library C.9.d.2.
By permission of the British Library.

The Nativity

15

<table>
<tr><td></td><td>Blissid be that lady bryght</td><td>*Blessed*</td></tr>
<tr><td></td><td>That bare a chyld of great myght,</td><td>*Who bore*</td></tr>
<tr><td></td><td>Withouten peyne, as it was right,</td><td>*Without pain; proper*</td></tr>
<tr><td></td><td>Mayd mother Marye.</td><td></td></tr>
<tr><td>5</td><td>Goddys Sonne is borne;</td><td>*God's*</td></tr>
<tr><td></td><td>His moder is a maid,</td><td></td></tr>
<tr><td></td><td>Both after and beforne,</td><td></td></tr>
<tr><td></td><td>As the prophycy said,</td><td></td></tr>
<tr><td></td><td>With ay;</td><td>*(see note)*</td></tr>
<tr><td>10</td><td>A wonder thyng it is to se</td><td>*wondrous; see*</td></tr>
<tr><td></td><td>How mayden and moder on may be.</td><td>*one*</td></tr>
<tr><td></td><td>Was there never nonne but she,</td><td>*There was never such a one but she*</td></tr>
<tr><td></td><td>Maid moder Mary.</td><td></td></tr>
<tr><td></td><td>The great Lord of heaven</td><td></td></tr>
<tr><td>15</td><td>Owr servant is becom</td><td>*Our*</td></tr>
<tr><td></td><td>Thorow Gabriels stevyn,</td><td>*Through Gabriel's utterance/voice*</td></tr>
<tr><td></td><td>Owre kynd have benom,</td><td>*Our nature has taken*</td></tr>
<tr><td></td><td>With ay;</td><td></td></tr>
<tr><td></td><td>A wonder thyng it is to se</td><td></td></tr>
<tr><td>20</td><td>How lord and servant on may be.</td><td>*one*</td></tr>
<tr><td></td><td>Was ther never nonne but he,</td><td></td></tr>
<tr><td></td><td>Born of maid Marye.</td><td></td></tr>
<tr><td></td><td>Two sons togyther, they</td><td>*suns*</td></tr>
<tr><td></td><td>Owght to shyne bryght;</td><td>*Ought*</td></tr>
<tr><td>25</td><td>So did that fayer ladye</td><td>*fair*</td></tr>
<tr><td></td><td>Whan Jesu in her light,</td><td>*When Jesus became incarnate/shone*</td></tr>
<tr><td></td><td>With ay;</td><td></td></tr>
<tr><td></td><td>A wonder thyng is fall:</td><td>*befallen*</td></tr>
</table>

	The Lord that bought fre and thrall	*bought (redeemed) free and slave*
30	Is found in an assis stall	*discovered/made; ass'*
	By his moder Mary.	

	The sheperdes in her region,	*their*
	Thei lokyd into heaven;	*They looked*
	Thei se an angell commyng doun	*saw; down*
35	That said with myld steven,	*Who; mild voice*
	With ay,	
	Joy be to God almyght,	
	And pece in therth to man is dyte,	*peace; the earth; ordained*
	For God was born on Chrismes nyght	*Christmas*
40	Of his moder Marye.	

	Thre kynges of great noblay,	*Three; nobility*
	Whan that child was born,	
	To hym they tok the redy wa	*took the direct way*
	And kneled hym beforn,	*knelt before him*
45	With ay;	
	These three kynges cam fro fare	*came from afar*
	Thorow ledyng of a stare	*Through guidance of a star*
	And offered hym gold, encence, and mure,	*incense, myrrh*
	And to hys modere Mary.	

16

	Nu this fules singet and maket hure blisse,	*Now the birds sing and rejoice*
	And that gres up thringet and leved the ris;	*the grass grows; branch puts forth leaves*
	Of on ic wille singen that is makeles:	*one I; matchless/mateless (see note)*
	The king of halle kinges to moder he hire ches.	*all; for his mother he chose*

5	Heo his wituten sunne and wituten hore,	*She is without sin; corruption*
	Icumen of kinges cunne of Gesses more;	*Come; kin of Jesse's root*
	The Loverd of monkinne of hire was yboren	*Lord; mankind; her; born*
	To bringen us hut of sunne, elles wue weren forlore.	*out of sin, or else we were lost*

	Gabriel hire grette and saide hire, "Ave!	*greeted her; said [to] her*
10	Marie, ful of grace, ure Lover be uit thee;	*our Lord be with you*

The Nativity

The frut of thire wombe ibleset mot id be.   *fruit; your; blessed may it*
Thu sal go with chide, for sout ic suget thee."   *You shall; child; truth I tell you*

And thare gretinke that angle havede ibrout,   *the greeting that angel*
He gon to bithenchen and meinde hire thout.   *She began to think; mind her thoughts*
15   He saide to then angle, "Hu may tiden this?   *She; the angel; How may this happen*
Of monnes ymone nout y nout iuis."   *I know nothing of man's company, truly*

Mayden heo was uid childe and maiden her biforen   *Virgin she; with; here before*
And maiden ar sothent hire chid was iboren;   *is since her child was born*
Maiden and moder nas never non wimon boten he: *was never any woman but she*
20   Wel mitte he berigge of Godes Sune be.   *might she bearer of God's Son*

Iblessed beo that suete chid and the moder ec   *Blessed be; sweet child; also*
And the suete broste that hire sone sec;   *sweet breast, sucked*
Ihered ibe the time that such chid uas iboren,   *Praised be; was born*
That lesed al of pine that aree was forlore.[1]

17

Alleluya!

Now wel may we merthis make: *mirth*
For us Jesus manhode hath take,   *human form*
Only for our synnes sake,   *sins'*
5   Gaudeamus.   *Let us rejoice*

A kynge of kynges now forth is brought
Of a maide that synned nought   *sinned not*
Nother in ded, nother in thought,   *Neither in deed, nor*
Res miranda.   *Wonderful thing*

10   An angel of cunsel this day is borne   *counsel; born*
Of a maide y seide beforne,   *I said before*
For to save that was forlorne,   *what was lost*
Sol de stella.   *The sun from a star*

---

[1] *Who released all from suffering who before were lost*

That sunne hath never doun goynge,   *never goes down*
15 Nother his lyght no tyme lesynge;   *Nor ever loses his light*
The sterre is evermore shynynge,   *star; shining*
   Semper clara.   *Ever bright*

Right as the sterre bryngeth forth a bem   *brings; beam*
Of whom ther cometh a mervelus strem,   *From; marvelous stream*
20 So childede the maide withoute wem,   *gave birth; blemish*
   Pari forma.   *In like manner*

18

Mary so myelde of hert and myende   *mild; heart; mind*
   Hath borne a child to save mankyende.

Mary so myelde and good of fame,   *reputation*
   By vertu of the Holy Goost,   *virtue*
5 Hath borne a chielde, Jhesus by name,   *child*
   To save mankyende, the whiche was lost.   *which*

Marie so myelde in hert and myende,
   As Gabriell to her behight,   *promised*
Hath borne a chielde to save mankyende,
10   The Son of God and king of myght.

Marie so myelde, that quene of grace,
   Hath borne a chielde — scripture seith soo —   *child; says so*
To bringe mankyende out of that place
   Where is bothe peyne and endeles woo.   *pain; endless woe*

15 Mary so myelde in worde and thought
   Hath borne a chielde, Jhesus soo good,   *so*
The whiche ayene mankyende hath bought   *Who has bought humankind back*
   On the roode tree with his hert bloode.   *cross; heart's blood*

Mary so myelde in dede and wille   *deed*
20   Hath borne a chielde that made alle thing,

The Nativity

To whom al thing obeyeth by skille   *everything obeys by reason*
    As to theire prince, theire lorde and king.

Mary so myelde, so pure and clene,
    Unto hir chielde, that hath no pere,   *peer*
25 By hir mekenes she is a meane   *mediator*
    That we shalle come to heven quere.   *Whereby; to the chancel of heaven*

Mary so myelde, moder and may,   *maiden*
    Hath borne a chielde by hir mekenesse
That shall bringe us at Domes Day   *deliver; Judgment Day*
30 Fro thraldom, peyn, woo, and distresse.   *slavery, pain, woe*

19

My Fader above, beholdying thy mekenesse,   *meekness*
As dewe on rosis doth his bawme sprede,   *roses; its balm spread*
Sent his Gost, most soverayne of clennes,   *Spirit; purity*
Into thy brest, a rose of wommanhede,   *breast; womanhood*
5 Whan I for man was borne in my manhede;   *humanity*
For whiche with rosis of hevenly influence
I me rejoyse to pley in thy presence.   *rejoice; play*

Benyng moder, who first dide inclose   *Gracious; did enclose*
The blessed budde that sprang out of Jesse,   *bud*
10 Thow of Juda the verray perfite rose,   *You; Judea; perfect*
Chose of my Fader for thyn humylité   *Chosen by; humility*
Without fadyng most clennest to bere me;
For whiche with roses of chast innocence,   *chaste*
I me rejoyse to pley in thi presence.

15 O Moder, Moder, of mercy most habounde,   *abundant*
Fayrest moder that ever was alyve:
Though I for man have many a bloody wounde,
Among theym alle there be rosis fyve,   *five*
Agayne whos mercy fiendis may nat stryve;   *Against whose*
20 Mankynde to save, best rosis of defence,   *defense*
Whan they me pray for helpe in thy presence.   *to me pray for help*

20

Ther is no rose of swych vertu	*such virtue*
As is the rose that bare Jesu.	*bore*

Ther is no rose of swych vertu	
As is the rose that bar Jesu,	*bore*
5 *Alleluia.*	

For in this rose conteynyd was	*contained*
Heven and erthe in lytyl space,	*little*
Res miranda.	*Wonderful thing*

Be that rose we may weel see	*By; well*
10 That he is God in personys thre,	*three*
Pari forma.	*In like manner*

The aungelys sungyn the sheperdes to:	*sang to the shepherds*
Gloria in excelsis Deo!	*Glory to God in the highest*
Gaudeamus.	*Let us rejoice*

15 Leve we al this wordly merthe	*worldly mirth*
And folwe we this joyful berthe;	*birth*
Transeamus.	*Let us go*

21

Holy moder, that bere Cryst,	*mother; bore*
Buggere of monkunde,	*Buyer (redeemer) of mankind*
Thou art gat of hevene blisse	*gate of heavenly*
That prest wey gyfst and bunde.[1]	
5 Thou sterre of se, rer op the volk	*star; sea, raise up; people*
That rysing haveht in munde.	*have; mind*
In thee thou bere thyn holy Vader,	*yourself you bore; Father*
That mayden were after and rather,	*before*
Wharof so wondreth kunde.	*At which wonders nature*

---

[1] *Who gives [us] the accessible (straight, swift) and certain (stable, secure) way*

10	Of Gabrieles mouthe	*From*
	Thou vonge thylke *Ave*;	*caught (received) that*
	Lesne ous of sunne nouthe,	*Release us from sin now*
	So woe bisecheth thee.	*we beseech you*
	Amen.	

22

	Syng we, syng we,	
	Regina celi, letare!	*Rejoice, queen of heaven*
	Holy maydyn, blyssid thu be,	*blessed are you*
	Godes Sone is born of thee;	
5	The Fader of hevene worchepe we:	*worship*
	Regina celi, letare!	*Rejoice, queen of heaven*
	Heyl wyf, heyl maydyn, heyl brytgh of ble,	*mother; bright of countenance*
	Heyl dowter, heyl suster, heyl ful of peté,	*daughter; sister; pity*
	Heyl chosyn to tho personys thre:	*chosen of the Trinity*
10	*Regina celi, letare!*	
	Thu art empresse of hevene so fre,	*noble*
	Worthi maydyn in magesté;	
	Now worchepe we the Trenyté.	
	Regina celi, letare!	
15	Lady, so lovely, so goodly to se,	*see*
	So buxsum in thi body to be,	*obedient*
	Thu art his moder for humylité,	*in humility*
	Regina celi, letare!	
	These ben curteys kynges of solumnté;	*are courteous; solemnity*
20	They worchepyd thi sone with umylité,	*humility*
	Milde Mary, thus rede we:	*proclaim (see note)*
	Regina celi, letare!	
	So gracius, so precyows in ryalté,	*precious; royalty*
	Thus jentyl, thus good, thus fynd we,	*gentle; find*

25 Ther is non swych in non cuntré.   *no such; country*
      Regina celi, letare!

      And therfore knel we doun on our kne,   *kneel; knee*
      This blyssid berthe worchepe we,   *birth worship*
      This is a song: humylyté!
30   *Regina celi, letare!*

23

      Lullay, myn lykyng, my dere sone, myn swetyng,   *my delight; dear; beloved*
      Lullay, my dere herte, myn owyn dere derlyng.   *heart; darling*

      I saw a fayr maydyn syttyn and synge;   *sit and sing*
      Sche lullyd a lytyl chyld, a swete lordying.   *lulled; little; lord*

5   That eche Lord is that that made alle thinge;   *eternal; he who; things*
      Of alle lordis he is Lord, of all kynges Kyng.   *lords*

      Ther was mekyl melody at that chyldes berthe;   *much; child's birth*
      Alle tho wern in hevene blys, thei made mekyl merth.   *who were; heavenly; much*

      Aungele bryght, thei song that nyght and seydyn to that chyld,   *Angels; sang; said*
10   "Blyssid be thou, and so be sche that is bothe mek and myld."   *meek; gracious*

      Prey we now to that chyld, and to his moder dere,
      Grawnt hem his blyssying that now makyn chere.   *Grant them; make cheer*

24

      "Ler to loven as I love thee;   *Learn*
      On al my limes thu mith i-se   *limbs; might see*
      Hou sore thei quaken for colde;   *How sorely*
      For thee I suffre michil wo.   *great woe*
5   Love me, suete, an no mo;   *and nothing else*
      To thee I take an holde."   *cling*

The Nativity

Jesu, swete sone dere,   *sweet; dear*

In porful bed thu list nou here,   *poor; lie*

And that me grevet sore.   *grieves sorely*

10 For thi credel is als a bere,   *your cradle is like a bier*

Ox and asse ben thi fere;   *are your companions*

Wepen mai I ther fore.   *I weep therefore*

Jesu, swete, beo nout wroth;   *be not angry*

I have neither clut ne cloth   *rag nor cloth*

15 Thee inne for to folde,   *To wrap you in*

I ne have but a clut of a lappe;   *patch; rag*

Therfore ley thi fet to my pappe

And kepe thee fro the colde.   *keep*

Cold thee taket, I may wel se,   *afflicts you*

20 For love of man it mot be

Thee to suffren wo;

For bet it is thu suffre this

Than man forbere hevene blis.   *deny*

Thu most him bighen therto.   *redeem in this way*

25 Sithen it most nedes that thu be ded

To saven man for the qued,   *from evil*

Thi suete wil be do.   *done*

But let me nouth duellen her to longe   *not abide here too long*

After thi det me underfonge   *death take me to you*

30 To ben for everemo.

      Amen.

25

    Lullay, lullay, la, lullay,

    My dere moder, lullay.

Als I lay upon a nith   *As; night*

   Alone in my longging   *desire*

5 Me thouthe I sau a wonder sith,   *I thought I saw a wondrous sight*

   A maiden child rokking.   *rocking her child*

The Nativity

The maiden wolde withouten song
    Hire child o slepe bringge;[1]
The child thouthte sche dede him wrong   *she did*
10   And bad his moder sengge.   *bade; sing*

"Sing nou, Moder," seide that child,   *now; said*
    "Wat me sal befalle   *What will happen to me*
Here after wan I cum to eld;   *when; adulthood*
    So don modres alle.   *All mothers do so*

15   "Ich a moder treuly   *Each*
    That kan hire credel kepe   *knows how to; cradle*
Is wone to lullen lovely   *Is accustomed to*
    And singgen hire child o slepe.   *to sleep*

"Suete moder, fair and fre,   *Sweet; noble*
20   Sithen that it is so,   *Since*
I preye thee that thu lulle me
    And sing sumwat therto."   *something*

"Suete sone," seyde sche,
    "Weroffe suld I singge?   *What should I sing about*
25   Wist I nevere yet more of thee   *Know*
    But Gabrieles gretingge.   *(i.e., the Annunciation)*

"He grette me godli on is kne   *greeted; courteously; his knee*
    And seide, 'Heil Marie,
Ful of grace, God is with thee!
30   Beren thu salt Messye.'   *You shall bear the Messiah*

"I wondrede michil in my thouth,   *much; thought*
    For man wold I rith none.   *For I would have no man*
'Marie,' he seide, 'drede thee nouth: *dread you not*
    Lat God of hevene alone.   *Let God take care of it*

35   "'The Holi Gost sal don al this.'
    He seyde withouten wone   *delay*

---

[1] Lines 7–8: *The maiden wanted to bring her child to sleep without song*

That I sulde beren mannis blis,		*should bear man's bliss*
Thee, my suete sone.		

"He seide, 'Thu salt beren a king | *shall*
40   In King Davitis see | *David's city*
In al Jacobs woniing | *dwelling place*
Ther king suld he be.' | *should*

"He seyde that Elizabeth,
That baraine was before, | *barren*
45 A child conceyved hath;
To me leve thu the more. | *believe*

"I ansuered blethely, | *gladly*
For his word me paiyede, | *pleased me*
'Lo, Godis servant her am I;
50   Be et as thu me seyde.' | *Let it be*

"Ther, als he seide, I thee bare | *Then; bore you*
On midwenter nith, | *midwinter night*
In maydened withouten kare | *maidenhood; pain*
Be grace of God almith. | *By; almighty*

55 "The sepperdis that wakkeden in the wolde | *shepherds; watched; open country*
Herden a wonder mirthe | *Heard; wondrous celebration*
Of angles ther, as thei tolde, | *angels; foretold*
In time of thi birthe.

"Suete sone, sikirly | *surely*
60   No more kan I say
And if I koude fawen wold I | *But; fain would I*
To don al at thi pay." | *do; pleasure*

"Moder," seide that suete thing,
"To singen I sal thee lere | *I shall teach you*
65 Wat me fallet to suffring | *What I will suffer*
And don wil I am here. | *And do while*

The Nativity

"Wanne the sevene daiyes ben don,   *When; days are done*
    Rith as Habraham wasce,   *Just as Abraham ordained*
Kot sal I ben with a ston   *Cut (circumcised)*
70   In a wol tendre place.   *very tender*

"Wanne the tuelve dayyes ben do,   *twelve*
    Be leding of a stere   *leading; star*
Thre kingges me sul seke tho   *Three kings shall seek me then*
    With gold, ensens, and mirre.

75 "The fourti day, to fille the lawe,   *fortieth; fulfill*
    We solen to temple ifere   *We shall go to the temple together*
Ther Simeon sal thee sey a sawe   *Where; shall speak a saying to you*
    That changen sal thi chere.   *shall change; mood*

"Wan I am tuelve yer of elde,   *twelve years old*
80   Joseph and thu, murningge,   *anxious*
Solen me finden, Moder milde,   *Shall find me*
    In the temple techingge.   *teaching*

"Til I be thretti at the leste   *thirty years old at least*
    I sal nevere fro thee suerve,   *from you swerve*
85 But ay, Moder, ben at thin heste,   *be at your command*
    Joseph and thee to serve.

"Wan the thretti yer ben spent,
    I mot beginne to fille   *I must begin to fulfill*
Werfore I am hidre sent,   *hither*
90   Thoru my Fadres wille.   *By my Father's*

"Jon Baptist of merite most
    Sal baptize me be name;
Than my Fader and the Holi Gost
    Solen witnessen wat I ame.   *Shall bear witness to what I am*

95 "I sal ben tempted of Satan,   *shall be*
    That fawen is to fonde,   *fain; tempt*
The same wise that was Adam,   *In the same manner*
    But I sal betre withstonde.   *shall better withstand*

The Nativity

"Disciples I sal gadere   *gather*
100   And senden hem for to preche   *them forth*
The lawes of my Fader
   In al this werld to teche.

"I sal ben so simple   *innocent*
   And to men so conning   *wise*
105 That most partiye of the puple   *the majority; people*
   Sal wiln maken me king."   *want to*

"Suete sone," than seyde sche,   *Sweet; she*
   "No sorwe sulde me dere,   *sorrow; suffer*
Miht I yet that day se   *Might; see*
110   A king that thu were."

"Do wey, Moder," seide that suete,   *Stop; sweet [one]*
   "Therfor kam I nouth,   *That is not why I came*
But for to ben pore and bales bete   *humble; suffering's remedy*
   That man was inne brouth.   *into which; born*

115 "Therfore wan to and thretti yer ben don *when thirty-two*
   And a litel more,
Moder, thu salt maken michil mon   *much mourning*
   And seen me deyye sore.   *die painfully*

"The sarpe swerde of Simeon   *sharp sword*
120   Perse sal thin herte,   *Shall pierce your heart*
For my care of michil won   *much strife*
   Sore thee sal smerte.   *Sorely shall hurt you*

"Samfuly for I sal deyye,   *Shamefully shall I die*
   Hangende on the rode;   *Hanging on the cross*
125 For mannis ransoun sal I payye   *man's ransom; pay*
   Myn owen herte blode."   *My own heart's blood*

"Allas, Sone," seyde that may,   *maiden*
   "Sithen that it is so,   *Since*
Worto sal I biden that day,   *Why must I live to see that day*
130   To beren thee to this wo?"   *bear you for; woe*

"Moder," he seide, "Tak et lithte,   *Make light of it (take it easy)*
   For liven I sal ageyne,   *I shall live again*
And in thi kinde thoru my mith,   *(see note)*
   For elles I wrouthte in weyne.   *worked in vain*

135 "To my Fader I sal wende   *shall go*
   In myn manhed to hevene;   *earthly form*
The Holigost I sal thee sende   *shall [to] you send*
   With hise sondes sevene.   *his seven gifts*

"I sal thee taken wan time is   *when it is time*
140   To me at the laste
To ben with me, Moder, in blis;   *be*
   Al this than have I caste.   *foreordained*

"Al this werld demin I sal   *judge*
   At the dom risingge.   *doom (Judgment Day)*
145 Suete moder, here is al
   That I wile nou singge."   *will now*

Serteynly, this sithte I say   *sight; saw*
   This song I herde singge
Als I lay this Yolisday   *Christmas Day*
150   Alone in my longingge.   *desire*

26

"Modyr, whyt os lyly flowr,   *white as lily*
   Yowr lullyng lessyth my langour."   *Your; relieves*

As I up ros in a mornyng,   *rose one morning*
My thowth was on a mayd yyng   *thought; young*
5 That song aslep with hyr lullyng   *sang to sleep*
Her swet son, owr savowr.   *savior*

As sche hym held in hyr lape,   *lap*
He toke hyr lovely by the pape,   *lovingly; breast*

The Nativity

	And therof swetly he toke a nappe,	*draught*
10	And sok hys fyll of the lycowr.	*sucked; liquid*
	To hys modyr gen he seye,	*he began to say*
	"For this mylke me must deye;	*I must die (see note)*
	It ys my kynd therwith to playe,	*nature/station (see note)*
	My swet modyr, paramowr."	*darling*
15	The maydyn frely gen to syng,	*freely (unrestrainedly) began*
	And in hyr song she mad mornyng,	*made mourning*
	How he that is owr hevyn kyng	
	Shuld shed hys blod with gret delowr.	*great dolor*
	"Modyr, thi wepyng grevyth me sor;	*weeping grieves*
20	But I wold dey, thu haddys be lor;	*Unless I die, you must be lost*
	Do awey, modyr, and wep no more;	*Stop, mother; weep*
	Thy lullyng lessyth my langowr."	*relieves*
	Swych mornyng as the maydyn mad,	*Such lament; made*
	I can not tell it in this howr,	*hour*
25	Therfor be mery and glade,	*merry; glad*
	And make us mery for owr saviowr.	

27

	Lullay, my fader, lullay, my brother,	
	Myn owyn dyre sone, lullay.	*own dear*
	Ye ben my fader by creacion;	*You are; creation*
	My brother ye ben by nativité;	*birth*
5	Of Adam we coome bothe al and summ;	*come; all and some*
	My owyn dyre sone, lullay.	
	Ye ben my fader that made me of nowght,	*nothing*
	And with youre blode us all dyre bowght;	*blood; dearly bought*
	I am youre moder; knowe ye me nowght?	*not*
10	My owyn dyre sone, lullay.	

77

Ye ben my fader and I youre chyld;
I am youre moder undefyld;   *undefiled*
Loke on youre moder that ys so myld;   *is*
Myn owyn dyre sone, lullay.

15   Ye ben my fader eternally;
My sone ye ben, so most ye drey   *suffer*
For Adamys gylt — ye know wel why;   *Adam's guilt*
Myn owyn dyre sone, lullay.

Ye ben my fader that may nowght dey;   *not die*
20   With yow, my sone, thus schal I playe;   *shall I play*
Youre payne myn herte perschyth in tweye; *pain; pierces in two*
My owyn dyre sone, lullay.

28

I passud thoru a garden grene;   *passed through*
   I fond a herbere made full newe.   *discovered a garden*
A semelyor syght I haff noght sene: *seemlier; I have not seen*
   O ylke tree sange a tyrtull trew;   *On each; turtledove*
5   Theryn a mayden bryght of hew,   *Therein; hue*
And ever sche sange, and never sche sest.   *ceased*
   Thies were the notus that sche can schew: *These; notes; did utter*
Verbum caro factum est.   *The word is made flesh*

I askud that mayden what sche mentt;
10   Sche bad me byde and I schuld here.   *stay; should hear*
What sche sayd I toke gude tent;   *paid close attention to*
   Yn hyr songe had sche voice full clere.   *clear*
   Sche said, "A prynce withouten pere   *peer*
Ys borne and lyde betwene to best;   *laid between two beasts*
15   Therefore I synge as ye mey here   *so you might hear*
Verbum caro factum est."

And thoroght that frythe, as I can wend,   *forest; did go*
   A blestfull song yit hard I mo, *blissful; yet heard; more*
And that was of three scheperdus hend: *gentle*

20 "*Gloria in excelsis Deo.*" *Glory to God in the highest*
   I wold noght they had faren me fro, *I did not want them to leave me*
  And efthyr them full fast I prest. *after; hurried*
   Then told thei me that thei sange soo
  For *verbum caro factum est.*

25 They said that songe was this to sey:
   "To God abovun be joy and blysse, *above*
  For pece yn erth also we pray, *peace*
   Tyll all men that yn goodnesse ys.
   The may that is withouten mysse *maid; fault*
30 Hasse borne a child betwene to best: *two beasts*
   Sche is the cause therof iwysse *surely*
  That *verbum caro factum est.*"

  I fared me furthe yn that frythe; *traveled forth; wood*
   I mett three commely kyngis with crone; *crown*
35 I spod me furth to speke them with, *propelled myself forth*
   And on my knees I kneled done. *down*
   The ryalest of home to me con rone *most royal of them; did speak*
  And said, "We farred wele at the fest; *fared; feast*
   Fro Bethleem now ar we bone *From; bound*
40 For *verbum caro factum est.*

  "For we seo God becomun yn mannus flech *saw*
   That bote hasse broght of all oure bale, *relief has brought for; suffering*
  Awey oure synnus for to wesche. *sins; wash*
   A mey hym harburd yn hur hall; *A maid harbored him in her hall (womb)*
45   Sche socourd hym sothly yn hur sale *sustained; truly; chamber*
  And hel that hend yn hur arest. *healthy that noble one in her rested*
   Foll trewly mey sche tell that tale *Full; may*
  That *verbum caro factum est.*"

  Untyll that prences wyll we pray, *Unto; princess*
50   Als sche is bothe moder and mayd: *As*
  Sche be oure helpe, als sche wele mey, *may*
   To hyme that yn hur lappe was layde.
   To serve hyme we be prest and payd, *eager; pleased*
  And therto make we oure behest; *promise*

55	For I hard when sche sange and said,	*heard*
	"*Verbum caro factum est.*"	

29

	Als I lay upon a nith	*one night*
	I lokede upon a stronde.	*looked; land*
	I beheld a mayden brith;	*bright*
	A child sche hadde in honde.	*in [her] hands*

5	Hire loking was so loveli,	*gaze*
	Hire semblant was so suete,	*appearance; sweet*
	Of al my sorwe sikerli	*sorrow surely*
	Sche mithte my bales bete.	*might; troubles relieve*

	I wondrede of that suete with,	*about; sweet creature*
10	An to myself I sayde	*And*
	Sche hadde don mankindde unrith	*done; wrong (see note)*
	But yif sche were a mayde.	*Unless she; virgin*

	Be hire sat a sergant	*By; man (attendant)*
	That sadli seide his sawe;	*solemnly; told his story*
15	He sempte be is semblant	*seemed by his appearance*
	A man of the elde lawe.	*old law (a Jew)*

	His her was hor on hevede,	*hair; gray; head*
	His ble began to glide:	*face; burn (i.e., he blushed)*
	He herde wel wat I seyde	*what; said*
20	An bad me faire abide.	*And bade me stay*

	"Thu wondrest," he seyde, "skilfuli,	*You wonder; reasonably*
	On thing thu hast beholde,	*On what you have seen*
	An I dede so treuli	*And I did likewise*
	Til tales weren me told	*Until*

25	"Hou a womman sulde ben than	*How; should be*
	Moder an maiden thore,	*and; there*

The Nativity

An withouten wem of man *blemish*
   The child sulde ben bore. *should; born*

"Althou I unworthi be,
30   Sche is Marie, my wif; *She*
God wot sche hadde nevere child be me. *knows; by*
   I love hire as my life. *her*

"But or evere wiste I, *before; knew*
   Hire wombe began to rise —
35 I telle thee treuthe treuli,
   I not nevere in wat wyse. *I do not know how*

"I troste to hire goodnesse *trust*
   Sche wolde no thing misdo; *She would do no wrong*
I wot et wel iwisse *know it with certainty*
40   For I have founden et so, *it*

"That rathere a maiden sulde *sooner; should*
   Withouten man conceyve
Than Marie mis don wolde *would do wrong*
   An so Joseph deceyve. *deceive*

45 "The child that lith so poreli *lies so poorly (in poverty)*
   In cloutes al bewent *rags; wrapped*
An bounden so misesli, *bound (dressed) so miserably*
   Fro hevene he is isent; *From; sent*

"His fader is king of hevene
50   An so seide Gabriel
To wam that child is evene *whom*
   O Emanuel." *(see note)*

But this child that I sau than *saw then*
   An as Joseph seyde
55 I wot the child is God an man *I know*
   An is moder mayde. *his; virgin*

The Nativity

I thankid him of his lore	*him (Joseph) for his instruction*
With al myn herte mith.	*my heart's might*
That this sith I say thore	*sight I saw there*
60 Als I lay on a nyth.	
This child thanne worchipe we	
Bothe day an nith	*night*
That we moun his face se	*might; see*
In joyye that is so lith. Amen.	*Serene*

30

Ecce quod natura mutat sua iura:	*Behold that nature changes her laws*
Virgo parit pura dei filium.	*A virgin pure gives birth to the Son of God*
Beholde and see how that nature	
Chaungith here lawe: a mayden pure	
5 Shalle bere a chielde (thus seith scripture),	*bear; child; says*
Jhesus, oure savyour.	
Beholde, the flease of Gedeon	*fleece*
Wexed wete, that no dewe fel on;	*Grew wet*
Beholde, the yerde of Aaron	*rod*
10 Unmoysted bare a floure.	*Unwatered; flower*
The prophete Isay seith thus:	*Isaiah*
"A mayde shall bere a childe to us	
Whose name shall be called Jhesus,	
Oure helpe and our socour.	
15 "A yerde shall goo oute of Jesse rote	*branch*
Wherof a floure shall ascende full soote."	*truly*
This floure is Crist, oure helth and boote,	*aid*
This yerde, Mary, his boure.	*bower*
Seynt Mathew seith in the gospell,	
20 "A mayde shall bere Emanuell,	

The Nativity

That is to sey, God with us to dwell,
   That lovely paramour."   *darling*

Forsoth, to us is borne a chielde;   *Truly; child*
A sonne is yeven to us full myelde   *given*
25   Of virgyne Marie undefielde
     To cease oure grete langoure.

This is the stone cutte of the hille,
Criste borne of Marie us untille   *unto us*
Without synne in thought, dede, and wille
30   To save us fro dolour.   *from*

This chielde shall be the Prince of Peas,   *Peace*
Whose kingdome shall ever encrease,
Wherof the peas shall nevir ceas   *peace*
     But encreace day and houre.

35   Seint Anselme seith, "So Criste did pas
Thurgh Marie myelde, as his wille was,
As the sonne beame goth thurgh the glas,   *goes through*
     That mayde full of honoure."

Mary at the Foot of the Cross

31

Heir followis the houris of oure ladyis dollouris.	*hours; sadness (see note)*

Quhat dollour persit our ladyis hert	*What dolor pierced*
Quhan scho hard hir sone was tane and bund,	*When she heard; taken; bound*
Syne led to Annas that of syn had na part,	*Then; [he] who; no*
Quhair fals witnes agane him sone wer fund.[1]	

At prime · *6 a.m.*

5	At prime scho followit him to Pilotis place	*she; Pilate's*
	With sobing, siching, lik to fall in swone;	*sobbing, sighing; swoon*
	Thair the Jowis spittit in his face	*There; Jews spit*
	And fals witnes spak fast to put him doun.	*witnesses spoke*

At terce

	At terce, "Crucify him!" the Jowis can cry;	*did*
10	The quhit coit and purpour claith gaif him for scorne.[2]	*(see note)*
	Thai scurgit him, and our lady that stude by	*They scourged; stood*
	Saw him beir the croce and crownt with thorne.	*bear; cross; crowned [him]*

At sext

	At sext thai him nakit nalit on a tre;	*naked nailed; tree*
	For drink thai gaif him bitter gall.	*gave*
15	The blud droppit doun on his moder Mary,	*dropped*
	The erd trimblit, and cragis begouth to fall.	*earth trembled; rocks began*

At none

	At none he commendit his moder to Sanct Johnne,	*commended; Saint John*
	Syne with gret dolour scho saw him decese.	*Then; she; die*

---

[1] *Where false witnesses against him soon were found*

[2] *Who gave him quoits and purple cloth for scorn (see note)*

The sone tynt licht fra the sext till none.[1]

20 His passioun betuix God and ws maid peace.   *between; us made*

At ewinsang   *evensong*

Oure lady saw his syd oppinnit with a speir   *side opened; spear*

At ewinsang; syne his body thai tuk doun,   *evensong; then*

And laid him with mony salt tere   *many; tears*

In our ladyis bowum, of glore the crowne.   *bosom; glory*

At compling   *compline*

25 Our lady saw thame to graif his body beir,   *them; grave; bear*

And clois him thairin with a gret stane;   *close; therein; great stone*

To keip him the Jowis put men of weir,   *keep; Jews; war (soldiers)*

And the faith of Crist remanit in our lady allane.   *remained; alone*

O Mary, moder of mercy and of grace,

30 This houris to thi honour I refer,   *These hours*

To be my advocat in every cais   *case*

And stand with me at the bar.   *in court [at Judgment Day]*

Grant me of thi sonne to have compassioun   *from your son*

And ay be ane servand to thee,   *also be a servant*

35 And for my synnis do satisfactioun,   *sins; penance*

Syne be tane to the blis of hevin finalie.   *Then be taken; heaven finally*

32

Jesu Cristes milde moder   *Christ's*

Stud, biheld hire sone o rode   *Stood, beheld her son on cross*

That he was ipined on.   *tortured*

The sone heng, the moder stud   *son hung; stood*

5 And biheld hire childes blud,   *her; blood*

Wu it of hise wundes ran.   *How it from his wounds*

Tho he starf that king is of lif,   *When; died who; life*

Dreriere nas neverre no wif   *More sorrowful; woman*

Than thu were, levedi, tho.   *you were, lady, then*

---

[1] *The sun darkened its light from the sixth hour to the ninth hour*

Mary at the Foot of the Cross

10	The brithe day went into nith;	*bright; night*
	Tho Jhesu Crist, thin herte lith,	*Then; your heart's light*
	Was iqueint with pine and wo.	*quenched; pain; woe*
	Thi life drei ful harde stundes	*Your life endured; difficult hours*
	Tho thu seye hise bludi wundes	*When you saw his bloody wounds*
15	And his bodi o rode don.	*on the cross mounted*
	Hise wundes sore and smerte	*wounds; smarting*
	Stungen thureu and thurw thi herte	*Stung through and through*
	As te bihichte Simeon.	*[to] you promised*
	Nu his heved with blud bisprunken,	*head; blood besprinkled*
20	Nu his side with spere istungen	*spear pierced*
	Thu bihelde, levedi fre.	
	Nu his hondes sprad o rode,	*hands spread on cross*
	Nu hise fet washen wit blode	*washed with blood*
	An inaillet to the tre.	*And nailed; tree (cross)*
25	Nu his bodi with scurges beten,	*scourges beaten*
	And his blud so wide hutleten	*blood; let out*
	Maden the thin herte sor;	*Made your heart sore*
	Warso thu castest thin eyen	*Wherever you cast your eyes*
	Pine strong thu soie im dreien;	*Pain; you saw him suffer*
30	Ne mithte noman tholie mor.	*Nor might anyone endure more*
	Nu is time that thu yielde	*Now*
	Kende that thu im witheld.	*Child; [from] them withheld*
	Tho thi child was of thee born;	*Then*
	Nu he hoschet wit goulinge	*Now they demand with shouting*
35	That thu im in thi chiltinge	*He whom you in your child-care*
	Al withelde thar biforn.	*withheld from them before*
	Nu thu fondest, moder milde,	*Now; find*
	Wat wyman drith with hir childe,	*What; suffer; their children*
	Thei thu clene maiden be.	*Though you are a pure virgin*
40	Nu thes thiolden arde and dere	*you have suffered hard; dearly*
	The pine werof thu were	*pain you suffered*
	Ine ti chilthing quite and fre.	*In giving birth, free and clear (see note)*

	Sone after the nith of sorwen	*Soon; night of sorrow*
	Sprong the lith of edi morwen;	*Sprang; light of blessed morning (Easter)*
45	Ine thin herte, suete may,	*In your; sweet maiden*
	Thi sorwen wende al to blisse,	*sorrows turned*
	Tho thi sone al mid iwisse	*When; with complete certainty*
	Aros hupon the tridde day.	*Arose upon; third*
	Welle wat thu were blithe	*Indeed you were joyful*
50	Tho aros fram deth to live,	*When [he] arose from death*
	Thur the hole ston he glod.	*Through; whole [tomb]stone (see note); glided*
	Al so he was of the boren;	*Just as; of you born*
	Bothen after and biforen,	*Both*
	Hol bilof thi maidenhod.	*Whole remained your virginity*
55	Neue blisse he us broute	*New bliss*
	That mankin so dere boute	*Who mankind so dearly bought*
	And for us gaf is dere lif.	*gave his dear life*
	Glade and blithe thu us make,	*Glad; joyful*
	For thi suete sones sake,	
60	Edi maiden, blisful wif.	*Blessed; woman*
	Quen of evene, for thi blisse	*Queen; heaven*
	Lithe al hure soriness	*Lighten all our sorrow*
	And went hur yvel al in to gud.	*turn our evil into good*
	Bring hus, moder, to thi sone,	*us*
65	Mak hus evre with im wone	*Make us ever; him dwell*
	That hus boute wit his blud.	*us bought with; blood*
	Amen.	

33

	"Stond wel, Moder, under rode,	*Stand; cross*
	Bihold thi child wyth glade mode;	*glad spirit*
	Blythe, Moder, mittu ben."	*Happy; might you be*
	"Sune, quu may blithe stonden?	*Son, who*
5	Hi se thin feet, hi se thin honden	*I see your feet, I see your hands*
	Nayled to the harde tre."	*tree (cross)*

Mary at the Foot of the Cross

"Moder, do wey thi wepinge: *cease your weeping*
Hi thole this ded for mannes thinge;   *I suffer death; mankind's sake*
For owen gilte tholi non."   *my own guilt suffer I none*
10   "Sune, hi fele the dede stunde;   *I sense; time of death*
The swerd is at min herte grunde,   *my heart ground*
That me byhytte Symeon."   *promised*

"Moder, reu upon thi bern: *have pity on your child*
Thu wasse awey tho blodi teren,   *wash; those bloody tears*
15   It don me werse than mi ded."   *pains me worse; my death*
"Sune, hu mitti teres wernen?   *how may I stop my tears*
Hy se tho blodi flodes hernen   *I see these bloody streams run*
Huth of thin herte to min fet."   *Out; feet*

"Moder, ny y may thee seyn,   *now I say to you*
20   Bettere is that ic one deye   *I alone die*
Than al mankyn to helle go."
"Sune, y se thi bodi swngen,   *hanging (swung)*
Thi brest, thin hond, thi fot thur-stungen   *breast; hand; foot pierced*
No selli thou me be wo."   *wonder I am woeful*

25   "Moder, if y dar thee tellen,   *dare tell you*
Yif y ne deye, thu gost to helle;   *If I do not die, you go to hell*
Hi thole this ded for thine sake."   *I suffer this death*
"Sune, thu best me so minde.   *Son, you are for me such a concern*
With me nout; it is mi kinde   *Blame; not; my nature*
30   That y for thee sorye make."   *I make sorrow for you*

"Moder, merci, let me deyen,   *die*
For Adam ut of helle beyn   *To redeem Adam from hell*
And al mankin that is forloren."   *all mankind; lost*
"Sune, wat sal me to rede?   *what will prepare me*
35   Thi pine pined me to dede;   *Your suffering pains me to death*
Let me deyn thee biforen."   *die before you*

"Moder, mitarst thi mith leren   *first you might learn*
Wat pine tholen that childre beren,   *What suffering they endure who bear children*
Wat sorwe haven that child forgon."   *sorrow they have; lose*
40   "Sune, y wot y kan thee tellen,   *I know I can tell you*

Bute it be the pine of helle, *Unless it be*
More sorwe ne woth y non." *More sorrow know I none*

"Moder, reu of moder kare, *pity of motherly sorrow*
Nu thu wost of moder fare, *Now you know; mother's experience*
45 Thou thu be clene mayden man." *Though you are a virgin*
"Sune, help alle at nede, *all in need*
Alle tho that to me greden — *they who to me cry out*
Mayden, wyf, and fol wyman." *unchaste woman*

"Moder, y may no lenger duellen; *longer dwell*
50 The time is cumen y fare to helle, *The time has come [that] I go to hell*
The thridde day y rise upon." *third*
"Sune, y wyle withe funden. *I want to go with you*
Y deye ywis of thine wnden; *I die, I know, of your wounds*
So reuful ded was nevere non." *sorrowful [a] death*

55 When he ros than fel thi sorwe: *ended your sorrow*
The blisse sprong the thridde morewe *sprang; third day*
Wen blithe, Moder, wer thu tho. *When joyful, Mother, were you then*
Moder, for that ilke blisse *same bliss*
Bisech ure God, ure sinnes lesse, *Beseech our God, our sins forgive*
60 Thu be hure chel ayen hure fo. *our shield against; foe*

Blisced be thu, quen of hevene,
Bring us ut of helle levene *out of hell's flame*
Thurth thi dere sunes mith. *Through; dear son's might*
Moder, for that hithe blode *comforting(?) blood*
65 That he sadde upon the rode *shed; cross*
Led us into hevene lith. Amen. *heaven's light*

34

Suete sone, reu on me, and brest out of thi bondis: *Sweet son, have pity; burst*
For nou me thinket that I se thoru bothen thin hondes *see through; hands*
Nailes dreven into the tre; so reufuliche thu honges. *driven; ruefully you hang*
Nu is betre that I fle and lete alle these londis. *better; flee; leave; lands*

5   Suete sone, thi faire face droppet al on blode,   *drips; blood*
    And thi bodi dounward is bounden to the rode;   *bound; cross*
    Hou may thi modris herte tholen so suete a fode,   *heart suffer; child*
    That blissed was of alle born, and best of alle gode?   *[most] blessed; good*

    Suete sone, reu on me, and bring me out of this live,   *life*
10   For me thinket that I se thi deth, it neyhit suithe.   *approaches swiftly*
    Thi fete ben nailed to the tre; nou may I no more thrive,   *feet*
    For al this werld withouten thee ne sal me maken blithe.   *world; never shall; happy*

35

    The angell sayde to thee that the fruyt off thi body sulde be blyssyde;
    Ande now, in the dome of the Jewys, Crist es a-cursede.   *court; is cursed*
    At hys burth thu harde angels syngynge;   *heard*
    Ande now thow seys hys frendis wepynge.   *see; friends weeping*
5   At hys burthe kyngis and schiperdys dyd hym omage and wyrschyppe;   *homage*
    And now al maner of men don hym despyte and schendschyppe.   *injury; harm*
    At hys burth thow wantyd womanes wo;   *lacked woman's woe (see note)*
    Bot, as thow wel fellys, now it ys noght so.   *you well feel; is not*
    Some tyme thou hadest cause for to synge "lullay,"
10   Bot now thi songh ys all off wylaway.   *song; "wellaway" (a cry of lament)*
    Somtym thou fed hym wyth thi sweet mylk to hys esse;   *his ease*
    Ande now the Jewys fedyng hyme wyt bitter gall to his dysesse.   *with; discomfort*
    Som tyme thou founde hym in the mydyl off the doctors in the temple;   *midst of*
    Ande now thou fyndyst hyme hangynge in the mydyl of the Jewes on the krosse.

36

    "A Son! tak hede to me whas sone thou was,   *Ah; take heed; whose*
    And set me uppe wyt thee on i crosse.   *with you upon the*
    Me her to leve, and thee thus hense go,   *Me here to leave; hence*
    Yt is to me gret kare and wo.   *It*
5   Stynt now, Son, to be harde to thi moder,   *Cease; harsh*
    Thou that ever was god to all other."   *good*

"Stynt now, Moder, and wepe no more;   *Stop; weep*

Thi sorow and thi dyssesse grevysse me fule sore.   *discomfort grieves*

Thou knowyse that in the I tok mannys kynde,   *took human nature*

10   In hyt for mannys syne to be the pynde.   *the afflicted [one]*

Be now glade, Moder, and have in thoghte   *thought*

That mannes hel is fondyn forwake, that I have soght. *mankind's salvation is found*

Thow salt noght now kare what thow salt done;   *shall not worry about*

Lo! Jone, thi kosyne, sall be thi sone."   *John; kinsman, shall*

37

"Womman, Jon I take to thee   *John; give to you*

Instede of me thi sone to be."

Allas, wo sal myn herte slaken?   *who; heart relieve*

To Jon I am towarde taken;

5   Mi blisful sone me hat forwaken,   *exhausted by vigilance (see note)*

And I have no mo.   *more*

Wel may I mone and murning maken,   *moan; mourning*

And wepen til myn eyne aken.   *eyes ache*

For wane of wele my wo is waken, *waning of happiness; woe; awakened*

10   Was nevere wif so wo.   *woman; woeful*

38

Nou goth sonne under wod;   *sun; wood*

Me reweth, Marie, thi faire rode.   *I have pity; [upon] your; face*

Nou goth sonne under tre;   *tree*

Me reweth, Marie, thi sone and thee.   *son*

39

Sodenly afraide, half waking, half slepyng,

And gretly dismayde, a wooman sate weepyng —   *dismayed; sat*

91

Mary at the Foot of the Cross

With favoure in hir face ferr passyng my reason,   *beauty; far*

And of hir sore weepyng this was the enchesone: *reason*

5   Hir soon in hir lap lay, she seid, slayne by treason.   *son*

Yif wepyng myght ripe bee, it seemyd than in season.   *be; then*

"Jhesu," so she sobbid,   *sobbed*

So hir soon was bobbid   *As; son; beaten/mocked*

And of his lif robbid,   *robbed*

10   Saying thies wordis as I say thee: *these words*

"Who cannot wepe come lerne at me."   *learn from*

I said I cowd not wepe, I was so harde-hartid.   *could; hard-hearted*

Shee answerd me with wordys shortly that smarted:

"Lo, nature shall move thee, thou must be converted;

15   Thyne owne Fader this nyght is deed," lo thus she thwarted.   *dead; argued*

"So my soon is bobbid   *son; cheated/derided*

And of his lif robbid."

Forsooth than I sobbid,   *Truly; sobbed*

Veryfying the wordis she seid to me.

20   "Who cannot wepe may lerne at thee."

"Now breke, hert, I thee pray; this cors lith so rulye,   *break, heart; corpse; pitifully*

So betyn, so wowndid, entreted so Jewlye.   *beaten; wounded, treated by Jews*

What wight may me behold and wepe nat? Noon truly,   *person; weep not? None*

To see my deed dere soone lygh bleedyng, lo, this newlye."   *dead dear son lie*

25   Ever stil she sobbid,

So hire soon was bobbid

And of his lif robbid,

Newyng the wordis as I say thee: *Renewing*

"Who cannot wepe com lerne at me."

30   On me she caste hire ey, said, "See, mane, thy brothir."   *eye; man*

She kissid hym and said, "Swete, am I not thy moder?"

In sownyng she fill there, it wolde be non othir;   *swooning; fell; no other*

I not which more deedly, the toone or the tothir.   *know not; deathlike; one; other*

Yit she revived and sobbid,

35   So hire soon was bobbid

And of his lif robbid;

"Who cannot wepe," this was the laye.   *song*

And with that word she vanysht away.

Mary at the Foot of the Cross

40

Thou synfull man of resoun that walkest here up and downe,

Cast thy respeccyoun one my mortall countenaunce.   *attention on*

Se my blody terys fro my herte roote rebowne,   *See; tears; heart's root spring*

My dysmayd body chased from all plesaunce,   *pleasure*

5   Perysshed wyth the swerd moste dedly of vengaunce.   *sword*

Loke one my sorofull chere and have therof pytee,   *Look on; countenance; pity*

Bewailynge my woo and payne, and lerne to wepe wyth me.   *woe*

Yf thu can not wepe for my perplexed hevynesse,

Yet wepe for my dere sone, which one my lap lieth ded   *who on; lies dead*

10   Wyth woundis innumerable, for thy wyckednesse,   *wounds*

Made redempcyoun wyth hys blood, spared not hys manhed.   *manhood (life)*

Then the love of hym and mornynge of my maydenhed   *mourning*

Schuld chaunge thyne herte, and thu lyst behold and see   *change; you desire to*

Hys deth and my sorow, and lerne to wepe wyth me.

15   Thyne herte so indurat is that thu cane not wepe   *hard; can*

For my sonnes deth, ne for my lamentacyoun?   *nor*

Than wepe for thy synnes, when thu wakest of thy slepe   *Then*

And remembre hys kyndnes, hys payne, hys passioun,

And fere not to call to me for supportacyoun.   *fear; support*

20   I am thy frend unfeyned and ever have be;   *unfeigned; been*

Love my sone, kepe well hys lawes, and come dwell wyth me.

41

Why have ye no reuthe on my child?   *pity*

Have reuthe on me, ful of murning,   *mourning*

Taket doun on rode my derworthi child,   *Take down from the cross; precious*

Or prek me on rode with my derling.   *crucify; cross; beloved*

5   More pine ne may me ben don   *More pain may not be inflicted on me*

Than laten me liven in sorwe and schame;   *[to] let me live; sorrow; shame*

Als love me bindet to my sone,   *As; binds me*

So lat us deyyen bothen i-same.   *let; alike*

42

Of alle women that ever were borne
That berys childur, abyde and se   *Who bear children, stay and see*
How my son liggus me beforne   *lies before me*
Upon my kne, takyn fro tre.   *knee; from [the] cross*
5   Your childur ye dawnse upon your kne   *children; dandle; knee*
With laghyng, kyssyng, and mery chere: *cheer*
Behold my childe, beholde now me,
For now liggus ded my dere son, dere.   *lies dead; dear*

O woman, woman, wel is thee,   *well are you*
10   Thy childis cap thu dose upon;   *child's; you put on*
Thu pykys his here, beholdys his ble;   *You comb his hair; appearance*
Thu wost not wele when thu hast done.   *You do not know (appreciate)*
But ever alas I make my mone   *lament*
To se my sonnys hed as hit is here: *see; son's head; it*
15   I pyke owt thornys be on and on   *pick out thorns one by one*
For now liggus ded my dere son, dere.

O woman, a chaplet choysyn thu has   *you have chosen a garland*
Thy childe to were, hit dose thee gret likyng   *wear, it pleases you greatly*
Thu pynnes hit on with gret solas;   *great satisfaction*
20   And I sitte with my son sore wepyng.
His chaplet is thornys sore prickyng;   *thorns sorely pricking*
His mouth I kys with a carfull chere.   *kiss; careful (woeful) face*
I sitte wepyng, and thu syngyng,
For now liggus ded my dere son, dere.

25   O woman, loke to me agayne   *look; again*
That playes and kisses your childur pappys   *Who; child's breast*
To se my son I have gret payne,
In his brest so gret gap is,   *hole (wound)*
And on his body so mony swappys.   *slashes*
30   With blody lippys I kis hym here;   *lips*
Alas, full hard me thynk me happys,   *my circumstances*
For now liggus ded my dere son, dere.

O woman, thu takis thi childe be the hand   *you take; by*

And seis, "My son, gif me a stroke!"   *give me a pat (see note)*

35   My sonnys handis ar sore bledand,

To loke on hym me list not layke.   *I do not like*

His handis he suffyrd for thi sake   *hands; suffered (permitted)*

Thus to be boryd with nayle and speyre;   *pierced; nail and spear*

When thu makes myrth, gret sorow I make,

40   For now liggus ded my dere son, dere.

Beholde, women, when that ye play

And hase your childur on knees daunsand: *bounce your children on your knees*

Ye fele ther fete, so fete are thay,   *touch; feet; comely*

And to your sight ful wel likand.   *pleasing*

45   But the most fyngur of any hande   *largest finger*

Thorow my sonnys fete I may put here   *Through; feet*

And pulle hit out sore bledand,   *it; sorely bleeding (i.e., the feet)*

For now liggus ded my dere son, dere.

Therfor, women, be town and strete,   *by town and way*

50   Your childur handis when ye beholde,   *When you behold your children's hands*

Theyr brest, theire body and theire fete   *breast; feet*

Then gode hit were on my son thynk ye wolde,[1]

How care has made my hert full colde,   *sorrow; heart*

To se my son, with nayle and speyre,   *see; nail and spear*

55   With scourge and thornys manyfolde,   *scourge; many thorns*

Woundit and ded, my dere son, dere.   *Wounded and dead*

Thu hase thi son full holl and sounde,   *You have your son whole and sound*

And myn is ded upon my kne;   *dead; knee*

Thy childe is lawse, and myn is bonde,   *free; bound*

60   Thy childe is an life and myn ded is he;   *alive; mine is dead*

Whi was this oght but for thee?   *Why did this happen but for you*

For my childe trespast never here.   *sinned*

Me thynk ye be holdyne to wepe with me   *are obligated; weep*

For now liggus ded my dere son, dere.

---

[1] *You would do well to think about my son*

65   Wepe with me, both man and wyfe:

        My childe is youres and lovys yow wele.   *yours; loves you well*

        If your childe had lost his life,

        Ye wolde wepe at every mele,   *occasion*

        But for my sone wepe ye never a del.   *not a bit*

70   If ye luf youres, myne has no pere;   *you love yours, mine has no equal*

        He sendis youris both hap and hele,   *sends yours; fortune; salvation*

        And for yow dyed my dere son, dere.   *you died*

        Now alle wymmen that has your wytte   *wit (mind)*

        And sees my childe on my knees ded,

75   Wepe not for yours, but wepe for hit,   *it (my child, i.e., Jesus)*

        And ye shall have ful mycull mede.   *great reward*

        He wolde ageyne for your luf blede   *bleed for love of you*

        Rather or that ye damned were.   *Rather than letting you be damned*

        I pray yow alle, to hym take hede,   *think of him*

80   For now liggus ded my dere son, dere.

        Fare wel, woman, I may no more

        For drede of deth reherse his payne.   *fear of dying; suffering*

        Ye may lagh when ye list, and I wepe sore,   *laugh when you please*

        That may ye se and ye loke to me agayne.   *may you see if you look to me*

85   To luf my son and ye be fayne,   *If you desire to love my son*

        I wille luff yours with hert entere,   *I will love yours with my whole heart*

        And he shall brynge your childur and yow sertayne   *you certainly*

        To blisse wher is my dere son, dere.

          Explicit fabula.   *End of story*

43

        O litel whyle lesteneth to me   *A; listen*

        Ententyfly, so have ye blys.   *Attentively; bliss*

        Gode ensaumple here schul ye,   *Good example hear you shall*

        Of noble mater wrought it is,   *matter*

5   How Mary spak to the Rode tre   *spoke; Rood tree (Cross)*

        Whan her sone was in anguys.   *son; anguish*

        The Cros answeryd that lady fre   *noble*

        Ful myldely, seiye clerkys wys,   *say wise clerks*

	That this tale have made couthe;	*well-known*
10	Thei have expouned it by sight,	*interpreted (see note)*
	A good ensaumple and a bryght.	*example; moral [one]*
	But apocrifum thei holde it right,	*fiction; rightly*
	For tre spak nevere with mouthe.	*tree spoke; mouth*

	Oure lady fre	*noble*
15	To the Rode tre	*Rood tree (Cross)*
	Sche made her mone	*lament*
	And seyde, "On thee	
	Is fruyt of me	*fruit*
	Full wo-bygone;	*woebegone*
20	With blody ble	*appearance*
	My fruyt I gan see	*fruit (child) I saw*
	Among hys fone.	*foes*
	Of sorewe I see	*In sorrow*
	Hys veynes fle	*veins flayed*
25	Fro blody bone.	*From*
	Tre, thou dost no treuthe	*do nothing true*
	On pilory my fruyt to pynne;	*pin*
	He hath no spot of Adam synne.	*Adam's*
	Flessche and veynes fle atwynne,	*Flesh and veins flayed both in two*
30	Wherfore I rede of reuthe.	*urge pity*

	"Cros, thi bondes schul be blamed:	*your bonds shall*
	My gode fruyt thou hast bigyled,	*beguiled*
	The fruytes moder was never famed,	*defamed*
	My wombe is faire, founde unfyled.	*undefiled*
35	Child, why art thou noght aschamed	*ashamed*
	On pilory to be ipyled,	*fastened*
	As grete thevys that were gramed,	*thieves; punished*
	That dyeden thorough her werkis wylde?	*died for their works wild*
	Blode from hede is hayled;	*drawn*
40	All to-fowled is my faire fruyte,	*befouled*
	That never dyd treget ne truyte	*trickery nor wrong*
	With thevys that love ryot unrighte.	*thieves; unjust riot*
	Why schal my sone be nayled?	

"Thee grete thevys galowes were greyd,   *[For] you great thieves' gallows; built*
45 That evere to robbe ronnen ryfe;   *run in great numbers*
Why schal my sone theron be leyde?
He noyyed never man ne wyfe.   *injured; nor*
A drynk of deep, sothely seyde,   *deep drink, truly said*
Cros, thou gevys the Lord of lyfe;   *you give*
50 Hys veynes breke with thi breyde,   *break; assault (see note)*
My fruyte stont in stroke and stryfe.   *stands; buffetting; strife*
The faire fruyte of my flessche,
My leve childe, withoute lak,   *beloved; fault*
For Adam Goddis biddyng brak,   *Because Adam broke God's command*
55 The blood ran on my briddes bak,   *bird's back (see note)*
Droppynge as dewe on ryssche.   *dew; rushes*

"The jugement have thei joyned   *imposed (enjoined upon you)*
To bere fooles full of synne;   *bear criminals*
Yet scholde my sone fro thee be soyned   *excused*
60 And never hys blood on thee rynne.   *run on you*
But now is truthe with tresoun twyned, *truth; treason intertwined*
With a theef to henge fer in fenne.   *thief; far out; fen*
With fele nayles hys feet be pyned.   *many; pinned*
A careful modir men may me kenne;   *sorrowful; know*
65 In balys I am bounde.   *suffering*
The brid that was of a mayde borne   *bird*
On this tree is all fortorne: *torn apart*
A broche torow hys breest was borne;   *spear through; breast*
Hys hert now hath a wounde.

70 "Tre, thou art loked by lawe   *ordained*
That a theefe and a traytour on thee schal deye: *traitor on you shall die*
Now is truthe with tresoun drawe,   *drawn*
Vertu is falle by vicys weye.   *fallen; vicious means*
Love and truthe and sothefast sawe   *truthful speech*
75 On a tre traytours do teye;   *tie traitors to a tree*
Now is vertue with vyces slawe.   *virtues; vices slain*
Of all vertues Cryst is keye;   *key*
Vertue is swetter than spyces.   *sweeter*
In foote and honde he bereth blody prykke,   *bears; wounds*
80 The heed is full of thornes thikke,

Mary at the Foot of the Cross

The goode hangeth among the wikke: *wicked*
Vertue thus deieth with vyces. *dies*

"Cros, unkynde thou schalt be kyd; *you shall be known*
My sonys stepmoder I thee calle. *son's*
85 My bridde was borne with beeste on bedde, *beasts*
And by my fleissche my fruyt gan falle, *flesh; was born*
And with my breestys my brid I fedde. *breasts; bird; fed*
Cros, thou gyvest hym eysell and galle. *vinegar*
My white rose rede is spred, *red [with blood]*
90 That floryssched was in fodders stalle. *bloomed; barn*
Feet and faire handes
That now be croysed, I kissed hem ofte, *crucified; them often*
I lulled hem and leyde hem softe; *sang lullabies to; folded them softly*
And thou, Cros, haldes hym highe alofte, *holds him*
95 Bounde in blody bandes.

"My love I lulled uppe in hys leir, *bed*
With cradel bande I gan hym bynde; *did bind him*
Cros, he stiketh uppon thi steir, *is nailed; frame*
Naked in the wylde wynde. *wild wind*
100 Fowles formen her nest in the eyr, *Birds make their nests; aerie*
Foxes in den rest thei fynde, *dens find rest*
But Goddys Sone and hevenys eir, *God's Son; heaven's heir*
Hys hede holdeth on thornes tynde; *Holds his head; sharp (tined)*
Of moornyng I may mynne. *For mourning; be remembered*
105 My sones hed hath reste none, *head has no rest[ing place]*
But leneth on the schuldre bone. *leans; your shoulder*
The thornes thorow the panne is gone: *through; brain*
Thys woo I wyte synne. *know [to be] sin*

"Cros, to sle hym is thi sleithe; *kill; trick*
110 My blody brid thou berest for blysse. *with joy*
Cros, thou holdest hym highe on heithe; *height*
Hys faire feet I may not kysse.
My mouthe I putte, my swere I strecche, *neck I stretch*
Hys feet to kys:
115 The Jewes fro the Cros me kecche, *from; drive*
And on me make her mowe amys, *at; their taunts wicked*

99

Mary at the Foot of the Cross

	Her game and her gawdes;	*Their jests; devices*
	The Jewes wrought on me wo.	*woe*
	Cros, I fynde thou art my fo;	*foe*
120	My brid thou berist beten blo	*bear; blue*
	Among thes folys frawdys."	*fools dishonest*
	Crystys Cros than gaf answere,	*Christ's; gave*
	"Lady, to thee I owe honour.	
	Thi bryght palme now I bere;	*(see note)*
125	My schynyng scheweth of thi flour,	*beauty shows off (manifests)*
	Thy trye fruyt I to-tere.	*true (precious); rend*
	Thi fruyt me florysschith in blood colour	*adorns me*
	The worlde to wynne, as thou mayst here:	*may hear*
	This blossom blomed in thi bour	*bloomed; bower (womb)*
130	Not all for thee alone,	*Not all for you alone*
	But forto wynne all this werd,	*to redeem; world*
	That waltereth under the develes swerd.	*welters; devil's sword*
	Thorowe foote and honde God lete hym gerd	*Through; hand; be pinned*
	To amende mannys mone.	*To amend; lament*
135	"Adam dyd full grete harmes;	*did; harm*
	He bote a fruyt under a bowe.	*bit; branch*
	Therfore thi fruit spred hys armes	*your fruit (Jesus)*
	On tre that is tighed with tyndes towe.	*tree; tied; two spikes*
	Hys body is smyte ny the tharmes,	*smitten near the intestines*
140	He swelt with a swemely swow,	*sweats (bleeds); swaying swoon*
	Hys breest is bored with deethis armes,	*pierced; deadly weapons*
	And with hys deeth fro deeth us drowe,	*death from death us drew*
	And all hys goode freendys.	*friends*
	As Isayas spak in prophecye,	*Isaiah*
145	He seyde this sone, Seynt Marye,	*son, Saint*
	Hys dethe slowe dethe in Calvarye	*death slew death*
	And leveth withoute endys.	*cleanses*
	"Lady, love dothe thee alegge	*causes you [to] allege*
	Fruite prikkyd with sperys orde.	*Spear's point*
150	I Cros, withoute knyves egge,	*knife's edge*
	I kerve fruit beest of horde.	*cut; best of the lot*
	All is rede, ribbe and rigge,	*red; rib and back (i.e., completely)*

The bak bledeth agens the borde; *back bleeds against; board*
I am a pyler and bere a brigge. *pillar; bear a bridge*
155 God is the weye, witnesse one worde: *way*
God seith he is sothefast weye. *says; true way*
Many folk slode to hell slider; *slid; slipperily*
To hevene noman cowde thider, *no one could go*
Til God deighed and taught whider *died; where*
160 Men drawe whan thei deye. *go when*

"And Moyses fourmed hys figour, *Moses; figure*
A whyte lambe, and noon other beest; *no; beast*
He sacred so oure savyour *venerated as*
To be mete of myghtes meest. *food; most*
165 And chosen cheef in honour,
I bare fleissche to folkys feest, *flesh (meat, food); mankind's feast*
Jesu Cryst oure creatour;
Hys flessche fedeth leste and mest, *feeds least and most*
Rosted agens the sonne. *Roasted (scorched/tortured); sun*
170 On me lay the lambe of love; *lamb*
I was plater, hys body above, *platter*
Whan flessche and veynes all toclove, *When; severed*
With blood I was bironne. *covered*

"Yit Moyses this resoun rad, *Yet; counsel gave*
175 'Ete youre lambe with soure vergeous'; *Eat; bitter herbs (paschal lamb)*
Sowre saws make the sowle glad, *Sour sauces; soul*
Sorowe for synnes oures. *Sorrow for our sins*
That vergeous maketh the fende adrad, *herb; fiend dread*
And fer fleth fro Goddis spous. *far flees from God's spouse*
180 And bere a staaf and stonde sadde *bear; staff; solemnly*
Whan flessche thee fedith in Goddis hows. *you eat flesh; God's house*
This staf is Crystis crouche: *cross*
Stonde thou styf by this stake *Stand; stiffly*
Whan the fonge yowre fleissche in take; *When you receive the host*
185 Than may the devyll no maystryes make *power have*
Youre sowles to touche. *souls*

"Whan pardoun is schewed with a scryne, *betokened by a shrine (see note)*
With boke on bord with nayles smyte, *sign; board; driven*

	With rede lettres wryten blyne.	*written by line*
190	Blewe and blak among me pyte,	*Blue; upon me written (depicted)*
	My Lorde I likne to that signe:	*liken*
	The body was bored and on borde bete,	*pierced; board beaten*
	In bright blode oure boke gan schyne.	*book did shine*
	How woo he was no wight may wyte,	*woeful; person; know*
195	Ne rede in hys rode	*read; face (see note)*
	Youre pardoun boke fro top to too.	*book from; toe*
	Wryten it was full wonder woo,	*Written; [with] wondrous woe*
	Rede woundes and strokes bloo:	*Red/Read wounds; blows blue*
	Your boke was bounde in blode.	*book; bound*

200	"In holy write this tale I herde,	*writings; heard*
	How riche giftis God us gaf;	*gifts; gave*
	God seith hymself a good scheperde,	*calls*
	And every herde byhoveth a staf.	*shepherd needs; staff*
	The Cros I kalle the heerdys yerde;	*call; shepherd's staff*
205	Therwith the devyl a dent he gaf.	*he gave the devil a blow*
	With that yerd the wolfe he werid,	*defended against*
	With dyntes drofe hym all to draf."	*blows drove; chaff*
	The Cros this tale tolde,	
	How he was the staf in herdis hande,	*shepherd's*
210	Whan scheep borsten oute of bande;	*burst; flock*
	The wolfe he wered oute of lande,	*drove*
	That devouride Crystis folde.	*Christ's [sheep]fold*
	Oure ladye seyde, "Cros, of thi werk	*your work*
	Wonder naght, thei I be wrothe.	*Doubt not, though; angry*
215	Thus seyde Poule, Crystes clerk,	*St. Paul*
	To the fikell Jewes, withoute othe,	*fickle; oath*
	Jewes stone-hard, with synnes merke,	*sin's mark*
	Thei bete a lambe withoute lothe,	*beat; fault*
	Softer than water under serk,	*shirt*
220	Milk or mede melled bothe:	*mead blended*
	The Jewes were the hard stonys.	*stones*
	Softer than water or mylk lycour	*liquid*
	Or dew that lithe on lily flour	*lies; flower*
	Was Cristes body in blode colour —	*bloody hue*
225	The Jewes brisseden hys bonys.	*bruised; bones*

Mary at the Foot of the Cross

	"Sithe mannys sone was so nedy	*Since; compelled*
	To be lad as a lamb so mylde,	*led*
	Why were gylours so gredy	*jailors; greedy*
	To fowle so my faire chylde?	*defile*
230	And Cros, why were thou so redy	
	My fruite to foule fer in felde?"	*far off in a field*
	The Cros seyde, "To make the devyll dredy,	*fearful*
	God schope me schelde, schame to schelde.[1]	
	Sithe lombe of love dyede	*[the] lamb; died*
235	And on me yelde hys goost with voys	*yielded his spirit with his voice (see note)*
	Men chose me a relyk choys,	*choice relic*
	The signe of Jesu Crystis Croys.	*Christ's Cross*
	Ther dar no devyl abyde.	
	"Many folk I defende fro her foos,"	*from their foes*
240	Cristes Cros this sawe he syde,	*saying; spoke*
	"Hevene gate was keithed clos	*Heaven's gate; locked closed*
	Til lambe of love now he deyede.	
	It is write in tixt and glos,	*written; text; gloss*
	For Cristis deeth prophetes preyde,	*death prophets prayed*
245	Till lambe of love deyed and roos.	*died and rose*
	In hell pyne many folk was teyde;	*pain; tied*
	In the houre of highest noone	*high noon*
	The lambe of love seide his thought:	
	'All is fulfilled that well was wrought;	
250	Man is oute of bondys brought,	*bondage brought*
	And hevene dorys undone.'	*doors opened*
	"And I was Cros, and kepte that gifte	
	That geve was of Fadres graunt;	*given; Father's consent*
	I was loked I schulde uplifte	*ordained*
255	Goddis Sone and maydenes faunt.	*maiden's babe*
	Noman had schelde of scrifte:	*No one; shield; confession (see note)*
	The devyll stode as lyoun raumpaunt,	*lion rampant (see note)*
	Many folk he keighte to hell clifte,	*took; chasm*
	Till the dyntes of the Cros gan hym adaunte.	*blows; did him daunt*
260	My dede is founde and boked,	*judged and recorded*
	All the werke that I have wroughte,	

---

[1] *God made (shaped) me as a shield, to shield from shame*

Mary at the Foot of the Cross

It was in the Fadres forthoughte.
Lovely lady, lak me noughte,   *doubt me not*
I dyd as I was loked.   *did; ordained*

265 "In water and blood cristenyng was wrought,   *baptism*
     Holy writ witnessith it well;   *writing (the Bible)*
     And in the well of worthi thought,
     Man is cristened to soule hele.   *for soul's healing*
     The blood that all the world hath bought,
270 A digne cristenyng he gan me dele.   *noble; did me give*
     Cryst in cristenynge forgat me nought,
     Hys fressche blood whan I gan fele,   *did feel*
     Mayde, modir, and wyve: *woman*
     Crystis blood gaf me bapteme;   *baptized me*
275 Bystreke I was with rede streme   *Bestreaked; red stream*
     Whan Jesu bled upon a beme   *beam*
     Of cipresse and olyve.   *cypress; olive*

     "Jesu seyde to Nichodemus,   *(see note)*
     But a barn be twies born,   *Unless a man is born twice*
280 Whan domesday schal blowe his bemys,   *Judgment Day; trumpets*
     He schulde lye as man lorn: *lie; lost*
     First bore of wombe where rewthe remys,   *born; sorrow cries out*
     Sith with font synne is schorn.   *Then; [baptismal] font [where]; shorn*
     And I was Cros to mannys quemys;   *for mankind's benefit*
285 I baar the fruyt thou bere aforn   *bore; bore before*
     For thi beryng alone;   *bearing*
     But I had born hym efte,   *Unless; after*
     Fro riche rest man had be refte,   *From; deprived*
     And in a lore logge lefte,   *lost home*
290 Ay, to grucche and grone.   *moan and groan*

     "Thou were crowned hevene queen
     For the birthen that thou bere;   *child; bore*
     Thi garlond is of gracious greene,   *garland*
     Of hell emperesse and hevene empere.   *empress; heaven's empire*
295 I am the relyk that schyneth schene;   *shines bright*
     Men wolde wyte where I were.   *will know where I was*
     At the pleyn parlement I schal been,   *final judgment; shall be*

104

At domesday prestly to pere — *eagerly; appear*
Whan God schal seye right there,
300 'Trewly on thee, Rode tre, — *Truly*
Man, I dyed for love of thee;
Man, what hast thou do for me — *done*
To be my frendly fere?' — *companion*

"At parlement I wil put pleynyng, — *make complaint*
305 How maydenes sone on me gan sterve, — *did die*
Spere and spounge and hard naylyng, — *sponge*
The hard hede the helme gan kerve; — *skull; helmet (crown of thorns) did cut*
And I schal crye, 'Rightful kyng!
Ilk man have as thee serve.' — *Each; as [he] serves you*
310 The right schul ryse to ryche reynynge; — *rise; rich reigning*
Truyt and treget to helle schal terve. — *Sin; trickery; fall*
Mayde meke and mylde,
God took in thee hys flessch trewe; — *his; true*
I bare thi fruyt lele and newe. — *bare; faithful*
315 It is right the Rode to Eve helpe schewe, — *Cross; show (see note)*
Man, woman, and chylde."

The queen, thus acorded with the Cros, — *reconciled*
Agens hym spak nomore speche. — *Against; spoke no more speech*
The lady gef the Cros a cosse; — *gave; kiss*
320 The lady of love, love gan seche, — *sought to love [the Cross]*
Theigh hire fruit on him were dight to dros, — *Though; condemned to death*
Whon rendyng ropus gan him reche. — *tearing ropes; grab*
Cristes Cros hath kept us from lose, — *loss*
Maries preyers and God ur leche. — *prayers; our healer*
325 The queen and the Cros acord: — *agree*
The queen bare first, the Cros aftirward,
To fecche folk fro hellward, — *fetch; from*
On holy styres to styghe upward — *stairs; rise*
And reigne with oure Lord. — *reign*

330 A clerk fourmed this figour — *composed; story*
Of Maries sorwe to seighe summe, — *tell some*
As he had see in scharp schour — *seen; sharp suffering/pain*
How Cristes armes were rent and rune. — *torn; slandered*

The Cros is a colde creatour, — *inanimate creature*
335 And ever yet was deef and dum; — *deaf; dumb*
This tale florissched with a faire flour, — *flower (message)*
This poynt I prove apocrifum. — *fiction*
Witnesse was never founden
That evere Crystis Cros spak, — *Christ's Cross spoke*
340 Ne oiure lady leyde hym no lak; — *Nor [that] Our Lady accused him of fault*
But for to dryve the devyll abak, — *back*
Men speke of Cristes wounden.

A clerk fourmed this fantasye
On Crists stervyng stok to stere, — *Toward; dying cross; direct*
345 That bare the body all blody,
Whan dethes dent gan hym dere. — *Death's blows; injure*
This apocrifum is no foly; — *fiction; folly*
In swich a lay dar thee naght dere, — *In such a poem lurks [for] you no harm*
That dothe man to seke mercy, — *causes; seek*
350 Wikked werkes awey to were, — *Wicked; scorn*
In tixte ful well is write. — *text; written*
A lombe hath larged all this glose, — *lamb (see note); elaborated [on]; commentary*
Plenté speche therin to prose, — *Rich; compose*
The counseill of the Cros to unclose, — *disclose*
355 Of Maryes woo to wite. — *woe; know*

In flesshly wede — *garment (i.e., human form)*
God gan hym hede, — *did conceal himself*
Of mylde may
Was born to blede,
360 As Cristes crede, — *creed*
Sothely to say.
On stokky stede — *stocklike steed*
He roode, men rede, — *rode; teach*
In rede aray. — *red array*
365 Fro develis drede — *From fear of the devil*
That Duk us lede — *Duke (Christ)*
At domesday,
Whan pepil schal parte and passe — *people shall divide and go*
To holy hevene and hell the wode. — *void*
370 Now Cristes crosse and Crystes blode

Mary at the Foot of the Cross

And Maries praier mylde and goode
Graunte us the lyfe of grace. Amen.

44

Upon my ryght syde y me leye;	*I; lay*
Blessid lady, to thee y pray:	
For the teres that ye lete	*tears; you cried*
Upon yowre swete sonnys feete,	*son's feet*
5 Sende me grace for to slepe,	*sleep*
And good dremys for to mete,	*dreams to dream*
Slepyng, wakyng till morowe daye bee.	*until morning comes*
Owre Lorde is the frwte, oure lady is the tree,	*fruit*
Blessed be the blossome that sprange, Lady, of thee.	*from you*
10 *In nomine Patris et Filii et Spiritus sancti.*[1] Amen.	

45

M and A and R and I,	
syngyn I wil a newe song.	
It wern fowre letterys of purposy:	*were; purpose*
M and A, R and I.	
5 Tho wern letteris of Mary	*They were*
Of hom al our joye sprong.	*From whom; sprang*
On the mownt of Calvory,	*mount; Calvary*
With M and A, R and I,	
There he betyn his bryte body	*they beat; untarnished (see note)*
10 With schorges that wern bothe scharp and long.	*scourges*
Our swete lady stod hym by,	*stood by him*
With M and A and R and I,	

---

[1] *In the name of the Father and the Son and the Holy Spirit*

Che wept water with here ey,   *She; her eye*
And alwey the blod folwyd among.   *always; blood flowed (see note)*

15   God, that sit above the sky,
     With M and A, R and I,
     Save now al this cumpany,
     And sende us joye and blysse among!

46

Mary myelde made grete mone   *lament*
For her dere sonne alone.

When fals Judas her son had solde
To the Jewes wikked and bolde,
5   As he before to hir had tolde,
     She was wofull alone.   *woeful*

When he came to Cayphas and An   *Annas (see note)*
To be juged for synfull man,   *as a*
In her hert she was woofull than
10   For hir dere son alone.

When that she sawe his flessh to-torn,
And on his hede a crowne of thorn,   *head*
And how the Jewes hym did shorn,   *scorn*
     She was wofull alone.

15   When hir dere son, Jhesus so goode,
     Was nayled fast uppon the roode,   *cross*
     She sobbed and wept watre and bloode   *water*
        For hir dere son alone.

Whenne hir dere son on the thirde day
20   With hir dide mete and thus did say,   *meet*
     "Hayle, holy moder, wyfe, and may,"
        She was joyfull alone.

47

	I syke when y singe,	*sigh*
	For sorewe that y se,	*sorrow; see*
	When y with wypinge	*weeping*
	Biholde upon the tre	*tree*
5	Ant se Jesu the suete,	*And see*
	Is herte blod forlete,	*His; pouring forth*
	For the love of me	
	Ys woundes waxen wete;	*His*
	Thei wepen stille ant mete.	*gently; fittingly (see note)*
10	Marie, reweth thee.	*have pity*
	Heghe upon a doune,	*High; hill*
	Ther al folk hit se may,	*Where all folks may see it*
	A mile from uch toune,	*each town*
	Aboute the midday,	
15	The Rode is up arered;	*Cross; raised*
	His frendes aren afered,	*are afraid*
	Ant clyngeth so the clay.	*shrink [in fear] like [dry] clay*
	The Rode stond in stone,	
	Marie stont hire one	*nearby*
20	Ant seith "Weylaway!"	*And says*
	When y thee biholde,	*I you*
	With eyghen bryhte bo,	*eyes; both*
	Ant thi bodi colde,	
	Thi ble waxeth blo,	*color turns blue*
25	Thou hengest al of blode	*bloody*
	So heghe upon the Rode	*high*
	Bituene theves tuo;	*Between two thieves*
	Who may syke more?	*sigh*
	Marie wepeth sore	
30	Ant siht al this wo;	*And sees*
	The naylles beth to stronge,	*are too strong*
	The smythes are to sleye,	
	Thou bledest al to longe,	*too long*
	The tre is al to heyghe,	*too high*

35	The stones beoth al wete.	*are all wet*
	Alas, Jesu the suete,	*sweet*
	For nou frend hast thou non	*now; none*
	Bote Seint Johan, mournynde,	*But; mourning*
	Ant Marie, wepynde,	*And; weeping*
40	For pyne that thee ys on.	*suffering; upon you*

	Ofte when y sike	*sigh*
	Ant makie my mon,	*lament*
	Wel ille thah me like,	*though*
	Wonder is hit non,	
45	When y se honge heghe	*hung high*
	Ant bittre pynes dreghe	*enduring bitter pains*
	Jesu my lemmon,	*beloved*
	His wondes sore smerte,	*hurt sorely*
	The spere al to is herte,	*spear pierces his*
50	Ant thourh is sydes gon.	*goes through his sides*

	Ofte when y syke	
	With care y am thourhsoht.	*pierced through*
	When y wake y wyke;	*lie awake I grow weak*
	Of serewe is al my thoht.	*sorrow; thought*
55	Alas men beth wode	*are insane*
	That suereth by the Rode	*swear*
	Ant selleth him for noht	*nothing*
	That bohte us out of synne:	*Who bought (redeemed)*
	He bring us to wynne	*bliss*
60	That hath us duere boht.	*dearly purchased*

48

Jhesus:

	Maiden and moder, cum and se,	
	Thi child is nailed to a tre.	*tree (cross)*
	Hand and fot he may nouth go,	*foot; not*
	His bodi is wonden al in wo.	*wounded; woe*
5	Al abouten he is to-toren,	
	His heved is wrethen with a thorn,	*head; wreathed*

His sides bothen on blode be,
With blod hes blent, he may nouth se.   *he is blinded; not*

Maria:
    Mi suete sone that art me dere,   *dear to me*
10   Wat has thu don, qui art thu here?   *why*
    This suete bodi that in me rest,
    That loveli mouth that I have kist,   *kissed*
    Nou is on rode mad thi nest.
    Mi dere child, quat is me best?   *what is best for me*

Jhesus:
15   Jon, this womman for my sake,   *John*
    Womman, to Jon, I thee betake.   *entrust*
    Alone I am withoten make,
    On rode I hange for mannis sake   *cross; man's*
    This gamen alone me must pleyye
20   For mannis soule this det to deyye.   *debt; die*
    Mi blod is sched, my fles is falle   *shed; fallen*
    Me thristet sore, for drink I calle   *thirst painfully*
    Thei geven me eysil medlid with galle.   *vinegar mixed*
    For mannis senne in wo I walle   *sin; wail*
25   Yef thei weren kende to loven me outh,   *If; taught; properly*
    Of al my peine me ne routh.   *I do not care*

    Fader, my soule I thee betake!   *give to you*
    My bodi deyghet for mannis sake.   *dies; man's*
    Senful soules in helle lake,   *Sinful; hell's lake*
30   To hem I go, awey to take.   *them*
    Mannis soule, thou art my make;   *Man's; mate*
    Love me wel, I thee nouth forsake,   *do not forsake you*
    And my moder herteliche,   *heartily*
    For sche helpet thee stedfasliche   *she helps you steadfastly*
35   An thou salt comen that blisse to   *And you shall come to that bliss*
    Ther my Fader is for evermo.   *Where; evermore*

Plate B: **The Assumption**. *The Hours of Catherine of Cleves*: Hours of the Virgin — Compline. Pierpont Morgan M.945, fol. 42a (c. 1435). By permission of the Pierpont Morgan Library.

The Assumption and Mary as Queen of Heaven

49

Crist sayde to hur:	*her (Mary's corpse)*
"Com, my swete, com, my flour,	*Come; flower*
Com, my culver, myn owne boure,	*dove; bower*
Com, my modyr, now wyth me:	*mother*
For hevyn qwene I make thee."	*queen of heaven*

Then the body sat up, and lowted to Crist, and sayde:	*bowed*
5 "My swete sonne, with al my love	
I com wyth thee to thyn above;	*with you*
Wher thou art now, let me be,	
For al my love ys layde on thee."	

50

The infinite power essenciall	
Me thoght I sawe verrement	*truly*
Procedyng from his trone celestiall	*throne*
To a dere damsell that was gent.	*dear lady; gentle*
5 Songes melodious was in their tent,	
Of angells synging with gret solemnyté	*great*
Before a quene whiche was present:	
Ecce virgo, radix Jesse.	*Behold a virgin, root of Jesse*

Tota pulcra, to the lillé like,	*All beautiful, like the lily*
10 She was set withe saphures celestiall;	*sapphires*
The odour of hir mowthe aromatike	*mouth aromatic*
Dyd coumford the world unyversall.	*Did comfort*
Moche clerer she was then the cristall;	*Much clearer; than*
She is the flowre of all formosité,	*beauty*

15	Devoide of actes crymynall:	*Without sin*
	Ecce virgo, radix Jesse.	
	Oleum effusum, to languentes medsyne,	*Oil poured out, medicine to the suffering*
	O Maria by denominacioun,	*name*
	Fulgent as the beame celestyne,	*Bright*
20	Called unto hir coronacioun:	
	Phebus persplendent made his abdominacioun,	*Phoebus; abdication*
	Devoidyng all in tenebrosité	*Eliminating all in darkness*
	For gret love of hir exaltacioun:	*exaltation*
	Ecce virgo, radix Jesse.	
25	Ryght diligent were the mynstrells divine	
	Trones and dominaciones for to expresse,	*Thrones; dominations*
	Angells, archangells, dubbit in doctryne,	*dubbed*
	To mynystre to that regall arayed in rychesse.	*regal [one]*
	The Prynce perpetuall spake to that pryncesse,	*eternal*
30	Smylyng in his suavyté,	*kindness*
	"*Columba mea*, the cloystre of clandnesse,	*My dove, the cloister of purity*
	Ecce virgo, radix Jesse.	
	"Surge, true tabernacle of virginité,	*Rise*
	Bothe mother and maiden inculpable:	
35	Cum furthe of thy consanguinité	*Come forth from your humanity*
	Unto glorie incomparable."	
	Then kneled this oryent and amyable	*pearl; amiably*
	Before the pellicane of perpetueté,	*pelican everlasting (see note)*
	And he crowned that regyent venerable:	*queen*
40	*Ecce virgo, radix Jesse.*	
	By the spectable splendure of hir fulgent face	*virtuous splendor; shining*
	My sprete was ravesshed and in my body sprent;[1]	
	Inflamed was my hert with gret solace	
	Of the luciant corruscall resplendent.	*shining shimmering resplendent [one]*
45	Then this curious cumpany incontynent	*immediately*
	Withe the seraphynnes in their solemnyté	*seraphim*

---

[1] *My spirit was ravished and leapt in my body*

Solemply sang this subsequent: *solemnly; following*
    Ecce virgo, radix Jesse.

     O Deifere delecate and doghter dyvyne,   *God-bearer; daughter divine*

50   Mother of mercy and meyden melleffluus,

     Devoide of dysseyte, dubbet in doctryne,   *Devoid of deceit, dubbed*

     Trone of the Trinité, treite thow for us.   *Throne; entreat*

     Us defende from the dongeon dolorous   *dungeon*

     And bring to abide in blisse withe thee,

55   There to love our Godd most glorious:
    Ecce virgo, radix Jesse.

51

     Hayle, luminary and benigne lanterne:

     Of Jerusalem the holy ordres nyne   *orders nine*

     As quene of quenes laudacion eerne   *eager praise*

     They yeve to thee, O excellente virgyne!   *give*

5   Eclypsyd I am for to determyne

     Thy superexcellence of *Cantica canticorum*;   *Song of songs*

     The aureat beames do nat in me shyne: *golden; not*

       Ave regina celorum!   *Hail queen of heaven*

     Hayle, verray *mater misericorde*,   *true mother of mercy*

10   And peereles pryncesse of excellence,

     Of aungelles aloft pray *Sol justicie*,   *Sun (Son) of justice*

     Thy swete son of most magnificence,

     That no perylous plage of pestilence,   *perilous plague of pestilence*

     Syth thow art *laus Apostolorum*,   *Since you are the glory of the Apostles*

15   Entyr in Englond, thy dower, with reverence: *Enter in[to]*

       Ave regina celorum!

     Hayle, holy maydyn, modyr and wyfe,

     That brought Israel out of captyvyté,

     As sterre of Jacob by a prerogatyfe

20   With the blessyd bawme of thy virginité,   *balm*

     The holyest roote that sprang out of Jesse,

     Prymrose of plesaunce, callyd *flos florum*,   *flower of flowers*

Thou were tryacle ageyn olde antiquité:	*antidote*
Ave regina celorum!	

25	Hayle, gloryous lady, *O rosa marina,*	*rose of the sea*
	Whyche hast fostryd lying in thy lappe	*fostered*
	Tetragramaton, that fed us with Manna,	*(see note)*
	Of Leviathan mawgre the sleyghty trappe,	*despite; deceptive*
	To thys worlde a lyghte sprong ys from thy lappe,	*a light is sprung*
30	With virginall mylke *ut castitas lilium,*	*milk as a chaste lily*
	So lyst the Holygost in thee hys wynges wrappe:	*desires; wrap you in his wings*
	Ave regina celorum!	

	Hayle, fayrest and fresshe of consolacion,	
	Us to conduct by the pathe of paradyse,	
35	Above all women, without comparyson,	
	Of bewté be thow blessyd floure delise,	*beauty; fleur-de-lis*
	A dew diamant, most precyous of pryse,	*diamond; worth*
	As Gabryell seyd, *Dominus tecum,*	*God is with you*
	O myrrour of mekenes most prudent and wyse:	*meekness*
40	*Ave regina celorum!*	

	Hayle, condute of comfort, with watyr crystall,	*conduit; clear*
	Perpetually our peynes to wasshe and repell,	
	Geyve sorow of sekenes, o sugor celestiall,	*divine sweetness*
	Pes, victory, and grace graunt with us to dwell,	*Peace*
45	Pray gentyll Jesu, of mercy the well,	*Pray to gentle Jesus, well of mercy*
	To blysse above that we may all come,	*That we may all come to bliss above*
	Where more joy ys then tung may telle:	*tongue*
	Ave regina celorum!	

52

	Lefdy blisful, of muchel might,	*Lady; great strength*
	Heyere thanne the sterres light,	*Higher; stars'*
	Hym the thee made wumman best	*who made you*
	Thou gove hym souken of thi brest.	*gave suck*
5	Thet thet Eve us hadde bynome	*That which; deprived us of*
	Thow hast iholde thorw thy sone.	*regained through*

116

The Assumption and Mary as Queen of Heaven

Thow art in hevene an hole imad — *in heaven a hole made*
Thorw which the senful thorwgeth glad. — *sinful pass (glide) through*
Thow art the kynges gate idyght; — *called*
10 Brightore thow art than eny light.
Lif thorw Marye us is iwrought, — *accomplished for us*
Alle ben glade thet Crist hath ibought. — *Be glad, all whom Christ has redeemed*

53

Haill, quene of hevin and steren of blis: — *star of bliss*
Sen that thi sone thi Fader is, — *Since your son is your Father*
How suld he ony thing thee warn, — *should he deny you anything*
And thou his mothir and he thi barne? — *child*

5 Haill, fresche fontane that springis new, — *fountain; springs*
The rute and crope of all vertu, — *root; crop; virtue*
Thou polist gem without offence: — *polished; flaw*
Thou bair the Lambe of Innocence. — *bore*

Mary Mediatrix

54

I pray thee, lady, the moder of Crist,
Praieth youre sone me for to spare   *Ask; to spare me*
With al angels, and John Baptist,
And all youre company that now ys thare.   *(i.e., in heaven)*
5   Al holichurch, for my welfare,
Graunt me of youre merites a participacioun,
And praieth oure Lorde for my salvacyon.   *pray to*

55

Sancta Maria, ora pro nobis.   *Saint Mary, pray for us*

O moder mylde, mayde undefylde,   *undefiled*
Thatte we so wylde be notte begylde   *wayward be not misled*
And evere exylde fro Crist and hys,   *exiled; his [elect]*
5   *Ora pro nobis.*   *Pray for us*

O quene of grace most fayre of face,
Of alle solace ledyng the trace,   *comfort excelling; pattern*
Of the highe place thatte we nott mys,   *So that we do not miss the high place*
Ora pro nobis.

10   O lady fre of high degré   *noble of high degree*
Thatte we may se thy sone and thee,   *see*
And ever to be where alle joy ys,
Ora pro nobis.

Thatte Crist us sende grace to amende
15   Oure tyme myspende or we hense wende,   *misspent before we go hence (die)*
And atte oure ende to graunte us blys,
Ora pro nobis.

Mary Mediatrix

56

<table>
<tr><td></td><td>Sancta Maria, ora pro nobis.</td><td>Holy Mary, pray for us</td></tr>
<tr><td></td><td>O tryclyn of the Trinité,</td><td>triclinium (see note)</td></tr>
<tr><td></td><td>Replete with alle divinité,</td><td></td></tr>
<tr><td></td><td>O flowre of alle virginité,</td><td></td></tr>
<tr><td>5</td><td>Ora pro nobis.</td><td>Pray for us</td></tr>
<tr><td></td><td>O blessid quene of heven blys,</td><td></td></tr>
<tr><td></td><td>Wherof the joye eternalle is,</td><td></td></tr>
<tr><td></td><td>Of the whiche blis thatte we not mys,</td><td>which (heaven's); miss</td></tr>
<tr><td></td><td>Ora pro nobis.</td><td></td></tr>
<tr><td>10</td><td>O emperesse of helle alsoo,</td><td></td></tr>
<tr><td></td><td>Into thatte place thatt we not goo</td><td></td></tr>
<tr><td></td><td>Where is derkenes and endles woo,</td><td>darkness; woe</td></tr>
<tr><td></td><td>Ora pro nobis.</td><td></td></tr>
<tr><td></td><td>O spowsesse of Crist, oure savyowre,</td><td>spouse (see note)</td></tr>
<tr><td>15</td><td>The whiche restyd in thy chast bowre,</td><td>Who rested; chaste bower</td></tr>
<tr><td></td><td>Thatte he kepe us fro alle dolowre,</td><td>from all sorrow</td></tr>
<tr><td></td><td>Ora pro nobis.</td><td></td></tr>
<tr><td></td><td>O sweete lady so meke and mylde,</td><td></td></tr>
<tr><td></td><td>Unto Jesu, thy blessid chylde,</td><td></td></tr>
<tr><td>20</td><td>Fro blysse thatt we be notte exylde,</td><td>From; not exiled</td></tr>
<tr><td></td><td>Ora pro nobis.</td><td></td></tr>
<tr><td></td><td>Holy moder of Crist Jesu,</td><td></td></tr>
<tr><td></td><td>Thatte is the Lorde of alle vertu,</td><td>virtue</td></tr>
<tr><td></td><td>Thatte he with grace may us renu,</td><td>renew</td></tr>
<tr><td>25</td><td>Ora pro nobis.</td><td></td></tr>
<tr><td></td><td>Holy virgyn of virgyns alle,</td><td></td></tr>
<tr><td></td><td>Thatt thy sweete sone Jesus may calle</td><td></td></tr>
<tr><td></td><td>Us unto hym, bothe grete and smalle,</td><td></td></tr>
<tr><td></td><td>Ora pro nobis.</td><td></td></tr>
</table>

30   Thatte we, which be terrestrialle,
        May leve this lyff so bestialle   *leave; life*
        And come to blysse celestialle,
            Ora pro nobis.

57

        Sainte Marie, virgine,
        Moder Jhesu Cristes Nazarene,
        Onfo, schild, help thin Godric,   *Receive, shield*
        Onfang, bring heghilich with thee in Godes riche.[1]

5   Sainte Marie, Cristes bur,   *bower*
        Maidenes clenhad, moderes flur,   *Maiden of maidens, flower of mothers*
        Dilie min sinne, rix in min mod,   *Deliver [me from] my sin; reign in my heart*
        Bring me to winne with the selfd God.   *bliss; God himself*

58

        Ave maris stella, the sterre on the see,   *Hail sea star (Mary Star); sea*
        Dei mater alma, blyssid mot ye be,   *Beloved mother of God, blessed are you*
        Atque semper virgo, prey thi sone for me,   *And ever virgin; beseech*
        Felix celi porta, that I may come to thee.   *Joyful gate of heaven*
5   Gabriel, that archangyl, he was massanger,   *messenger*
        So fayre he gret our lady with an *Ave* so cler.   *greeted; clear (pure)*
        Heyl be thu, Mary, be thu, Mary,
        Ful of Godis grace and qwyn of mercy.   *queen*
        Alle that arn to grete withoutyn dedly synne   *who pray to you without deadly sin*
10   Forty dayis of pardoun God grauntyt hym.   *them (see note)*

---

[1] Lines 3–4: *Receive (accept) your Godric, shield him, help him, / Received, bring him solemnly with you into God's kingdom*

59

Marie moder, wel thee be,
Marie mayde, thenk on me.
Moder and made was never non   *No one was ever mother and virgin*
Togeder, ladi, bote thou alon.   *but; alone*

5   Marie moder, mayde clene,   *pure*
Schilde me fro sorwe and tene;   *Shield; from sorrow; suffering*
Marie, out of synne help thu me,
And out of dette, for charité.   *debt*

Marie, for thine joies five,
10   Help me to leve in clene live,   *live; pure life*
For the teres thou lete under the rode,   *tears; shed; cross*
Sende me grace of lives fode,   *sustenance/Christ*

Wherwith I may me clothe and fede   *feed*
And in treuthe mi liif lede.   *life*
15   Help me, ladi, and alle myne,   *my kin*
And schilde us alle fro helle pyne.   *shield; hell's pain*

Schilde me, ladi, fro velanye,   *from villainy*
And fro alle wikkede companye;   *wicked*
Schilde me, ladi, fro widded schame   *cursed shame*
20   And fram alle widdede fame.   *cursed*

Swete ladi, thou me were   *protect*
That the fend noughth me dere   *fiend does not harm me*
Bothe bi day and bi nyghth,   *night*
Help me, ladi, with thi righth.   *righteousness*

25   For myne frendes I bidde thee,   *I pray to you for my friends*
That high mote amended be,   *they might*
Bothe to soule and to lyve,   *in soul and in living*
Marie, for thyne joies fyve.

For myne fomen I bidde also   *enemies; pray*
30   That they mote heer so do,   *might so do here*

That they in wrathe hy ne deye,   *do not die in wrath*
Swete lady, ich thee preye.   *I [to] you*

Hy that ben in goode lyve,   *They who live virtuously*
Marie, for thine joies fyve;
35   Swete ladi, therinne hem holde   *keep them*
Bothe the yonge and the olde.

And that ben in dedlich synne,   *they who are in deadly sin*
Ne lete hem nevere deie therinne   *Do not let them die therein*
Marie, for thine joies alle,
40   Lete hem nevere in helle falle.   *them; fall into hell*

Swete ladi, thou hem rede,   *counsel them*
That thei amendi of here misdede;   *they amend their wrongdoing*
Bysek thi sone, hevene kyng,   *Beseech*
That he me graunte good endyng,   *grant to me*

45   And sende me, as he wel may,
Schrift and hosel at myn endyng day,   *Confession; Holy Communion*
And that we mote thider wende   *might go there*
Ther joie is withouten ende.   *Where*
        Amen Amen.

60

Thou wommon boute vere   *without peer*
Thyn oune vader bere.   *own father bore*
Gret wonder thys was,
That on wommon was moder   *one*
5   To vader and hyre brother: *father; her*
So never other nas.   *was never any other*

Thou my suster and moder
And thy sone my brother:
Who shulde thoenne drede?   *then fear*
10   Whoso havet the kyng to broder   *has; as/for brother*

122

And ek the quene to moder   *also*
Wel auhte vor to spede.   *ought to prosper*

Dame, suster and moder,
Say thy sone my brother   *Tell*
15 That ys domes mon   *Who is judge*
That vor thee that hym bere   *for you who*
To me boe debonere;   *be gentle*
My robe he haveth opon.   *i.e., God wears man's flesh*

Soeththe he my robe tok   *Since; took*
20 Also ich finde in bok   *As I; book (Bible)*
He ys to me ybounde;   *bound/joined*
And helpe he wole, ich wot,   *will; know*
Vor love the chartre wrot,   *wrote*
The enke orn of hys wounde.   *ink flowed from*

25 Ich take to wytnessinge   *as witness*
The spere and the crounynge,
The nayles and the rode,   *cross*
That he that ys so cunde   *kind*
Thys ever haveth in munde   *mind*
30 That bouhte ous wyth hys blode.   *bought us*

When thou geve hym my wede,   *clothing/garment (the flesh)*
Dame, help at the noede: *[time of] need*
Ich wot thou myth vol wel   *know; might full well*
That vor no wreched gult
35 Ich boe to helle ypult;   *be dragged into hell*
To thee ich make apel.   *appeal*

Nou, dame, ich thee byseche   *beseech*
At thylke day of wreche   *that; misery*
Boe by thy sones trone   *Be; throne*
40 When sunne shal boen souht —   *sin; exposed*
In werk, in word, in thouht —
And spek vor me, thou one.   *you alone intercede for me*

	When ich mot nede apere,	*must needs appear*
	Vor mine gultes here,	
45	Tovore the domesmon,	*Before the judge*
	Suster, boe ther my vere	*companion*
	And make hym debonere	*him (Jesus the judge)*
	That mi robe haveth opon.	

	Vor habbe ich thee and hym	
50	That markes berth wyth hym,	*bears*
	That charité him tok,	
	The woundes al blody,	
	The toknes of mercy	
	Ase techeth holy bok.	*As*
55	Tharf me nothing drede;	*Suffer me; to fear*
	Sathan shal nout spede	*not succeed*
	Wyth wrenches ne wyth crok.	*By hook or by crook*
	Amen.	

61

	Marie, yow quen, yow moder, yow mayden briht,	*queen*
	Yow wilt, yow canst, yow art of miht:	*You will, you can, you are able*
	Yow lyf, yow love, yow hope of blisse,	*You [are] life; you [are]*
	In sinne, in sorwe, in nede, us wisse.	*sorrow; guide us*

62

	Levedie, ic thonke thee	*Lady, I thank you*
	Wid herte suithe milde,	*With; so very mild*
	That gohid that thu havest idon me	*[For] that good; done*
	Wid thine suete childe.	*With your beloved*

5	Thu ard god and sute and brit,	*You are good; delightful; bright*
	Of alle otheir icorinne;	*others chosen*
	Of thee was that suete wight	*From you; sweet one*
	That was Jesus iboren.	*Who; born*

Mary Mediatrix

Maide milde, biddi thee	*I pray you*
10 Wid thine suete childe	*with*
That thu herdie me	*shelter*
To habben Godis milce.	*have God's mercy*
Moder, loke one me	*look upon me*
Wid thine suete eyen;	*beloved (gracious) eyes*
15 Reste and blisse gef thu me,	*Give me rest and joy*
Mi levedi, then ic deyen.	*when I die*

63 (Egerton MS)

Blessed beo thu, lavedi, ful of hovene blisse,	*lady; heavenly*
Swete flur of parais, moder of mildernisse.	*mildness*
Thu praie Jesu Crist thi sone, that he me iwisse	*pray [to]; know*
Ware alond al swo ihc beo, that he me ne imisse.[1]	
5 Of thee, faire lavedi, min oreisun ich wile biginnen,	*orison (prayer) I will*
Thi deore swete sunnes love thu lere me to winnen.	*dear; son's; teach; enjoy*
Wel ofte ich sike and sorwe make, ne mai ich nevere blinnen,	*sigh; cease*
Bote thu, thruh thin milde mod, bringe me out of sunne.	*Unless you; sin*
Ofte ihc seke merci, thin swete name ich calle,	*I seek*
10 Mi flehs is foul, this world is fals; thu loke that ich ne falle.	*flesh; watch*
Lavedi freo, thu schild me fram the pine of helle,	*free (noble); shield; from; pain*
And send me into that blisse that tunge ne mai tellen.	*tongue may not tell*
Mine werkes, lavedi, heo makieth me ful won;	*deeds; they make me full wan*
Wel ofte ich clepie and calle, thu iher me forthan	*I address; hear; then*
15 Bote ic chabbe the help of thee, other I ne kan,[2]	
Hel thu me ful wel thu mist; thu helpest mani a man.	*You may lead me full well*
Iblessed beo thu, lavedi, so fair and so briht,	
Al min hope is uppon thee, bi dai and bi nicht.	*by day and by night*

---

[1] *Wherever I am on earth, that he never fail me*

[2] *Unless I shall have help from you, I have no other*

Mary Mediatrix

Helpe thruh thin milde mod, for wel thu mist,   *might*

20 That ich nevere for feondes sake furgo thin eche liht.[1]

Briht and scene quen of hovene, ich bidde thin sunnes hore.

The sunnes that ich habbe icun, heo rewweth me ful sore;

Wel ofte ich chabbe thee fursaken; wilich never eft more,

Lavedi for thine sake, treuwen feondes lore,[2]

25 Iblessed beo thu, lavedi so feir and so hende: *virtuous*

Thu praie Jesu Crist thi sone, that he me isende,   *entreat; send*

Whare alond alswo ich beo er ich honne wende

That ich mote in parais wonien withuten ende.[3]

Bricht and scene quen of storre, so me liht and lere, *beautiful; illuminate; teach*

30 In this false fikele world so me led and steore,   *fickle; lead; guide*

That ich at min ende-dai ne habbe non feond to fere.

Jesu, mit ti swete blod thu bohtest me ful deore.[4]

Jesu, Seinte Marie sone, thu iher thin moder bone.   *hear; mother's prayer*

To thee ne dar I clepien noht; to hire ich make min mone;

35 Thu do that ich, for hire sake, boe imaked so clene

That ich noht at dai of dome beo flemed of thin exsene.[5]

---

[1] *That I never for fiend's sake forgo your true light*

[2] Lines 21–24: *Bright and radiant queen of heaven, I bid your mercy [for my] sins. / The sins that I have known, I regret them sorely; / I have often forsaken you; I will never do so again, / Lady, for your sake, true fiends forsake*

[3] Lines 27–28: *Wherever on earth I may be before I go on / That I might dwell eternally in Paradise*

[4] Lines 31–32: *That I have no fiend to fear at my ending-day. / Jesus, with your sweet blood you bought me full dearly*

[5] Lines 33–36: *Jesus, Saint Mary's son, you hear your mother's prayer. / I dare not call on you; to her I make my plea; / For her sake, make me so pure / So that I am not exiled from your sight at Judgment Day*

Mary Mediatrix

64 (MS Harley 2253)

Blessed be thou, levedy, ful of heovene blisse,	*lady; heavenly*
Suete flur of parays, moder of mildenesse,	*flower; paradise*
Preyghe Jesu thy sone that he me rede ant wysse	*Pray; guide; teach*
So my wey forte gon that he me never misse.	*lose/desert/leave*
5 Of thee, suete levedy, my song y wile byginne:	
Thy deore suete sones love thou lere me to wynne;	*dear; teach*
Ofte y syke ant serewe among, may y never blynne	*sigh and grieve; stop*
Levedi, for thi milde mod, thou shilde me from synne.	
Myne thohtes, levedy, maketh me ful wan,	*thoughts; gloomy*
10 To thee y crie ant calle, thou here me for thi man	
Help me, hevene quene, for thyn ever ycham;	*I am ever yours*
Wisse me to thi deore sone; the weies y ne can.	*Guide; ways I do not know*
Levedy, Seinte Marie, for thi milde mod	*countenance*
Soffre never that y ben so wilde ne so wod	*Suffer (Permit); I be; wild nor so mad*
15 That ich her forleose thee that art so god	*I here forfeit you; good*
That Jesu me to bohte with is suete blod.	*bought; his sweet blood*
Bryhte ant shene sterre cler, lyht thou me ant lere[1]	
In this false, fykel world myselve so to bere	*fickle; bear (conduct)*
That y ner at myn endyng have the feond to fere;	*never; fiend; fear*
20 Jesu, mid thi suete blod thou bohtest me so dere.	*bought; dearly*
Levedi, Seinte Marie, so fair ant so briht,	
Al myn help is on the bi day ant by nyht;	
Levedi fre, thou shilde me so wel as thou myht,	*free (noble); shield*
That y never forleose heveriche lyht.	*forfeit heavenly light*
25 Levedy, seinte Marie, so fayr ant so hende,	*noble*
Preye Jesu Crist, thi sone, that he me grace sende	
So to queme him ant thee er ich henne wende	*serve (please); go hence*
That he me bringe to the blis that is withouten ende.	

---

[1] *Bright and shining star clear, illuminate and teach me*

Mary Mediatrix

	Ofte y crie "Merci": of mylse thou art well;	*Often I cry; mercy; [the] well*
30	Alle buen false that bueth mad bothe of fleysh ant fell;[2]	
	Levedi suete, thou us shild from the pine of helle,	
	Bring us to the joie that no tonge hit may of telle.	*tongue*
	Jesu Crist, Godes Sone, Fader ant Holy Gost,	
	Help us at oure nede as thou hit al wel wost;	*all know best*
35	Bring us to thin riche, ther is joie most;	*kingdom; joy*
	Let us never hit misse for non worldes bost.	*not miss; any wordly boast*

65

	Mary, modur of grace, we cry to thee,	*mother; to you*
	Moder of mercy and of pyté,	*pity*
	Put us fro the fendes fondying,	*Keep us from the fiend's temptation*
	And help us at oure last endying,	
5	And to thi sone oure pes thou make,	*peace*
	That he of us no wreke take.	*So that he takes no vengeance on us*
	To yow I cri wyth mylde steven,	*humble voice*
	All the halowes that are in heven	*saints*
	Helpe that Criste my gylth forgyve,	*guilt forgive*
10	And will hym serve will I lyve.	*while*

---

[2] *All are sinful who are made of flesh and skin*

Penitential Poems

66

Hayl Mari,
Hic am sori;   *I am sorry*
Haf pité of me and merci.   *pity*
Mi levedi,   *lady*
5 To thee I cri:
For mi sinnis dred ham hi,   *fearful am I*
Wen hi thenke that hi sal bi,   *When I think about what I shall be*
That hi haf mis hi-don   *What I have misdone*
In worde, in worke, in thoith foli.   *foolish thought*
10 Levedi, her mi bon.   *hear my prayer*

Mi bon thu her,   *My prayer you hear*
Levedi der,   *Lady dear*
That hic aske wit reuful cher;   *What I ask with rueful heart*
Thu len me her   *You support me here*
15 Wil hic am fer.   *While I am far away*
Do penanz in mi praier;   *Cause penance*
Ne let me noth ler that thu ber   *Deny me not your countenance (see note)*
At min endin day.   *my final day*
The warlais, thai wil be her   *devils (warlocks); here*
20 Forto take thair pray.   *capture their prey*

To take thar pray,
Alse hi her say,   *As I hear*
Thai er redi boyt nite and day.   *They are ready both night*
So strange er thai   *strong are they*
25 That we ne may   *may not*
Agayneis thaim stond, so waylaway,   *Against them stand, alas*
But gif thu help us, mitteful may,   *Unless you; courageous maiden*
Wit thi sunes grace;   *With your son's*

129

	Wan thu comes thai flet awai,	*When you come, they flee away*
30	Dar thai not se thi face.	*Dare*
	Thi face to se,	*see*
	Thu grant hit me,	*Please grant me*
	Lefdi fulfillid of pité,	*full of pity*
	That hi may be	*I*
35	In joy wit thee	*with you*
	To se thi sone in Trinité,	
	That sufferid pine and ded for me	*Who; pain and death*
	And for al mankyn.	*mankind*
	His flesse was sprade on rode tre	*body; stretched; cross*
40	To leys us al of sine.	*release us all from sin*
	Of sine and kar	*sin; care*
	He maked us bar	*made us bare (stripped us)*
	Wan he thollid pines sar.	*When he suffered pains sore*
	To drupe and dar	*droop; remain still (see note)*
45	We athe wel mare,	*ought all the more*
	Alse for the hondis doyt the har,	*As the hare does for the hounds*
	Wan we thenke hu we sal far	*When we imagine how we should fare*
	Wan he sal dem us alle;	*shall judge*
	We sal haf ned thare	*shall have need there*
50	Apan Mari to calle.	*Upon*

67

	On hire is al mi lif ilong	*her; life's longing*
	Of hwam ich wule singe,	*whom I will sing*
	And herien hire ther among.	*praise her*
	Heo gon us bote bringe	*She has brought us remedy*
5	Of helle pine that is strong;	*From hell's suffering; fierce*
	Heo brohte us blisse that is long,	*She brought; endures*
	Al thurht hire chilthinge.	*through her birth-giving*
	Ich bidde hire one mi song,	*I pray [to] her in my song*
	Heo geove us god endinge	*[That] she give us good ending*
10	Thah we don wrong.	*Though we do*

	Thu art hele and lif ond liht,	*health; life and light*
	And helpest al monkunne;	*mankind*
	Thu us havest ful wel idight,	*You have; treated*
	Thu geve us weole and wunne.	*abundance; joy*
15	Thu brohtest dai, and Eve night;	*You brought*
	Heo broghte woht, thu broghtest right,	*She brought woe; you brought*
	Thu almesse and heo sunne.	*You charity; she sin*
	Bisih to me, lavedi bright,	*Look after me, lady*
	Hwenne ich schal wende heonne,	*When I shall go hence*
20	So wel thu miht.	*As well you might*
	Al this world schal ago	*shall go*
	With seorhe and with sore,	*sorrow; pain*
	And al this lif we schule forgo,	*life; shall give up*
	Ne of thunche hit us so sore:	*Nor think sorrowfully of it*
25	This world nis butent ure ifo.	*is nothing but our enemy*
	Tharfore ich thenche hirne at go	*Therefore I think of her always*
	And do bi Godes lore;	*according to God's teaching*
	This lives blisse nis wurth a slo.	*life's; is not worth a berry*
	Ich bidde, God, thin ore,	*I pray; your mercy*
30	Nu and everemo.	*Now; evermore*
	To longe ich habbe sot ibeo;	*Too long I have been a fool*
	Wel sore ich me adrede;	*sorely; fear*
	Iluved ich habbe gomen and gleo	*I have loved games and glee*
	And prude and feire wede.	*pride; fine clothing*
35	Al that is dweole, wel i seo;	*error, well I see*
	Tharfore ich thenche sunne fleo	*I think to flee [from] sin*
	And alle mine sot dede.	*my foolish deeds*
	Ich bidde hire to me biseo	*beg her to look after me*
	And helpe me and rede,	*counsel*
40	That is so freo.	*Who; noble*
	Agult ich habbe, weilawei;	*Guilt I have, alas*
	Sunful ich am an wrecche.	*I am sinful and wretched*
	Awrec thee nu on me, levedi,	*Chastise me now, lady*
	Er deth me honne fecche.	*Before death takes me hence*
45	Do nim thee wreche — ich am redi —	*Take your vengeance — I am ready*
	Other let me liven and amendi,	*Or; live and amend*

131

That no feond me ne drecche.   *no fiend torment me*
For mine sunnes ich am sori;   *sins; sorry*
Of this world ich ne recche.   *I do not value this world*
50   Levedi, merci. Amen.   *Lady, [have] mercy*

68

Worsshipful maiden to the world, Marie,
Modir moost lovynge unto al mankynde,   *Mother most loving*
Lady to whom al synful peple crie   *people cry*
In hir distresse, have us in thy mynde!   *their; mind*
5   Thurgh thy benigne pitee, us unbynde   *Through; kind pity unbind us*
Of our giltes, that in thy sones birthe   *sins, who; son's birth*
To al the world broghtest the joie and mirthe. *joy*

To whom shal I truste so sikirly,   *surely*
To axen help in my necessitee   *ask*
10   As unto thee, thow modir of mercy?
For to the world mercy cam in by thee: *came*
Thow baar the Lord of mercy, lady free;   *bore*
Who may so lightly mercy us purchace   *easily; obtain*
Of God thy sone as thow, modir of grace?   *you, mother*

15   Lady, right as it is an impossible   *just as; impossibility*
That thow sholdest nat have in remembrance   *should not remember*
Why thow baar God, so it is incredible   *you bore*
To any wight of catholyk creaunce,   *person of catholic (universal) belief*
Thee nat to reewe on our synful grevaunce.   *not to pity our sinfulness*
20   Forthy, lady benigne and merciable,   *Therefore; merciful*
Unto thy sone make us acceptable.   *son*

O God, that maad art sone unto womman,   *who is made son of woman*
For mercy, and thow womman which also
By grace art maade modir to God and man,
25   Outhir reewe on us wrecches ful of wo,   *Either pity us wretches; woe*
Thou sparyng and thow preyynge,   *You (God) sparing; you (Mary) praying (see note)*
Or elles wisse us whidir for to flee   *Or else advise us where to flee*
To hem that been mercyfullere than yee.   *To any who be more merciful than you*

	If it so be as wel I woot it is,	*know*
30	That so grevous is myn iniquitee	*grievous; sinfulness*
	And that I have wroght so moche amis,	*done so much wrong*
	So smal my feith, so slow my charitee,	*inadequate my faith*
	And, Lord, so unkonnynge is unto thee	*unpleasing*
	And thy modir my lewde orisoun,	*ignorant prayer*
35	So imparfyt my satisfaccioun,	*imperfect; satisfaction (see note)*
	That neithir of my giltes, indulgence,	*neither for my guilt forgiveness*
	Ne grace of helthe in no maner wyse	*Nor; salvation in any manner*
	Disserved have I for my greet offense,	*Deserved; great offense*
	Lo, that meene I that is my covetyse,	*by which I mean my covetousness*
40	That whereas my dissert may not souffyse,	*merit; suffice*
	The grace and mercy of yow bothe tweye	*you both two*
	Ne faille nat: that is it that I preye.	*Shall not fail*
	Mercyful Lord, have upon me mercy,	
	And lady, thy sone unto mercy meeve.	*move*
45	With herte contryt preye I thee meekly,	*heart contrite pray*
	Lady, thy pitee on me, wrecche, preeve;	*prove your pity on me, [a] wretch*
	Bisyly preye, for I fully leeve	*Busily; believe*
	For whom thow preyest, God nat list denye	*God will not deny*
	Thyn axynge, blessid maiden Marie!	*Your request*

69

	Salve	Hayl, oure patron and lady of erthe,	*(see note)*
	Regina	Qwhene of heven and emprys of helle:	*Queen; empress*
	mater	Moder of al blis thu art, the ferth	*bliss; estuary*
	misericordie	Of mercy and grace the secunde welle.	*second well (see note)*
5	*vita*	Lyfe come of thee as the sownde of a bell	*comes from; sound*
	Dulcedo	Swetnes thu art both moder and mayde,	*Sweetness*
	et spes nostra	Oure hope with thee that we may dwelle	
	Salve	Hayl, ful of grace, as Gabriel sayd.	
	Ad te	To thee oure socour, our helpe, our trust,	*you our aide*
10	*clamamus*	We crye, we pray, we make oure complaynt.	
	Exules	Exylde to pryson fro gostly lust,	*spiritual desire*
	filii	The childer of Adam that so was ataynte,	*children; tainted*

	Eve	Of Eve our moder here ar we dreynte.	*overwhelmed*
	Ad te	To thee that byndes the fendes whelpe	*binds; fiend's offspring*
15	*suspiramus*	We sighe, we grone; we wax al faynte,	*grow faint*
	gementes	Wepyng for sorow, gode lady, now helpe.	*good*
	Et flentes	Wepyng for syn and for oure payne	
	In hac	In this derknes oure tyme we spende;	*darkness*
	lacrimarum	Of teres the comforth is a swete rayne,	*tears; rain*
20	*valle*	In the wayle of grace it will discende.	*Into; valley*
	Eya	Hafe done, gode lady, grace is thi frende;	
	Ergo	Therfore send us sum of thi grace.	*some*
	advocata	Oure advocate make us afore our ende,[1]	
	nostra	Oure synnes to wesche whils we hafe space.	*wash [away]; have*
25	*Illos tuos miseri-*		
	cordes oculos	Thi mercyful eene and lufly loke	*eyes; lovely gaze*
	Ad nos converte	Cast opon us for oure disporte,	*pleasure*
	Et Ihesum	And Jesu, thi babe, that thi flesche toke,	*took*
	Benedictum	So blyssed a Lord make us supporte,	
	Fructum	That fruyt of lyfe may us comfort.	
30	*ventris tui*	Of thi wome the fruyt may suffyse	*womb; suffice*
	nobis	To us whorby we may resorte,	*whereby; return*
	post hoc	Aftyr this exyle to paradyse.	*After*
	exilium	Exyle is grevos in this derk werre;	*grievous; dark confusion*
	ostende	Schewe us thi luf, the stronger to fyght.	*show; love*
35	*Benignum*	Benygne lady and our se sterre	*Kind; sea*
	O clemens	O buxum lanterne, gyf us thi lyght.	*gracious; give*
	O pia	O meke, o chaste, o blistfull syght	*blissful*
	O dulcis	O swete, o kynde, o gentyll and fre,	*noble*
	maria	Mary, with Jesu that joyful knyght,	
40	*Salve*	Hayle and fare wele and thinke on me.	

Amen.

---

[1] *Be our advocate before we die*

70

Mayden moder milde,
Oiez cel oreysoun, — Hear this prayer
From shome thou me shilde — shame; shield
E de ly mal feloun. — And from the evil villain

5 For love of thine childe,
Me menez de tresoun: — Lead me from treachery
Ich wes wod ant wilde, — I was mad and wayward
Ore su en prisoun. — Now I am in prison

Thou art feyr ant fre — fair and noble
10 *E plein de doucour;* — And full of gentleness (sweetness)
Of thee sprong the ble, — person
Ly soverein creatour; — The sovereign creator
Mayde, byseche y thee, — I beseech you
Vostre seint socour, — Your holy aid
15 Meoke and mylde be with me,
Pur la sue amour. — For love of him

Tho Judas Jesum founde, — When Judas found Jesus
Donque ly beysa, — Then kissed him
He wes bete ant bounde, — beaten and bound
20 *Que nus tous fourma.* — Who made us all
Wyde were is wounde — Wide; his wounds
Qe le gyw ly dona; — Which the Jews gave him
He tholede hard stounde, — suffered great pain
Me poi le greva. — But little did he grieve

25 On stou ase thou stode, — In [the] place where you stood
Pucele, tot pensaunt, — Maiden, lost in melancholy
Thou restest thee under rode, — You pause (rest yourself) under the cross
Ton fitz veites pendant; — See your son hanging
Thou seghe is sides of blode, — You see his bloody sides
30 *L'alme de ly partaunt.* — The soul parting from him
He ferede uch an fode — caused fear in everyone
En mound que fust vivaunt. — Who lived in the world

	Ys siden were sore,	*His sides*
	Le sang de ly cora;	*The blood ran from them*
35	That lond wes forlore,	*That land (the world) was lost*
	Mes il le rechata.	*But he redeemed it*
	Uch bern that wes ybore	*Every child who was born*
	En enfern descenda;	*Descended to hell*
	He tholede deth ther fore,	*suffered death therefore [for them]*
40	*En ciel puis mounta.*	*Then rose to heaven*
	Tho Pilat herde the tydynge —	*When Pilate heard the news*
	Molt fu joyous baroun —	*He was a most joyful nobleman*
	He lette byfore him brynge	*commanded*
	Jesu Nazaroun.	*Jesus of Nazareth*
45	He was ycrouned kynge	*crowned*
	Pur nostre redempcioun;	*For our redemption*
	Whose wol me synge	*Whoever sings [with] me*
	Avera grant pardoun.	*Will receive great pardon*

The Joys of Mary

71

Mary, for thine joys fyve,
Teche me the vey to ryth lyve.   *way to live right*

72

Be glad, of al maydens flourre,   *flower of all maidens*
That hast in hevene swich honoure   *such*
To passe in hye blisse   *surpass; high*
Aungelys and othur seints also;
5   The joye is nought like therto
Of eny that ther isse.   *any; is*

Be gladde, Goddis spouse bright,   *God's*
That gevest ther gretter light   *greater*
To the hevenli place
10 Than evir dede sunne on erthe here   *did sun*
When hit was brightis and most clere   *it; brightest*
In the midday space.

Be glad, of vertues vessel clene,   *clean vessel of virtues*
To whom obeith as right quene   *obeys*
15 The court of heven on hyghe,
And worschipeth withoute stynting   *ceasing*
Thorwe thankinges and be blessing   *Through; by*
And endeles melodie.

Be glad, moder of Jesu dere,
20 That spedist alle way thi prayere   *perpetually sends forth prayers*
Byfore the Trinité.
As God wil, suich is thi wille;   *such*

137

The Joys of Mary

	There may no wight sinful spille	*one; perish*
	On whom thou has pité.	*pity*
25	Be glad, moder of hevene king,	*heaven's*
	Swich he wol, aftir plesing,	*Such he will, as it pleases him*
	To thi servaunt trewe	*true*
	Graunt bothe mede and reward	*reward and recompense*
	Here and also aftirward	
30	In joye that ever is newe.	
	Be glad, mayden and moder swete,	
	Next the Sone thou hast a sete,	*You have a seat next to the Son*
	Iglorified blisfulli.	*Blissfully glorified*
	And this we saddely beleve,	*solemnly*
35	But how, openly descrive	*plainly describe*
	Ne may no thing ertheli.	
	Be glad, of oure gladnesse welle,	*well (source) of our gladness*
	That art seker ay to dwelle	*sure always*
	In mirthe that hath non ende,	*endless joy*
40	Which schal never were ne wast;	*wear or waste*
	Therto bringe us, moder chast,	*chaste*
	When we hen wende.	*go hence*
	Thus, thou blessed quene of hevene,	
	I worschipe thee with joyes sevene	*honor you*
45	In alle that y may.	*I*
	When y schal leve this soreful lyf,	*sorrowful*
	Be to me redy in that strif,	
	Lady, y thee pray.	*I pray you*
	Lady, for these joyes sevene	
50	And for thi gladnesse five,	*five joys*
	Bringe me to the blisse of hevene	
	Thorwe grace of clene lyfe.	*Through*

73

Heyle be thou, ladye so bryght:
Gabriel that seyde so ryght,   *rightly*
   "Cryst ys wyth thee."
Swettyst and swotyst in syght,   *Sweetest and most fragrant*
5   Modyr and mayde of myght,
    Have mercy on mee.

Hayle be thou, fynest to fonde: *seek*
Jesu thy sone, y undyrstonde,   *I*
   Of thee borne he was.
10   Glad were thou, lef in londe,   *beloved on earth*
Tho thou haddyst in honde   *When; hand*
    The prynce of oure pees.   *peace*

Heyle, ladye, flower of alle thynges:
Ryally three ryche kynges,
15   Derely dyght,   *Richly arrayed*
Comely wyth knelynges,   *kneelings (respect)*
Broughten thi sone three thynges;
    The sterre was lyght.   *star*

Hayle, gladdyst of alle wyve: *women*
20   Aryse fro deth to lyve   *Arose from death to life*
   Thy sone, tho thou syghe.   *while you sighed*
Blyssyd be thoo woundys fyve   *those five wounds*
That made mannys soule to thryve   *man's; thrive*
   In heven so hyghe.   *high*

25   Heyle, joye in hert and in yghe: *heart; eye*
Wyth yghe thy sylf thoo thou syghe   *your own eyes though you sighed*
   On Holy Thursdaye,   *(see note)*
Jesu thi sone all upstyghe   *ascended*
Hoom into heven so hyghe,   *Home*
30   The apostles to paye.   *reward*

Heyle, ladye, full of all blys,
Tho that thou wentyst wysse   *When; went directly*

To blys soo bryght,   *so*
That blys God lete us never mysse,   *permit; to miss*
35   Marye; thou us wysely wysse   *guide*
Be daye and be nyght. Amen.   *By day*

74

Haile be thu, Mari maiden bright: *[to] you*
Thu teche me the wais right.   *You teach; ways*
I am a sorful, dreri wight,   *sorrowful, dreary one*
Als thu mai se,   *As you may see*
5   Quer I sal in the hard pine of hel be.   *Where I shall; suffering of hell*

Mi sinful saule sighes sare: *soul; sorely*
Lived I have in sin and care,
Leve I wil and do na mare.   *Cease; no more*
Mi levedi fre,   *lady noble*
10   Saul and bodi, liif and dede, biteche I thee.   *Soul; life and death, I commit to you*

Thar thu lay in thi bright boure,   *Where; bower*
Levedi, quite als lelé floure,   *white as lily flower*
An angel com fra hevene toure,   *from*
Sant Gabriel,   *Holy*
15   And said, "Levedi, ful of blis, ai worth thee wel!"   *grace, ever blessed*

Stil thu stod, ne stint thu noght,   *Quietly you kept watched, nor stopped not*
Thu said til him the bodword broght,   *You; to; message brought*
"Al his wil it sal be wroght,   *All his will it shall be done*
In his ancele."   *Through; handmaiden*
20   Levedi, bifor thi suete sun mak us lele.   *faithful*

The tother joy I wate it was,   *other (second); know*
Als sun schines thoru the glas,   *As; shines through the glass*
Sua ert thu, levedi, wemles,   *So are you, lady, spotless*
And ai sal be.   *ever shall*
25   Levedi, for that suete joy thu reu on me.   *have pity*

The Joys of Mary

	The thrid joy I understand,	*third*
	Thre kinges com of thrin land,	*three different lands*
	To fal thi suete sun til hand,	*fall before your sweet son*
	And gaf him gift:	*gave*
30	Mir, reclis, and gold red, als it was right.	*Myrrh, incense*
	The king was riche, the gold was rede,	
	The reclis fel til his goddhed,	*incense fell (was appropriate) to*
	Mir to man that sal be dede	*Myrrh for man who shall die (Christ)*
	For ur sake.	*our*
35	Levedi, to thi suete sun at ane us make.	*make us one with your sweet son*
	The feird it es al thoru his grace,	*fourth it is all through*
	Wuen he fra dede to liif ras,	*When he from death to life rose*
	Wuen he sua hard suongen was	*so hard scourged*
	On rode tre.	*cross*
40	Levedi, of ur sinnes al thu make us fre.	*free us from all our sins*
	The fiift, thu was til heven broght:	*fifth, you were brought to heaven*
	The Juus thee soght and fand thee noght,	*Jews sought you and did not find you*
	Als thi suete sun it wroght,	*As; wrought*
	Almighti king.	
45	Levedi Mari, be ur helpe at ur ending.	*our*
	Levedi, for thi joies five,	
	Thu kid thi might and help us suith,	*Exercise your power; sweetly*
	Levedi Mari, moder o live,	*of life*
	Wid flur and fruit,	*flower*
50	Rose and leli, thu sprede ay wide and helpe thi suite.	*lily; stretch*
	Levedi Mari, wele thu wast,	*well you know*
	The feindes fraistes me ful fast,	*fiends assail*
	Wele I hope I sal thaim cast	*I shall cast them [off]*
	Thoru might of thee,	*Through your might*
55	Quen I neven thi suete nam I ger thaim fle.	*When I name; name; make them free*
	Thir jois er said als I can sai	*These joys I tell as I can*
	Mi site, mi soru, I cast away,	*care; sorrow*
	Nu help me, levedi, wele thu may,	*Now*

	And be mi spere.	*hope*
60	Fra the har pain of hell thu me were.	*From; hard; protect*
	All that singes this sang	*who sing; song*
	And all that ligges in paines strang,	*lie; strong suffering*
	Thu lede thaim right thar thai ga wrang,	*You guide them*
	And have merci	
65	On all that trous that Godd was born of thee, fair levedi.	*believe*

75

	Heyl be thou, Marie, milde quene of hevene,	*[to] you; gentle*
	Blessed be thi name, and god it is to nevene;	*good; name*
	To thee I mene mi mone: I preie thou her mi stevene,	*intend; plaint; hear; voice*
	Ne let me nevere deie in none of the sennes sevene.[1]	
5	*Ave Maria gracia plena dominus tecum.*	*(Luke 1:28)*
	Heil, seinte Marie, quene cortas and hende,	*courteous; gracious*
	For the joye that thou haddest wan Crist the aungel sende,	*when*
	And seide that the holi gost scholde in thi bodi wende;	*into; pass*
	Thou bring me out of sinne and schuld me fram the fende.	*shield; from; devil*
10	*Ave Maria gracia plena dominus tecum.*	
	Joyful was thin herte withouten eni drede	*fear*
	Wan Jhesu Crist was of thee boren fayrest of alle thede;	*born; people*
	And thou mayde bifore and after as we in bok rede,	*book (Bible)*
	Lefdi, for that joie thou helpe me at nede.	*Lady; in [my] need*
15	*Ave Maria gracia plena dominus tecum.*	
	Ladi, ful of grace, gladful was thi chere	*countenance*
	Wan Jhesu Crist fram deth aros, that was thee lef and dere;[2]	
	Ladi, for the love of him that lay thin herte nere,	*near*
	Help me out of senne ther wile that I am here.	*sin during the time*
20	*Ave Maria gracia plena dominus tecum.*	

---

[1] *Nor let me ever die in any of the seven [deadly] sins*

[2] *When Jesus Christ arose from death, who was beloved and dear to you*

The Joys of Mary

Ladi, ful of myghte, mek and milde of mode,
For the love of swete Jhesu that don was on the rode,   *put; cross*
And for his woundes five that runnen alle ablode,   *bloody*
Thou help me out of senne, ladi fayr and gode.   *good*
25   *Ave Maria gracia plena dominus tecum.*

Ladi, seinte Marie, fair and goud and swete,
For the love of the teres that thiself lete   *tears; shed*
Wan thou seye Jhesu Crist nayled hond and fete,   *saw; feet*
Thou geve me grace in herte my sennes for to bete.   *amend*
30   *Ave Maria gracia plena dominus tecum.*

In counsayl thou art best, and trewe in alle nede,   *true; need*
To sinful men wel prest and redi in goud dede;   *very prompt*
Ladi, for the love of him thou seye on rode blede,   *saw; cross bleed*
Thou help me now and evere and save me at the nede.
35   *Ave Maria gracia plena dominus tecum.*

Ladi, flour of alle, so rose in erber red,   *flower; like; garden*
To thee I crie and calle, to thee I make my bed;   *prayer*
Thou be in stude and stalle ther I draue to ded[1]
Let me nevere falle in hondes of the qued.   *hands; devil (evil one)*
40   *Ave Maria gracia plena dominus tecum.*

Marie, for that swete joie that thou were than inne
Wan thou seie Jhesu Crist, flour of al mankinne,
Steye up to hevene ther joye is evere inne,   *Ascend; where*
Of bale be thou mi bote and bring me out of sinne.   *pain; relief*
45   *Ave Maria gracia plena dominus tecum.*

Marie, for that swete joye wan thou fram erthe was tan   *taken*
Into the blisse of hevene with aungeles mani an,   *many a one*
And iset bi swete Jhesu in fel and flecsch and ban,   *placed; skin; flesh; bone*
Thou bringe me to joyes that nevere schal be gon.   *shall; gone*
50   *Ave Maria gracia plena dominus tecum.*

---

[1] *You are in stable and stall where I draw near to death*

143

Marie, ful in grace, that sittest in trone,   *throne*
Now I thee biseche thou graunte me mi bone;   *prayer*
Jhesu to love and dred, my lif t'amende sone,   *to amend soon*
And bringe me to that heye kyng that weldeth sune and mone.   *high; wields*
55   *Ave Maria gracia plena dominus tecum.*

For thi joies five, ladi fair and bryght,
And for thi maydenhede and thi moche myght,   *great might*
Thou helpe me to come into tha iche lyght   *same*
Ther joye is withoute ende and day withote nyght.   *Where*
60   *Ave Maria gracia plena dominus tecum.*

Ladi, Seynte Marie, yif that thi wille were,   *if*
As thou art ful of joye and I am ful of care,
Thou help me out of sinne and lat me falle namare;   *no more*
And geve me grace in erthe my sinnes to reue sare.   *sorely rue*
65   *Ave Maria gracia plena dominus tecum.*

Ladi, quene of hevene, thou here me wit wille;   *hear; eagerly*
Y praye thou her mi stevene and let my soule nevere spille   *I; voice; die*
In non of the sinnes sevene thorw no fendes wille   *none; through; fiend's*
Nou bring my saule to hevene, therin a place to fille.   *soul*
70   *Ave Maria gracia plena dominus tecum.*

76

Levedy, for thare blisse   *that joy*
That thu heddest at the frume,   *you had; beginning*
Tho thu wistest myd iwisse   *When; knew with certainty*
That Jhesus wolde beo thi sune,   *be; son*
5   The hwile we beoth on lyve thisse   *While we are in this life*
Sunnen to don is ure wune;   *To sin is our custom*
Help us nu that we ne mysse   *now; do not lose*
Of that lif that is to cume.   *come*

Moder, blithe were thu tho,   *joyful; then*
10   Hwanne thu iseye heoven-king   *When you saw*
Of thee ibore withute wo   *Of you born; pain*

That scop thee and alle thing.	*Who created you*
Beo ure scheld from ure ivó,	*our shield; our foe*
And gef us thine blessying,	*give*
15 And biwyte us evermo	*protect; evermore*
From allekunnes suneging.	*human sin*
Levedi, al myd rihte	*rightfully*
Thu were gled and blithe	*glad; joyful*
Tho Crist thureh his myhte	*When; through his might*
20 Aros from dethe to lyve,	
That alle thing con dihte,	*Who did all things ordain*
And wes iboren of wyve.	*was born of woman*
He make us clene and bryhte	*made us pure; virtuous*
For his wundes fyve.	*By means of; five wounds*
25 From the Munt of Olyvete	*Mount of Olives*
Tho thi sone to heovene steyh,	*When; ascended*
Thu hit byheolde myd eye swete,	*beheld it with; loving*
For he wes thin heorte neyh.	*was near to your heart*
Ther he haveth imaked thi sete	*has prepared your seat*
30 In o stude that is ful heyh;	*a place; high*
Ther thee schulen engles grete,	*There angels shall greet you*
For thu ert bothe hende and sleyh.	*you are; courteous; prudent*
The king that wes of thee ibore,	*was; born*
To heovene he thee vette,	*he took you*
35 To thare blisse that wes forlore,	*the grace; was lost*
And bi hymseolve sette	*himself placed you*
Vor he hedde thee icore.	*For he had chosen you*
Wel veyre he thee grette;	*fairly; greeted*
Blythe were thu thervore,	
40 Tho engles thee imette.	*When angels met you*
Moder of milce and mayde hende,	*mercy; courteous*
Ich thee bidde as I con	*beseech you as I do*
Ne let thu noht the world us blende,	*Do not let the world blind us*
That is ful of ure ivon,	*our foes*
45 Ac help us at ure lyves ende,	*But; our lives'*
Thu that bere God and mon,	*You who bore God and man*

The Joys of Mary

	And us alle to heovene sende	
	Hwenne we schulle this lif forgon.	*When; depart*
	Jesus, for thire moder bene	*your good mother*
50	That is so veyr and so bryht,	*fair; pure*
	Al so wis, so heo is quene	*And so wise, that she is queen*
	Of heovene and eorthe, and thet is ryht:	*proper*
	Of ure sunnes make us clene,	*our sins; pure*
	And gef us that eche lyht,	*give; same light*
55	And to heovene us alle imene,	*together*
	Louerd, thu bryng, for wel thu miht.	*Lord; might*

146

Chansons d'Aventure and Love Quests

77

	Ase y me rod this ender day	*As I rode out the other day*
	By grene wode to seche play,	*wood to seek pleasure*
	Mid herte y thohte al on a may,	*With; entirely; maiden*
	Suetest of alle thinge.	*Sweetest; creatures*
5	Lythe ant ich ou telle may	*Listen and I may tell you*
	Al of that suete thinge.	*blessed one*
	This maiden is suete ant fre of blod,	*gracious and noble*
	Briht ant feyr of milde mod;	*Bright and fair; mind (temperament)*
	Alle heo mai don us god	*In every way she; good*
10	Thurh hire bysechynge.	*Through her intercession*
	Of hire he tok fleysh ant blod,	*took*
	Jhesus hevene kynge.	*heaven's*
	With al mi lif y love that may;	*life; maiden*
	He is mi solas nyht ant day,	*She; solace*
15	My joie ant eke my beste play,	*also; pleasure*
	Ant eke my lovelongynge.	
	Al the betere me is that day	*better [to] me*
	That ich of hire synge.	*I; her sing*
	Of alle thinge y love hire mest:	*most*
20	My dayes blis, my nyhtes rest;	
	Heo counseileth ant helpeth best	*She*
	Bothe elde ant yynge.	*old; young*
	Nou y may, yef y wole,	*if I will*
	The fif joyes mynge.	*five; recall*
25	The furst joie of that wymman:	
	When Gabriel from hevene cam	*came*
	Ant seide God shulde bicome man	*said*

147

	Ant of hire be bore	*her be born*
	Ant bringe up of helle pyn	*from Hell's torment*
30	Monkyn that wes forlore.	*Mankind; lost*
	That other joie of that may	*second joy; maiden*
	Wes o Cristesmasse day	*Was on*
	When God wes bore on thoro lay	*in perfect light*
	Ant brohte us lyhtnesse.	*brightness/light*
35	The ster wes seie byfore day;	*star was visible*
	This hirdes bereth wytnesse.	*These shepherds bear*
	The thridde joie of that levedy:	*lady*
	That men clepeth the Epyphany,	*call*
	When the kynges come wery	*weary*
40	To presente hyre sone	*her*
	With myrre, gold, ant encens,	*incense*
	That wes mon bicome.	*Who was man*
	The furthe joie we telle mawen:	*may*
	On Estermorewe wen hit gon dawen,	*Easter morning; began [to] dawn*
45	Hyre sone that wes slawen	*Her son; slain*
	Aros in fleysh ant bon.	*Arose; bone*
	More joie ne mai me haven,	*More joy one may not have*
	Wyf ne mayden non.	*Neither wife nor maiden*
	The fifte joie of that wymman:	
50	When hire body to hevene cam,	
	The soule to the body nam,	*returned*
	Ase hit wes woned to bene.	*it was accustomed to be*
	Crist leve us alle with that wymman	*grant us*
	That joie al forte sene.	*joy completely to see*
55	Preye we alle to oure levedy,	*lady*
	Ant to the sontes that woneth hire by,	*saints; live with her*
	That he of us haven merci	*they*
	Ant that we ne misse	*[do] not fail*
	In this world to ben holy	
60	Ant wynne hevene blysse. Amen.	*win/enjoy; bliss*

78

Nou skrinketh rose ant lylie flour,	*wither*
That whilen ber that suete savour,	*earlier bore; fragrance*
In somer, that suete tide;	*summer; sweet time*
Ne is no quene so stark ne stour,	*Nor; queen; strong nor powerful*
5 Ne no levedy so bryht in bour,	*lady; chamber*
That ded ne shal byglyde.	*Who shall not die*
Whose wol fleysh lust forgon	*Who will forgo physical pleasures*
And hevene blis abyde,	*live in heavenly bliss*
On Jesu be is thoht anon,	*his thought constantly*
10 That therled was ys side.	*Whose side was pierced*
From Petresbourh in o morewenyng,	*one morning*
As y me wende o my pleyghyng,	*went out for my pleasure*
On mi folie y thohte.	*I thought of my foolishness*
Menen y gon my mournyng	*Complaining I began my lament*
15 To hire that ber the hevene kyng;	*her who bore*
Of merci hire bysohte:	*Of her [I] sought mercy*
Ledy, preye thi sone for ous,	*us*
That us duere bohte,	*Who dearly bought us*
Ant shild us from the lothe hous	*And protect; hateful*
20 That to the fend is wrohte.	*for the fiend is built*
Myn herte of dedes wes fordred,	*My heart was terrified of death*
Of synne that y have my fleish fed	*I have fed my body*
Ant folewed al my tyme,	*And followed all my life*
That y not whider i shal be led,	*I do not know where I shall be led*
25 When y lygge on dethes bed,	*I lie*
In joie ore into pyne.	*Into joy or into pain*
On o ledy myn hope is,	*one*
Moder ant virgyne;	
We shulen into hevene blis	*shall [go] into heavenly bliss*
30 Thurh hire medicine.	*Through her*
Betere is hire medycyn	
Then eny mede or eny wyn;	*Than any mead or any wine*
Hire erbes smulleth suete.	*herbs smell sweet*
From Catenas into Dyvelyn	*Caithness; Dublin*

35	Nis ther no leche so fyn	*There is no physician so fine*
	Oure serewes to bete.	*sorrows; cure*
	Mon that feleth eni sor	*Man who feels any pain/sorrow*
	And his folie wol lete,	*wishes to abandon his folly*
	Withoute gold other eny tresor	*any other treasure*
40	He mai be sound ant sete.	*safe and content*

	Of penaunce is his plastre al;	*plaster (bandage)*
	Ant ever serven hire y shal	*I shall always serve her*
	Nou and al my lyve.	
	Nou is fre that er wes thral	*Now [everyone who] formerly was enslaved is free*
45	Al thourh that levedy gent and smal.	*through; lady gentle; slender*
	Heried be hyr joies fyve.	*Praised; five joys*
	Wherso eny sek ys,	*Where anyone is sick*
	Thider hye blyve,	*To there (her) let him hurry*
	Thurh hire beoth ybroht to blis	
50	Bo mayden ant wyve.	

	For he that dude is body on tre	*put his body on the cross*
	Of oure sunnes have pieté,	*sins; pity*
	That weldes heovene boures;	*rules; dwellings*
	Wymmon, with thi jolyfté,	*cheerfulness*
55	Thou thench on Godes shoures	*think; suffering*
	Thah thou be whyt and bryth on ble	*Though; bright*
	Falewen shule thy floures.	*Your flowers shall wither*
	Jesu have merci of us	
	That al this world honoures.	
	Amen.	

79

	In a tabernacle of a toure,	*niche; tower*
	As I stode musyng on the mone,	*moon*
	A crouned quene, most of honoure,	*greatest*
	Apered in gostly syght ful sone.	*Appeared in a vision*
5	She made compleynt thus by hyr one,	*on her own*
	For mannes soule was wrapped in wo,	

"I may nat leve mankynde allone,
   Quia amore langueo.   *Because I languish for love*

"I longe for love of man my brother,
10 I am hys vokete to voyde hys vyce;   *I am his advocate to eliminate his faults*
    I am hys moder — I can none other —   *I cannot do otherwise*
    Why shuld I my dere chylde dispyce?   *despise*
    Yef he me wrathe in diverse wyse,   *If; anger*
    Though flesshes freelté fall me fro,   *flesh's frailty fall from me*
15 Yet must me rewe hym tyll he ryse,   *pity; arises*
       Quia amore langueo.

"I byd, I byde in grete longyng,   *pray; wait*
    I love, I loke when man woll crave,   *look; ask (desire)*
    I pleyne for pyté of peynyng;   *lament; suffering*
20 Wolde he aske mercy, he shuld hit have.   *If he would ask; should have it*
    Say to me, soule, and I shall save,
    Byd me, my chylde, and I shall go;
    Thow prayde me never but my son forgave,   *You never prayed to me*
       Quia amore langueo.

25 "O wreche in the worlde, I loke on thee,   *miserable [people]*
    I se thy trespas day by day,   *see*
    With lechery ageyns my chastité,   *against (in contrast to)*
    With pryde agene my pore aray;   *against my humble array*
    My love abydeth, thyne ys away;
30 My love thee calleth, thow stelest me fro;   *calls you; steal away from me*
    Sewe to me, synner, I thee pray,   *Sue (Pray)*
       Quia amore langueo.

"Moder of mercy I was for thee made;   *I was made mother of mercy for you*
    Who nedeth hit but thow allone?   *needs it but you alone*
35 To gete thee grace I am more glade   *win you grace*
    Than thow to aske hit; why wylt thou noon?   *Than you to ask it; none*
    When seyd I nay, tel me, tyll oon?   *to anyone*
    Forsoth never yet, to frende ne foo;   *nor foe*
    When thou askest nought, than make I moone,   *then I complain*
40   *Quia amore langueo.*

"I seke thee in wele and wrechednesse,   *prosperity*
I seke thee in ryches and poverté;
Thow man beholde where thy moder ys,
Why lovest thou me nat, syth I love thee?   *since*
45   Synful or sory how evere thow be,
So welcome to me there ar no mo;   *more*
I am thy suster, ryght trust on me,
    Quia amore langueo.

"My childe ys outlawed for thy synne,
50   Mankynde ys bette for hys trespasse;   *made better despite*
Yet prykketh myne hert that so ny my kynne   *grieves; near*
Shuld be dysseased, o sone, allasse!   *distressed/afflicted*
Thow art hys brother, hys moder I was;   *Thou (sinner)*
Thow sokyd my pappe, thow lovyd man so;   *Thou (Jesus)*
55   Thow dyed for hym, myne hert he has,
    Quia amore langueo.

"Man, leve thy synne than for my sake;   *leave; then*
Why shulde I gyf thee that thou nat wolde?   *what you do not want*
And yet yef thow synne, som prayere take   *if you sin*
60   Or trust in me as I have tolde.
Am nat I thy moder called?   *not*
Why shulde I flee thee? I love thee soo,   *you so*
I am thy frende, I helpe beholde,
    Quia amore langueo.

65   "Now, sone," she sayde, "wylt thou sey nay,   *refuse*
Whan man wolde mende hym of hys mys?   *correct himself; wrong-doing*
Thow lete me never in veyne yet pray: *vain*
Than, synfull man, see thow to thys,   *see to this*
What day thou comest, welcome thow ys,   *you are welcome*
70   Thys hundreth yere yef thow were me fro;   *Were you away from me a hundred years*
I take thee ful fayne, I clyppe, I kysse,   *gladly; embrace*
    Quia amore langueo.

"Now wold I syt and sey nomore,
Leve and loke with grete longyng;   *Cease and wait*
75   When a man woll calle, I wol restore;   *will call; will restore*

	I love to save hym, he ys myne hosprynge;	*offspring*
	No wonder yef myne hert on hym hynge,	*hang*
	He was my neyghbore — what may I doo?	*do*
	For hym had I thys worshippyng,	
80	And therefore *Amore langueo.*	
	"Why was I crouned and made a quene?	
	Why was I called of mercy the welle?	
	Why shuld an erthly woman bene	*be*
	So hygh in heven above aungelle?	
85	For thee, mankynde, the truthe I telle;	
	Thou aske me helpe, and I shall do	
	That I was ordeyned, kepe thee fro helle,	*That which; appointed*
	Quia amore langueo.	
	"Nowe, man, have mynde on me forever,	*be mindful of*
90	Loke on thy love thus languysshyng;	
	Late us never fro other dissevere:	*Let; each other separate*
	Myne helpe ys thyne oune; crepe under my wynge.	*own*
	Thy syster ys a quene, thy brother ys a kynge,	
	Thys heritage ys tayled; sone, come therto,	*tallied (guaranteed in writing)*
95	Take me for thy wyfe and lerne to synge,	
	Quia amore langueo."	

80

	Upon a lady my love ys lente,	*bestowed (lent)*
	Withowtene change of any chere,	*Without; mood (i.e., steadfast)*
	That ys lovely and contynent	*temperate*
	And most at my desyre.	*the center of; desire*
5	Thys lady ys yn my herte pyght;	*is placed in my heart*
	Her to love y have gret haste.	*I; great*
	With all my power and my myghth	*might*
	To her y make myne herte stedfast.	*I make my heart*
	Therfor wyll y non othur spowese,	*I desire no other spouse*
10	Ner none othur loves for to take,	*Nor other love to take*

153

	But only to here y make my vowes,	*her I*
	And all othur to forsake.	*others*
	Thys lady ys gentyll and meke;	*is gentle and meek*
	Moder she ys and well of all.	*is; well*
15	She ys nevur for to seke	*never far to seek*
	Nothur to grete ner to small.	*Neither too great nor*
	Redy she ys nyght and day,	*Ready*
	To man and wommon and chylde ynfere,	*together*
	Gyf that they wyll awght to here say,	*If; will only to her*
20	Our prayeres mekely for to here.	*meekly; hear*
	To serve thys lady we all be bownde	*are bound*
	Both nyghth and day yn every place,	*night*
	Where evur we be, yn felde or towne,	*in field*
	Or elles yn any othur place.	*else*
25	Pray we to thys lady bryghth	*bright*
	In the worshyp of the Trinité	
	To brynge us alle to heven lyghth:	*heaven's light*
	Amen, say we, for charyté.	

81

	Maiden in the mor lay,	*moor*
	In the mor lay,	
	Sevenyst fulle,	*Seven nights*
	Sevenist fulle.	
5	Maiden in the mor lay,	
	In the mor lay,	
	Sevenistes fulle ant a day.	*and*
	Welle was hire mete:	*Good; her food*
	Wat was hire mete?	
10	The primerole ant the,	*primrose and*
	The primerole ant the,	
	Welle was hire mete:	

Wat was hire mete?
The primerole ant the violet.

15 Welle was hire dryng: *drink*
Wat was hire dryng?
The chelde water of the,   *cold*
The chelde water of the,
Welle was hire dryng:
20 What was hire dryng?
The chelde water of the welle spring.

Welle was hire bour: *bower*
Wat was hire bour?
The red rose an te,   *and the*
25 The red rose an te,
Welle was hire bour:
Wat was hire bour?
The rede rose an te lilie flour.   *lily flower*

82

Lulley, lulley, lully, lulley,
The fawcon hath born my mak away.   *falcon; mate/maker*

He bare hym up, he bare him down,   *bore*
He bare hym into an orchard brown.

5 In that orchard ther was an hall,
That was hanged with purpill and pall.   *rich curtains*

And in that hall ther was a bede,   *bed*
Hit was hangid with gold so rede.   *It; hung*

And yn that bed ther lythe a knyght,   *in; there lay*
10 His wowndes bledyng day and nyght.

By that bedes side ther kneleth a may,   *kneels; maiden*
And she wepeth both nyght and day.   *weeps*

And by that bedes side ther stondith a ston,	*bed's side; stands; stone*
"Corpus Christi" wretyn theron.	*"Body of Christ" written*

83

	Of on that is so fayr and bright,	*one*
	Velud maris stella,	*As the star of the sea*
	Brighter than the dayis light,	*day's*
	Parens et puella,	*Mother and maiden*
5	Ic crie to thee, thou se to me;	*look upon*
	Levedy, preye thi sone for me,	*Lady, beseech*
	Tam pia,	*So devoted*
	That ic mote come to thee,	*I might*
	Maria.	
10	Levedi, flour of alle thing,	*flower; all creation*
	Rosa sine spina,	*Rose without thorn*
	Thu bere Jhesu hevene king,	
	Gratia divina;	*By divine grace*
	Of alle thu berst the pris,	*are most excellent*
15	Levedi, quene of parays,	
	Electa,	*Chosen one*
	Mayde, milde Moder,	
	Es effecta.	*Made (Created)*
	Of kare, consell thou ert best,	*consolation*
20	*Felix fecundata;*	*Joyfulness made fruitful*
	Of alle wery thou ert rest,	
	Mater honorata;	*Honored mother*
	Bisek him with milde mod	*Beseech*
	That for ous alle sad is blod	*Who; shed his blood*
25	*In cruce,*	*On the cross*
	That we moten komen til him	*might come to*
	In luce.	*In the light*
	Al this world was forlore	*lost*
	Eva peccatrice,	*By the sinner Eve*
30	Tyl our Lord was ybore	*born*

	De te genitrice:	*By you his mother*
	With *Ave* it went away	*Hail*
	Thuster nyth and comet the day	*Dark night; comes*
	Salutis,	*Of salvation*
35	The welle springet hut of thee	*springs out of you*
	Virtutis.	*Of virtue*
	Wel he wot he is thi sone,	*knows*
	Ventre quem portasti;	*Whom you bore in your womb*
	He wyl nout werne thee thi bone,	*refuse; prayer*
40	*Parvum quem lactasti.*	*The little one you suckled*
	So hende and so god he his	*courteous; good; is*
	He havet brout ous to blis	*has brought*
	Superni,	*Of heaven*
	That haves hidut the foule put	*closed; pit*
45	*Inferni.*	*Of hell*

Plate C: **Vierge ouvrante** (fourteenth century). Paris, Musée national du moyen âge — Thermes et hôtel de Cluny. © Photo RMN.

84

Adam lay ibowndyn, bowndyn in a bond,	*(see note)*
Fowre thowsand wynter thowt he not to long;	*too*
And al was for an appil, an appil that he tok,	*apple; took*
As clerkis fyndyn wretyn in here book.	*written; their*

5	Ne hadde the appil take ben, the appil taken ben,	*Had not*
	Ne hadde never our lady a ben hevene qwen.	*have been heaven's queen*
	Blyssid be the tyme that appil take was,	*taken*
	Therfore we mown syngyn, "*Deo Gracias!*"	*may; Thanks be to God*

85

Swete and benygne moder and may,	
Turtill trew, flowre of women alle,	*Turtledove true; flower*
Aurora bryght, clere as the day,	*clear*
Noblest of hewe, thus we thee calle;	*hue*
5 Lylé fragrant eke of the walle,	*Lily*
Ennewid with bemys of blys	*Renewed (Revived)*
In whom never was founden mys:	*found sin*

So fayre, so good, was never non;	
Transcendyng is therfor thi place	*Your place therefore transcends*
10 Aungels alle and seyntis echone;	*Angels all and saints each one*
Next unto God, such is thi grace.	
Lo, thi mekenes thee did purchace	*did purchase [for] you*
Ever in joy so to endure	
In thi grete lande, o princes pure.	*great; princess*

15 Surmountyng is thin excellence,	*your*
Thou rose of prys, thou flowre of May,	*great value*

159

And Phebus lyke in his ascence,   *like Phoebus in his rising*
Natyff of blys where thou art ay,   *Inherent; always*
Lady saunzpere, this is no nay,   *without peer, undeniably*
20 Empres of helle also of righte,   *Empress; justice*
In thee is eke owre anker pight   *In you is also our anchor placed*

Stormys ageyne of cruell syn   *Against storms of cruel sin*
That puyssauntlye us do assayle;   *strongly*
And hwile we this world be yn   *while; are in*
25 Now, lady fayre, thou us not fayle.   *do not fail us*
Lat never vice on us prevayle;   *sin*
Entrete thi babe so, quene on hie   *your son; high*
In whom to thee is no denye.   *Who will not deny you*

Sith here is nought but myserie,   *Since; nothing*
30 The fende, the fleish, the world also   *fiend; flesh*
Assaute us ay withoute mercy,   *Assault; ever*
Not comfortles yit is owre wo: *yet; our woe*
Lady, to thee resorte we do,   *to you we resort*
Evyr tristying thi grace and ayde,   *trusting; aid*
35 In whom fully owre trist is layde.   *trust*

Sewte and service we owe, pardé,   *Suit (Following); indeed (by God)*
To thi highnesse of very due,
As royall most by pedigré
None lyke of grace ne of vertu.   *nor of virtue*
40 Lovely lady, thi servauntes trew,   *true*
Entrikid with passiouns wylde,   *Ensnared*
In tyme of nede socour and shilde;   *strengthen and protect*

Save hem fro syn and worldly shame   *them from sin*
That thee worship with humble herte;   *Who worship you*
45 And to thi son, Jesus by name,
Not sete to pray that we not smert.   *cease; suffer*
Lord, thi jugement we may not sterte   *escape*
Evere therfor thi grace us hight   *we hope for*
In worship of thi modere bright.   *mother*

86

O hie emperice and quene celestiall,   *high empress*
Princes eterne and flour immaculate,   *Princess eternal; flower*
Oure soverane help quhen we unto thee call,   *when*
Haile, ros intact, virgyne inviolate,   *rose*
5   That with the Fader was predestinate   *predestined*
To bere the floure and makar of us all,   *bear; flower; maker*
And with no spue of crime coinquinate,   *spew; co-defiled*
Bot virgyne pure, clerare than cristall.   *clearer*

O blissit ros, o gemme of chastitee,   *blessed rose; gem*
10   O well of beautee, rute of all gudenace,   *root; goodness*
O way of bliss, flour of virginitee,
O hede of treuth, o sterr without dirknace,   *head; star; darkness*
Graunt me, synfull, lyving in unclennace,   *impurity*
To sew the path of parfyte cheritee   *pursue; perfect charity*
15   And to forsake my synnis more and less,   *great and small*
Ay serving him that sched his blud for me.   *Ever; shed; blood*

O blissit lady, fillit of all gudenace,   *filled with; goodness*
Sen all my hope and traist is in your grace,   *Since; trust*
Beseke your sone for your hie gentilnace   *Beseech; son; high gentleness*
20   To grant me laisar or I dee, and space,   *opportunity (leisure) before I die*
All vicious lyf out of my saule to race,   *soul erase*
And ever to lyve in vertew and clenace.   *virtue; purity*
Out of the fendis bandis and his brace   *fiend's bondage; embrace*
Now, glorious lady, help of your gudenace.   *goodness*

25   For rycht as Phebus with his bemys brycht   *just as Phoebus; beams bright*
Illuminate all this erd in longitude,   *earth*
Rycht so your grace, your beautee, and your mycht   *Just so; beauty; might*
Anournyt all this warld in latitude.   *Adorns*
Tharfore to me now schaw your gratitude   *show*
30   Of your magnificence, that day and nycht
Your benigne grace be to me lyvis fud,   *life's food*
And me to save from every maligne wicht.   *evil creature*

	For though Leviathan, the ald serpent,	*old*
	Dissavit had oure parenes prothoplaust,	*Deceived; first parents (Adam and Eve)*
35	That in this warld doune has indigent,	*Who; world have done poorly*
	Maid him to be put till the last	*Made them*
	Eternale deth, quhilk ever suld have last.	*death, which should have lasted forever*
	Knawing your pure and incorrupt entent	*Knowing; intent*
	Incomparable, the Holy Gast als fast	*as*
40	Into your innocence doune has sent,	*down*

	And you illumynit with that blisful lycht;	*illuminated; light*
	I mene the Sone of the hie Deitee,	*mean; high Deity*
	That on a croce suspendit was on hicht	*cross suspended; high*
	For the redemption of humanité.	
45	Quharfor throu yow, my soverane lady free,	*Wherefore through*
	Mankynde redempt was; tharefore day and nycht	
	In every place blissit mote ye be	*may you*
	Eternaly, abufe all erdly wicht.	*above; earthly creatures*

87

	Glade us, maiden, moder milde,	*Make us glad*
	Thurru thin herre thu were wid childe —	*Through; ear; with*
	Gabriel he seide it thee —	
	Glad us, ful of gode thine,	*your goodness/God*
5	Tham thu bere buten pine	*Whom; without pain*
	With thee, lilie of chasteté.	

	Glade us of Jesu thi sone	
	That tholede deit for monis love;	*Who suffered death; man's*
	That dehit was, quiic up aros	*Who [when he] was dead, living*
10	Glade us maiden, Crist up stey	*ascended*
	And in hevene thee isey	*saw*
	He bar him selven into is clos.	*his heavenly mansion*

	Glade us Marie, to joye ibrought,	
	Muche wrchipe Crist hav thee iworut,	*created*
15	In hevene brit in thi paleis;	*bright*
	Ther that frut of thire wombe	*fruit; your*

He igefin us forto fonden   *gave; learn*
   In joye that is endeless.

88

Marye, mayde mylde and fre,   *gracious; noble*
Chambre of the Trynyté,
One wyle lest to me   *Listen for a moment*
Ase ich thee grete wyth songe;   *As I greet you*
5   Thagh my fet onclene be,   *Though; vessel*
My mes thou onderfonge.   *Receive my dish (see note)*

Thou art quene of paradys,
Of hevene, of erthe, of al that hys;   *is*
Thou bere thane kynge of blys   *bore the/that*
10   Wythoute senne and sore;   *sin; pain*
Thou hast yryght that was amys,   *righted what was amiss*
Ywonne that was ylore.   *Won what was lost*

Thou ert the colvere of Noe   *You are; dove of Noah*
That broute the braunche of olyve tre,   *brought*
15   In tokne that pays scholde be   *peace*
Bytuexte God and manne.   *Between*
Suete levedy, help thou me   *Sweet lady*
Wanne ich schal wende hanne.   *go hence (i.e., die)*

Thou art the bosche of Synay,   *bush of Sinai*
20   Thou art the rytte Sarray,   *true Sarah*
Thou hast ybrought ous out of cry   *brought us; calling range*
Of calenge of the fende.   *challenge (see note); devil*
Thou art Crystes oghene drury   *own beloved*
And of Davyes kende.   *David's kin*

25   Thou ert the slinge, thy sone the ston   *You are; son; stone*
That Davy slange Golye opon;   *David slung at Goliath*
Thou ert the yerd al of Aaron,   *rod*
Me dreye isegh spryngynde.   *[That] I saw living, though dry (dead)*

163

	Wytnesse at ham everechon	*You bear witness to all*
30	That wyste of thyne chyldynge.	*knew; childbearing*
	Thou ert the temple Salomon;	*[of] Solomon*
	In thee wondrede Gedeon;	*you wondered Gideon*
	Thou hest ygladed Symeon	*have delighted*
	Wyth thyne swete offrynge	
35	In the temple atte auter-ston	*altar-stone*
	Wyth Jhesus hevene kynge.	
	Thou ert Judith, that fayre wyf,	
	Thou hast abated al that stryf;	*strife*
	Olofernes wyth hys knyf	*Holofernes*
40	Hys hevede thou hym bynome.	*You took his head from him*
	Thou hest ysaved here lef	*their life*
	That to thee wylle come.	*wish to*
	Thou ert Hester, that swete thynge,	*Esther*
	And Assever the ryche kynge	*Assuerus*
45	Thee heth ychose to hys weddynge	*Has chosen to wed you*
	And quene he heth avonge;	*taken*
	For Mardocheus thy derlynge	*Because of Mardochai; favorite*
	Syre Aman was yhonge.	*Haman; hanged*
	The prophete Ezechyel,	
50	In hys boke hyt wytnesseth wel:	*it*
	Thou ert the gate so stronge so stel	*as strong as steel*
	Ac evere yschet fram manne;	*But ever shut from man*
	Thou erte the ryghte vayre Rachel,	*fair*
	Fayrest of alle wymman.	
55	By ryghte toknynge thou ert the hel	*sign; hill*
	Of wan spellede Danyel;	*Of which Daniel told*
	Thou ert Emaus, the ryche castel	
	Thar resteth alle werye;	*Where all the weary rest*
	In thee restede Emanuel,	
60	Of wan yspeketh Ysaye.	*whom Isaiah speaks*

Ine thee hys God bycome a chyld,   *In you has*
Ine thee hys wreche bycome myld;   *vengeance; merciful*
That unicorn that was so wyld
Aleyd hys of a cheaste: *Is appeased by one so chaste*
65 Thou hast ytamed and istyld   *tamed and pacified (calmed)*
Wyth melke of thy breste.   *milk*

Ine the Apocalyps Sent John   *Saint John*
Isey ane wymman wyth sonne bygon,   *Saw; sun, clothed*
Thane mone al onder hyre ton,   *The moon; toes*
70 Icrouned wyth tuel sterre: *Crowned; twelve stars*
Swyl a levedy nas nevere non   *Such; was never any like her*
Wyth thane fend to werre.   *the devil; combat*

Ase the sonne taketh hyre pas
Wythoute breche thorghout that glas,[1]
75 Thy maydenhod onwemmed hyt was   *virginity unstained*
For bere of thyne chylde.   *By birth/bearing*
Nou, swete levedy of solas,   *lady; solace*
To ous senfolle be thou mylde.   *us sinful; merciful*

Have, levedy, thys lytel songe   *Take*
80 That out of senfol herte spronge;   *sinful heart*
Agens the feend thou make me stronge   *Against the devil*
And gyf me thy wyssinge,   *give; guidance*
And thagh ich habbe ydo thee wrange,   *though I have done you wrong*
Thou graunte me amendynge.   *Grant me amends*

89

Ros Mary, most of vertewe virginall,   *pristine*
Fresche floure in quhom the hevinlie dewe doun fell;   *on whom; heaven's*
O gem joynit in joye angelicall,   *joined*
In quhom Jhesu rejosit for to dwell,   *whom; rejoiced*
5 Rute of refute, of mercy spring and well,   *Root of refuge*

---

[1] Lines 73–74: *As the sun passes through glass without breaking it*

Of ladyis chois as is of letteris A, — *choice (best)*
Emprys of hevyne, of paradys, and hell,
O mater Jhesu, salve Maria! — *O mother of Jesus, hail Mary*

O sterne that blyndis Phebus bemes bricht, — *blinds Phoebus' beams bright*
10 With cours abone the hevinis circulyne; — *course above; heavens circular*
Abone the speir of Saturn hie on hicht, — *Above; sphere; high; height*
Surmonting all the angell ordouris nyne; — *Surmounting; orders nine*
Haile, lamp lemand befor the trone devyne, — *beloved; throne*
Quhar cherubim sweit syngis osanna, — *Where; sing sweet praises*
15 With organe, tympane, harpe, and symbalyne; — *cymbal*
O mater Jhesu, salve Maria!

O cleir conclaif of clene virginité, — *pure conclave*
That closit Crist but curis criminale; — *enclosed; without harmful harborage*
Tryumphand tempill of the Trinité,
20 That torned ws fra Tartar eternale; — *turned us from Devil (see note)*
Princes of pes and palme imperiale, — *Princess; peace*
Our wicht, invinsable Sampson sprang thee fra, — *strong, invincible; from*
That with ane buffat bure doune Beliale; — *one blow beat down Belial*
O mater Jhesu, salve Maria!

25 Thy blissit sydis bure the campioun, — *sides bore; champion*
Quhilk, with mony bludy woundis, in to stowr, — *Who; many bloody; assault*
Victoriusly discomfit the dragoun
That redy wes his pepill to devoure; — *was ready to devour his people*
At hellis gettis he gaf tham no succour, — *hell's gates; gave*
30 Syne brak the barmekyn of that bribour bla, — *Then broke; rampart; angry thief (devil)*
Quhill all the feyndis trymblit for raddoure: — *While; fiends; trembled; fear*
O mater Jhesu, salve Maria!

O madyn meike, most mediatrix for man, — *meek, best intermediary*
O moder myld, full of humilité,
35 Pray thy sone Jhesu, with his woundis wan, — *pale wounds*
Quhilk denyeit him for oure trespas to de, — *Who sacrificed himself; sins; die*
And as he bled his blude apon a tre, — *bled; cross*
Us to defend fra Lucifer oure fa, — *from; foe*
In hevyne that we may syng apon our kne: — *upon; knee*
40 *O mater Jhesu, salve Maria!*

	Hail, purifyet perle, Haile, port of paradys;	*purified pearl*
	Haile, redolent ruby, riche and radyus;	*radiant*
	Haile, clarifyet cristale, haile, qwene and emperys;	
	Haile, moder of God, haile, virgin glorius;	
45	O gracia plena tecum Dominus,	*O full of grace, God is with you*
	With Gabriell that we may syng and say,	
	Benedicta tu in mulieribus:	*Blessed are you among women*
	O mater Jhesu, salve Maria!	

90

	All haile, lady, mother, and virgyn immaculate;	
	Haile, Mary, most precious that bare our savyour Jesu;	*bore*
	Haile, clarified cristall, haile, wife mundificate;	*pure*
	Haile, rote of grace, our joy thow did renewe,	*root*
5	For the Holy Gost did clerely in the yssue.	*purely; issue (see note)*
	Our soles for lacke had ells perresshed sore	*souls; lack; otherwise perished*
	Nere throgh the helpe of our highe redemptour.	*Without the help*

	All haile, whose solempne glorious concepcioun	*solemn; conception*
	Full of glorie and hye joye tryumphaunte:	*high*
10	Bothe celestyall and terrestriall gif laude with Jubilacioun	*give praise*
	Of new joy and gladnesse with solace incessaunte.	*comfort everlasting*
	Alhaile, whose nativité to us is solempnysaunte	*birth; festival*
	Ferens lucem ut Lucyfer, lux oriens,	*Bearing light like Lucifer, light of the east*
	Dyademe angelicall, *verum solem preveniens.*	*going before the true sun (see note)*

15	Alhaile be thy mekenes, *sine viro fecunditas*	*fruitfulness without man*
	Whose amyable Annunciacioun to us was redempcion.	
	Joye therfore be to thee, *tu summa suavitas,*	*you, most sweetness*
	And glorified be the houre of thy incarnacioun,	*incarnation [of Christ]*
	By whome we advoyde the infernall dampnacioun.	*avoid; damnation*
20	So dulcour was the ground in whom Crist hym planted	*sweet; planted himself*
	O mater most illuminate, we myght not the have wanted.[1]	

---

[1] *O mother most illuminate, we might not have done without you*

167

Haile, true chast virgyn and mother immaculate,   *chaste*
Whose pure purificacion to us was purgacion: *purgation*
Haile, replete with all virtue angelicate,
25   Whose celestiall hye ascendaunte Assumpcion
Was oure gret joye and glorificacion.
Wherfore, dere lady, solistrice be for grace,   *solicitress*
That we with thy son in heyven may have a place.

91

Hale, sterne superne; hale, in eterne   *Hail, high star; eternity*
In Godis sicht to schyne;   *God's sight*
Lucerne in derne, for to discerne   *Light in darkness to be discerned*
Be glory and grace devyne;   *By; divine*
5   Hodiern, modern, sempitern,   *[Of] present, recent, everlasting time*
Angelicall regyne: *queen*
Our tern inferne for to dispern   *infernal trouble; disperse*
Helpe, rialest rosyne.   *most royal rose*
Ave Maria, gracia plena: *Hail Mary, full of grace*
10   Haile, fresche floure femynyne;   *flower feminine*
Yerne us guberne, virgin matern,   *Desire to govern us, virgin mother*
Of reuth baith rute and ryne.   *pity both root and rind (fruit)*

Haile, yhyng, benyng, fresche flurising,   *young; good; flourishing*
Haile, Alphais habitakle: *Alpha's dwelling (see note)*
15   Thy dyng ofspring maid us to syng   *worthy child made*
Befor his tabernakle;
All thing maling we doune thring   *evil we do push [away]*
Be sicht of his signakle,   *By sight; sign*
Quhilk King us bring unto his ryng   *Which; reign*
20   Fro dethis dirk umbrakle.   *From death's dark shade*
Ave Maria, gracia plena:
Haile moder and maide but makle,   *without spot*
Bricht syng gladying our languissing   *Bright sign gladdening*
Be micht of thi mirakle.   *By might*

25   Haile, bricht be sicht in hevyn on hicht;   *bright by sight; high*
Haile, day sterne orientale;   *star of the east*

	Our licht most richt in clud of nycht,	*light; right; cloud; night*
	Our dirknes for to scale;	*darkness; scatter*
	Hale, wicht in ficht, puttar to flicht	*strong in fight, putter-to-flight*
30	Of fendis in battale,	*fiends*
	Haile, plicht but sicht; hale, mekle of mycht;	*hidden security; great of might*
	Haile, glorius virgin, hale!	
	Ave Maria, gracia plena:	
	Haile gentill nychttingale,	*nightingale*
35	Way stricht, cler dicht, to wilsom wicht	*straight; clearly spoken; wandering person*
	That irke bene in travale.	*Who is weary of travail*
	Hale, qwene serene; hale, most amene;	*queen; pleasant*
	Haile, hevinlie hie emprys;	*high empress*
	Haile, schene unseyne with carnale eyne;	*brightness unseen with fleshly eyes*
40	Haile, ros of paradys;	*rose*
	Haile, clene bedene ay till conteyne;	*(see note)*
	Haile, fair fresche floure delyce;	*fleur-de-lis*
	Haile, grene daseyne; haile fro the splene,	*green daisy; from; heart*
	Of Jhesu genitrice!	*mother*
45	*Ave Maria, gracia plena*:	
	Thow baire the prince of prys;	*You bore; worth*
	Our teyne to meyne and ga betweyne	*misery to pity; mediate*
	As humile oratrice.	*humble pleader*
	Haile, more decore than of before,	*beautiful*
50	And swetar be sic sevyne,	*seven times sweeter*
	Our glore forlore for to restore	*Our lost glory to restore*
	Sen thow art qwene of hevyn;	*Since*
	Memore of sore, stern in Auror,	*Mindful of sorrow; star; Aurora*
	Lovit with angellis stevyne;	*Praised; voices*
55	Implore, adore, thow indeflore,	*undefiled*
	To mak our oddis eveyne.	*make our odds even*
	Ave Maria, gracia plena,	
	With lovingis lowde ellevyn,	*loud praises raised/eleven (see note)*
	Quhill store and hore my youth devore	*While trouble; old age; devour*
60	Thy name I sall ay nevyne.	*shall ever name*
	Empryce of prys, imperatrice,	*Empress; excellence, royal intercessor*
	Bricht polist precious stane,	*Bright polished; stone*

Victrice of vyce, hie genitrice   *Victoress over; high mother*
Of Jhesu, Lord soverayne;
65   Our wys pavys fro enemys   *Pave our ways from enemies*
Agane the feyndis trayne;   *Against; fiend's trap*
Oratrice, mediatrice, salvatrice,   *Pleader*
To God gret suffragane.   *assistant*
Ave Maria, gracia plena:
70   Haile, sterne meridiane,   *star [of the] meridian*
Spyce, flour delice of paradys   *fleur-de-lis*
That baire the gloryus grayne.   *bore; grain*

Imperiall wall, place palestrall
Of peirles pulcritud;   *peerless beauty*
75   Tryumphal hall, hie trone regall   *high throne*
Of Godis celsitud;   *God's heavenly greatness*
Hospitall riall, the Lord of all   *Royal inn*
Thy closet did include;   *enclose*
Bricht ball cristall, ros virginall,   *Bright; rose*
80   Fulfillit of angell fude.   *Fed by angels (see note)*
Ave Maria, gracia plena:
Thy birth has with his blude   *son; blood*
Fra fall mortall origianall   *From the mortal first fall*
Us raunsound on the rude.   *ransomed; cross*

Notes

§1

In that time, als was ful wel. Index no. 1536. MS: Bodl. 2325 (Bodley 425), fols. 67b–68a (fourteenth century; West Midlands, with some northern features; Heuser suggests that the Psalter in which this poem appears originated in the West Midlands and was copied by a Northern scribe who uses *sal* for *shall, salt* for *shalt*, or occasionally *a* for *o* as in *knaw* or *hali*). Edition: W. Heuser, *Anglia* 29 (1906), 401–02.

This poem is a close translation of Luke 1:26–38. The translator adds only a few formulaic phrases (at lines 1 and 45). The poem appears in a mid-fourteenth-century MS which contains an English verse Psalter. Between Psalms 108 and 109 we find English versions of the four sequences (sung before the Alleluia in the liturgy) from the Gospels (often included in Books of Hours); this poem is one. Marian materials are often linked with the Psalms of David in that she is seen to be the flower that his songs proclaim. The MS also contains an English translation of *Ave maris stella*, "Heile sterne on the se so bright" (*Index* no. 1082, printed in B14, pp. 58–59).

2   *Gabriel.* Gregory of Nazianzus, a fourth-century commentator whose interpretations are incorporated into the *CA*, notes that Gabriel's name means "strength of God." Bernard of Clairvaux writes that Gabriel is the appropriate messenger because he announces the "coming of power" and comforts Mary: "Perhaps it would be better to say that he had the right to so great a name because he was to carry out so great a mission" (Homily 1, p. 7). Gabriel also appears to Zachariah with the news that Elizabeth will bear a son (Luke 1:5–25) and to the Old Testament prophet Daniel, to whom he shows visions (Daniel 8:16 and 9:21).

5   *maiden.* See Isaias 7:14, "a virgin shall conceive. . . ."

7   *Josep of the house of Davi.* St. Bernard writes: "Not only Joseph, but Mary as well, we must suppose, descended from the house of David. She would not have been engaged to a man of the house of David if she herself had not also been of this royal house" (Homily 2, p. 29). The apocryphal Gospel of the Birth of Mary attributed to St. Matthew (and once thought to have been translated by Jerome), claims that Mary

was "sprung from the royal race and family of David" (1:1, in *Lost Books of the Bible* [Cleveland and New York: World Publishing Company, 1926]), p. 17.

11   *ful of hape.* The word *hape* is rich in meaning. For this poet, grace — the advent of conception — is an event, that which happens (MED 2.a). The word also suggests Mary's worthiness (MED 1.e: "favor, graciousness") and, more importantly, her good fortune, prosperity, and happiness (MED 1.c) as she receives this blessing.

29   *in Jacob hous rike sal he.* See 2 Kings (RSV 2 Samuel) 7:13–16 and Isaias 9:6–7.

32   *Hou mai this be?* Bernard of Clairvaux comments that Mary "does not doubt the event, but wonders how it shall occur. She is not asking *whether* it will happen, but *how*" (Homily 4, p. 48).

34   *ful of miht.* See note to line 2.

36   *miht and heighest inshadw thee sal.* According to Bernard, this mysterious explanation implies that only God and Mary are to know the means by which she will conceive (Homily 4, pp. 49–50).

37   *heli.* Bernard: "Why does he say simply the 'Holy' and nothing else? I think that it must have been because there was no name by which he could correctly or worthily qualify that extraordinary, that magnificent, that awesome being who was going to unite the Virgin's most chaste flesh to his own soul in the only begotten Son of the Father. Had he said the 'holy flesh' or the 'holy man' or 'the holy child', whatever he might have found to say would have seemed to him inadequate" (Homily 4, p. 50).

§2

From heovene into eorthe. Index no. 877. MS: Jesus College Oxford 29, fols. 188b (first eleven lines) and 181a (last seven lines) (thirteenth century, Southwest Midlands). Edition: Morris, *An Old English Miscellany*, p. 100.

This fragment is one of the oldest extant vernacular Annunciation lyrics; Morris believes the poems in this MS were composed before 1250. The poem was apparently meant to be sung: the note *Item cantus* appears next to the first line, and the points in the MS seem to indicate rhythmic rather than syntactic breaks.

Notes

2   The name *Gabryel* has been written above *that* in a smaller hand.

5   *wunyinde*. This term is not easily glossed. "Dwelling" or "sojourning" are implied, or perhaps "living." The sense seems to point up the transience of Mary's life on earth.

12   This section of the poem begins on an earlier leaf of the MS. The sense of the poem suggests the omission of some lines paraphrasing Luke 1:35–37; now Mary is the speaker, but there is no clear physical evidence for this in the misbound MS.

13   *wenche*. The word, which originally meant "girl" or "young woman," connoted "servant" or "handmaid" in the Middle Ages (see OED *wench*, sb.1 and 3). There is no connotation of promiscuity in the usage.

15–18   Narrative poems about Mary often close in a prayer, either asking Christ to have mercy for his mother's sake, as in this case, or to Mary herself.

§3

Gabriel, fram evene kingh. Index no. 888. MS: BL Arundel 248, fol. 154a (c. 1300; East Anglian — Dobson identifies it as Norfolk — dialect). In the MS, the Latin text appears under musical notes, in five twelve-line stanzas; the English text follows. The poem "Jesu Cristes milde moder" (§32), possibly by the same author, also appears in the MS. Editions: Frederick J. Furnivall, *The Harleian MS 7334 of Chaucer's Canterbury Tales,* Chaucer Society first series 73 (Ludgate Hill: Trübner, 1885), pp. 695–96; Furnivall, *Cambridge MS Dd. 4. 24. of Chaucer's Canterbury Tales* (London: Chaucer Society, 1902), pp. 687–88; M. Jacoby, *Vier Mittelenglische Geistliche Gedichte des XIII Jahrhunderts* (Berlin: G. Bernstein, 1890), p. 35; B13, no. 44; Friedrich Gennrich, *Formenlehre des Mittelalterlichen Liedes* (Halle: Max Niemeyer, 1932), p. 179 (music with Jacoby's lyrics); J. B. Trend, *Music and Letters* 9 (1929), 114; Hughes and Abraham, p. 116 (with music from Cambridge University Addit. 710, which gives Latin but not English lyrics); Davies, no. 32; Sisam, *Oxford*, no. 39; DH, no. 15 (with music); Weber, pp. 29–31 (Brown's ed.). Wenzel compares the poem to its Latin source in *Preachers, Poets, and the Early English Lyric* (pp. 35–42). Weber discusses the poem's structure (and that of its music) on pp. 32–46, noting that the movement of the poem toward a final petition "and the way the petition is formed in terms of sacred history is analogous to the Mass liturgy. Just as the Mass is the re-enactment of the crucifixion to unite the present congregation to God, so the poem which relates the event of the annunciation to the crucifixion of Christ is made by the poet into a prayer in order to apply the events to himself and his listeners for their 'god won'" (p. 40).

This piece is a free translation of the thirteenth-century Latin hymn *Angelus ad Virginem* (the song sung by Nicholas in Chaucer's The Miller's Tale). On the Latin source (and music) see DH, pp. 178–83.

Furnivall indicates that the initial þ is to be read as *h*. Following Brown, I have emended the text accordingly, replacing *the* with *he* at lines 4, 47, 53, and 60.

3   *hire*. MS reads *thire*, which Brown glosses as "this," but Dobson emends to *hir* on the grounds that *thire*, which would mean "these," is inconsistent with the dialect of the text (p. 180).

26   *herde*. MS: *therde*.

29   *theumaiden*. Furnivall reads *thenmaiden* (*then*=*hen*=hand?); if *theu*=*theow*, however, then the word means "servant-maiden" (compare OE *þeowe*).

35   *withhuten lawe*. An exception to the law of nature (according to which a virgin cannot conceive a child).

38   *sithte*. The word may be, as Furnivall reads, *sichte*.

39   MS: *And* crossed out at beginning of line.

49   *Maiden moder makeles*. Compare §13, lines 1–2.

51   *thee*. Corrected from *be* (Brown's emendation).

§4

The angel to the vergyn said. By John Audelay. *Index* no. 3305. MS: Bodl. 21876 (Douce 302), fol. 24a–b (fifteenth century; West Midlands Shropshire dialect). Edition: Ella Keats Whiting, ed., *The Poems of John Audelay*, EETS o.s. 184 (1931; rpt. New York: Kraus, 1971), pp. 159–60.

Notes

This lyric appears in the works of John Audelay, in a group of four Marian poems. Audelay may have been a priest; he spent the last years of his life at Haghmond, an Augustinian abbey, and wrote for the monks there. The poem is a closer translation of *Angelus ad virginem* than §3. Though it is written in carol form, Dobson does not believe this version was meant for singing (p. 179).

At the head of the poem, the MS reads: *Hec salutacio composuit Angelus Gabrielus.*

2   *Entreng into here boure.* In the *Protevangelium*, Gabriel first visits Mary at a well, then reappears in her room.

3–4   *Fore drede . . . He said, "Haile!"* Gabriel uses a familiar greeting to avoid frightening Mary.

6   MS: *s* deleted after *Lord.*

9   *gate of heven.* This is a common image from the liturgy. Its source is Ezekiel 44:1–4, in which God shows Ezekiel a closed gate and explains: "This gate shall be shut, it shall not be opened, and no man shall pass through it: because the Lord the God of Israel hath entered in by it, and it shall be shut for the prince. The prince himself shall sit in it, to eat bread before the Lord: he shall enter in by the way of the porch of the gate, and shall go out by the same way." Medieval commentators interpret this as a prefiguring of the Immaculate Conception and virgin birth: only the Holy Spirit would have access to Mary's womb. Compare Lydgate's *Life of our Lady*, Book 2, line 568, and "Marye, mayde mylde and fre" (§88), lines 49–52. See the order for Sext of the Divine Office for the Feast of the Immaculate Conception; note also the *Biblia Pauperum* leaf for the Annunciation. Frederick Warren's introduction to the Sarum mass of the B.V.M. explains that one reason for celebrating her mass is that Saturday is "a door and entrance" to Sunday (*Sarum*, Part 2, p. 74).

12   *No syn never I knew.* The word refers to carnal sin — Mary is a virgin — and it implicitly affirms the Immaculate Conception, the absence of all human sin. The double negative form, used for emphasis, is common.

14   *stedfast.* Whiting's emendation of MS *sedfast.*

16   *boost.* Written in a different hand in MS. Whiting believes the second hand may reflect corrections and additions supervised by Audelay himself (p. ix).

17   *serten* and *sere* appear on a separate line in the MS.

19   *pere*. Whiting glosses this "pure," comparing the spelling of *sere* for "sure" (a fifteenth-century West Midlands form) in line 17. It could, however, be "peer," Christ dwelling as a human; compare *dere* for "dear" in line 36).

23   *as odur do*. Written in a different hand.

24   *burthe*. In a different hand and repeated in margin.

27   *the*. MS: þ.

29   *holé*. MS: *hohole*.

        kene. The MED gives two definitions for *kenen* (v.) that seem appropriate: "to engender" (a), and "to generate (sth.), develop" (c).

30–50   These lines are written in a different hand.

34   *wombe and waast*. A trope for physicality — not simply incarnate but with a belly that consumes and digests earthly food. As confirmation of this physicality, after the Resurrection Jesus will eat food and permit Thomas to touch the hole in his side ("wombe and waast," so to speak).

37   *For thay ther that thay nyst nott hwat, in law as we fyende*. I.e., the Bible (the law) indicates that God sent Christ for the sake of sinners, those who "know not what they do" (compare Luke 23:34).

39   *agaynes al monkynde*. I.e., against all laws of human nature — but, ironically, *for* the sake of humankind. Compare §3, line 35.

45   *thy*. Corrected in MS from *thou*.

§5

Nowel el el el . . . . Index no. 2113. MS: BL Sloane 2593, fol. 10a (mid-fifteenth century). Editions: Wright, *Specimens*, no. 6; Wright, *Songs* (Warton Club), p. 29; Sandys, p. 7; *EEC*, no. 242; Rickert, p. 13; Greene, *Selection*, no. 54.

Notes

Songs, meditations, and carols on the Joys of Mary are common in medieval literature. In England (particularly in the carol form), the number of joys is usually five (the Annunciation, the Nativity, the Resurrection, the Ascension, and Mary's Assumption); some continental poetry describes seven or twelve, and Lydgate often expands the number to fifteen. The number five (associated with the five senses and thus with the flesh) is frequently associated with Mary, and many songs in her honor employ a five-stanza form.

The Latin lines are the final lines of each stanza of the hymn *Gaude virgo, mater Christi*; for the text see §87, below. The English lines do not translate the hymn, but they treat the same material.

1   *Nowel.* From a French word meaning "birth." According to the OED, the first recorded use of this word in English occurs in the late fourteenth century, in *Sir Gawain and the Green Knight.* Perhaps the twelve *els* have revelational significance.

2   *gret with.* This may be a pun on *greeted/great*: Mary was greeted (MED *greten*, v.2) by Gabriel, and Mary was great with child (MED *greten*, v.1, to become pregnant) by means of Gabriel's announcement — conception by the Word (for this sense, compare lines 5 and 6).

17   *To helle he tok the ryghte way.* Compare the Apostles' Creed: "he descended into hell."

§6

Unto Marie he that love hath. By James Ryman. *Index* no. 3725. MS: Cambridge University Ee.1.12, fols. 26a–27b (1492). Editions: Zupitza, *Archiv* 89, 189–90; *EEC*, no. 257. The text is based on the *Magnificat*, found in Luke 1:46–55. Mary's song of praise to God is used as a hymn in the vespers liturgy. In the context of the biblical story, translations of the song also appear in several Corpus Christi cycles, e.g., the Wakefield "Salutation of Elizabeth." See *DBT*, "Magnificat."

1–2   These lines appear in large letters — Ryman's burdens are approximately double the size of the verses. The burden, addressed to the "audience," clearly encourages participation; by *synge* he means "sing along with me."

6   *verily.* MS: *verify.* Zupitza's emendation.

7   *he.* Added above the line.

20   *By his swete Sonne.* Luke reads: "He has shown might with his arm." Here and at line 26, Ryman makes interpretive adaptations to the scripture in order to call attention to Christ as the embodiment of strength and help. His interpretation agrees with those of Bede and Theophylact (d. 750) in the *CA,* who equate the Son with God's arm. Theophylact writes: "For in His arm, that is, His incarnate Son, He hath shewed strength, seeing that nature was vanquished, a virgin bringing forth, and God becoming man" (*CA*, Luke 1:51).

28–29   *He toke nature in Ysraell / And became man to save mankynde.* Luke reads "He has given help to Israel" (1:54).

31–34   *Joy be to God . . . .* Compare the *Gloria Patri* of the liturgy.

§7

Nowel, nowel, nowel / Syng we with myrth. Index no. 3822. MS: Bodl. 29734 (Eng. Poet e.1), fols. 47b–48a (mid-fifteenth century). Editions: Wright, *Songs* (Percy Society), no. 61; *EEC*, no. 261; Rickert, pp. 20–21; Silverstein, no. 92; Greene, *Selection*, no. 56; Davies, no. 133.

The MS, consisting of seventy-six religious and secular songs, written on paper in several hands, may be a minstrel's collection. The heading in the MS, *A song upon (now must I syng &c.),* must refer to a now-lost carol tune.

The carol resembles carols and *chansons d'aventure* in which a betrayed maiden laments her pregnancy (see *EEC* nos. 452–57); as Greene notes, "The blessed state of the Virgin and her rejoicing would have the effect of a striking contrast to hearers familiar with the type of song parodied" (*EEC*, p. 408).

Rickert writes that although the vision poem is popular in the fifteenth century, this one is "alone in representing Mary as prophesying the event, and picturing herself as singing the lullaby" (p. 149).

31   *lyghtnesse.* Perhaps a play on "heaviness," as in "heavy with child," but also suggesting illumination.

33   *fod*. Greene glosses the word as "child." But the metaphor suggests Christ's role as source of spiritual nourishment (food) as well. (The older meaning of *fode* is "food"; MED *fode*, n.2, "child," seems to come from the idea that a child is one who is fed or nurtured.)

§8

Edi beo thu, hevene quene. Index no. 708. MS: Corpus Christi College Oxford 59, fol. 113b, with music (late thirteenth century; Southeast Midlands; see below). Editions: R. Morris, *Old English Homilies of the Twelfth Century*, vol. 2, EETS o.s. 53 (1873; rpt. New York: Kraus, 1973), pp. 255–57, music, p. 261; Patterson, no. 30; B13, no. 60; Davies, no. 12; M. Bukofzer, "The Gymel, The Earliest Form of English Polyphony," *Music and Letters* 16 (1935), 79; DH, no. 13.

The MS comes from Llanthony, an Augustinian Priory, in Gloucestershire. Brown believes the poem was composed there. Dobson disagrees. He believes lines 41–64 are not part of the original poem: the first five stanzas, concluding in a prayer to Mary, constitute a unified religious love poem, in the first person (and Marian lyrics frequently employ a five-stanza structure). The last three stanzas are more impersonal. While stanza 6 elaborates on what has come before, 7 and 8 shift into an "explicitly doctrinal" mode and employ none of the courtly love conventions of the earlier stanzas. The prayer that ends stanza 8 simply reiterates the earlier prayer, in a new rhyme scheme. Furthermore, based on the features of dialect and orthography, Dobson believes the first five stanzas are a Southwest Midlands scribal copy of a poem composed in the Southeast Midlands. He theorizes that the scribe recorded these stanzas from memory (there are apparent errors), and he dismisses the last three stanzas as later additions.

The poet borrows numerous phrases (as well as metrical form) from Latin hymns. Yet he combines the traditions of that genre with conventions from secular French poetry: each stanza ends in a kind of refrain; the speaker declares himself Mary's knight (line 16) and her man (line 22), describes his "love bond" and worships her as the finest of women, noble in lineage.

1   *beo*. Dobson identifies this as a Southwest Midlands spelling of a Southeast Midlands form.

         hevene quene. An epithet from the liturgy. See, for example, the Sarum Office of the Blessed Virgin Mary in the Prymer (Maskell, 2:78). See also the "Queen of Heaven" poems in this volume.

1–2   Brown notes the similarity of these lines to a Latin antiphon found in Mone's collection: *Salve mundi domina / regina caelorum / Sanctorum laetitia / vita beatorum* (Mone, 2:210).

9–10   Brown notes the similarity to the beginning of a Latin hymn: "to SS. Tiberius, Modestus, and Florentia [Chevalier, No. 1620]: '*Aurora caeli praevia / a nocte lucem separat / divisa divina clare*'" (p. 213).

10   Morris and Patterson add *daiʒ* in brackets after *from*.

17   *Spronge blostme of one rote.* "And there shall come forth a rod out of the root of Jesse, and a flower shall rise up out of his root. And the spirit of the Lord shall rest upon him" (Isaias 11:1–2). If Mary is the flower, Jesus is the fruit.

20   *heore.* MS: *hore.* So emended by Morris and Patterson.

25 ff.   *eorthe to gode sede.* Compare *The Myroure of oure Ladye*: "Blyssed be thow moste worthy sower that haste sown a grayne of the beste whete in the best lande, wette wyth the dew of the holy goste" (p. 201).

26   *On thee lighte the heovene deugh.* An allusion to Gideon's fleece. The wet fleece in the desert was a sign to Gideon of God's purpose (Judges 6:36–40). Commentators regularly gloss the fleece as a sign of the Virgin Mary's immaculate conception. The *Biblia Pauperum* Annunciation leaf includes this image; compare also Psalm 71 (RSV 72):6.

36   *draucht.* This word conveys a host of applicable connotations: desire, motion, attraction, inclination, education, and draught/drink, like a love potion with Mary as the full vessel.

37   *sschildghe.* Morris, Patterson, and Dobson separate the word: *schild ʒe* ("shield, yea"), Dobson declaring Brown's *schildʒe* an impossible form.

41–42   *heghe kunne, / Of David.* See §1, note to line 7.

44   *evening.* MS: *evenig.* Emended by Morris.

45   *derne.* Commonly used in Middle English love poems to designate secrecy or private, personal love.

46   *swete*. Dobson emends to *trewe*; see note to line 49.

46–58   The lower right corner of the MS is gone; missing line-ends are supplied from earlier editions.

47   *Thi love us brouchte.* As corrected in margin. Text reads *Thus bring us in to.*

49   *Seolcudliche.* Text reads *swetelic*; margin reads *Seolcudliche*, with *i.e., trewe* above (next to the first letters of *swete* from line 46). All editors except Dobson read *i.e., treuwe* as a gloss on *Seolcudliche*.

51   *That al this world bicluppe ne mighte, / Thu sscholdest of thin boseme bere.* Patterson cites the third lesson for Matins in the Prymer: "Hooli modir of god, that deseruedist worthili to conceyue him that al the world myghte not holde" (Maskell, 2:10).

§9

Heyl, levedy, se-stoerre bryht. Attributed to William Herebert. *Index* no. 1054. MS: BL Addit. 46919, fol. 207a–b (Herebert's commonplace book; early fourteenth century, Southwest Midlands). Editions: Wright and Halliwell 2:228–29; Patterson, no. 42; B14, no. 17; Silverstein, no. 25; LH, no. 185; Reimer, pp. 120–21.

This poem recalls the Annunciation by echoing the "hail" or *Ave* in a prayer for Mary's protection, guidance, and intercession. It is a translation of the Latin hymn *Ave maris stella*, sung at the canonical hour of Nocturns, the Saturday Office of the Blessed Virgin Mary, and the Feast of the Annunciation. The Latin text is as follows:

Ave maris stella,	Mala nostra pelle,	Vitam praesta puram,
Dei mater alma	Bona cuncta posce.	Iter para tutum,
Atque semper virgo,		Ut videntes Iesum
Felix coeli porta.	Monstra te esse matrem,	Semper collaetemur.
	Sumat per te precem,	
Sumens illud Ave	Qui pro nobis natus	Sit laus Deo patri
Gabrielis ore,	Tulit esse tuus.	Summo Christo decus
Funda nos in pace,		Spiritui sancto
Mutans nomen Evae.	Virgo singularis,	Honor trinus et unus.
	Inter omnes mitis,	
Solve vincla reis,	Nos culpis solutos	(Daniel 1:204)
Profer lumen caecis,	Mites fac et castos.	

For later variations on the hymn, see §10, §58, B14, no. 45, and B15, no. 19.

1   *se-stoerre*. As David Jeffrey notes, the image of Mary as *stella maris*, star of the sea, originated in a scribal error; St. Jerome (*Liber Interpretationis Nominorum Hebraicorum)* translated the Hebrew name *Miriam* (in Exodus) as "drop of the sea," but *stilla* (drop) became *stella* (*DBT*, "Stella Maris," p. 735). Bede, for example, perpetuates the error as he glosses Mary's name in Luke: "Maria, in Hebrew, is the star of the sea" *(CA* Luke 1:26–27). The epithet found its way into poetry and hymns, e.g., *Ave maris stella* (Daniel 1:204), the antiphon for the None hour, and the Evensong hymn "Hail, sterre of the see." Numbers 24:17, Balaam's fourth oracle, provides support for the image: "A star shall rise out of Jacob and a sceptre shall spring up from Israel."

Bernard elaborates on the idea:

> Surely she is very fittingly likened to a star. The star sends forth its ray without harm to itself. In the same way the Virgin brought forth her son with no injury to herself. . . . She it is whose brightness both twinkles in the highest heaven and pierces the pit of hell, and is shed upon earth, warming our hearts far more than our bodies, fostering virtue and cauterizing vice. . . . O you, whoever you are, who feel that in the tidal wave of this world you are nearer to being tossed about among the squalls and gales than treading on dry land, if you do not want to founder in the tempest, do not avert your eyes from the brightness of this star. (Homily 2, p. 30)

The incipit *Ave maris stella, etc.* appears in the right margin.

3   *vurst and late*. A gloss on the Latin *semper virgo*. Voiced labial fricatives (*v* for *f*) are typical of the Southern dialect Herebert uses.

late. The *a* appears above the line.

4   *Of heveneriche sely gate*. A translation of the common Latin epithet *Felix coeli porta*. See note to §4, line 9. Joseph Connelly's note is useful here: "Mary is the gate of heaven primarily because, through her, *God* came on earth; but she is also the gate of heaven in relation to men since she is our mother as well; cf. John 19:26" (p. 161).

5   *Ave*. Luke 1:28.

In margin: *Sumens illud Ave.*

7   *In gryht*. The Latin hymn reads *in pace.*

8	*That turnst abakward Eve's nome.* I.e., Eva/Ave. The second-century commentator Irenaeus glossed *Ave* as *a vae* or *ab vae* (without woe) and elaborated on the pairing (see *Adversus Haereses*, 3.22.4 and 5.19.1), as did later writers. Just as Satan (the fallen angel) visited Eve, so Gabriel visited Mary; Mary's obedience made possible Christ's atonement for Eve's disobedience; the pain of childbirth (Eve's punishment) is balanced by the painless birth of one child who will provide "bote for bale"; the tree of Eden bore forbidden fruit, but the tree of Calvary (the cross) bore Christ and salvation. Jacobus de Voragine discusses the parallels between the Fall and the Annunciation, even citing the legend that the Fall, the Annunciation, and the Crucifixion all took place on Friday, March 6 (*Golden Legend* 1:208–09). See also John Donne's poem "Upon the Annunciation and Passion Falling upon One Day, 1608."
9	In margin: *Salve vincla reis.*
13	The Latin line *Monstra te esse matrem* appears in the margin.
17	Margin: *Virgu singularis.*
21	Margin: *Vitam presta puram.*
24	*ever.* The *r* is written above the line.
25	MS: *To þe uader cryst and to þe holy gost*, with *þe* and *to þe* marked for deletion.
25–26	Patterson notes that the *Gloria Patri* "was regularly appended to all hymns in the services" (p. 185).

§10

Blessed Mary, moder virginall. Index no. 534. MS: Bodl. 21575 (Douce 1), fol. 77a–b (fifteenth century). Editions: B15, no. 44; Davies, no. 107.

Another version of *Ave maris stella* (see §9), this poem appears in a small parchment book of offices, prayers, and hymns for private devotion.

2	*Integrate.* The word means "intact," "whole," "entire," suggesting chastity, purity, honesty.

2   *sterre of the see.* See note to §9, line 1.

5   *Myrroure without spot.* Compare Wisdom 7:26: "For she [Wisdom] is the brightness of eternal light, and the unspotted mirror of God's majesty, and the image of his goodness." The unspotted mirror is an iconographic symbol of the Immaculate Conception.

        rose of Jerico. See Ecclesiasticus 24:18 (Sirach 24:14), in which Wisdom says of herself: "I was exalted like a palm tree in Cades, and as a rose plant in Jericho." Compare "Of on that is so fayr and bright" (§83), line 11, and "Hale, sterne superne" (§91), line 8.

6   *Close gardyn.* The *hortus conclusus* image comes from Canticles (RSV Song of Solomon) 4:12, and appears in the liturgy. On the allegorical significance of gardens in medieval literature, see D. W. Robertson, Jr., "The Doctrine of Charity in Mediaeval Gardens: A Topical Approach through Symbolism and Allegory," *Speculum* 26 (1951), 24–49.

§11

Ave: Hayle mayden of maydyns, thorgth worde consaywyng. Index no. 1059. MS: Bodl. 21700 (Douce 126), fol. 92a–b (early fifteenth century, Northwest Midlands). Edition: Heuser, pp. 320–23.

This poem is found in a MS which also contains Bernard of Clairvaux's dialogue with Mary on the Passion.

The rhetorical technique employed here is *anaphora*, though it might also be described as *epimone*, which Richard Lanham defines as "frequent repetition of a phrase or question, in order to dwell on a point" (*A Handlist of Rhetorical Terms*, second ed. [Berkeley: University of California Press, 1991], p. 68).

The *Ave Maria* came into general use during the twelfth century; the prayer combines Gabriel's greeting (Luke 1:28) with Elizabeth's (Luke 1:42):

> Hail Mary, full of grace,
> The Lord is with thee.
> Blessed art thou among women,
> And blessed is the fruit of thy womb.

Compare B14, no. 131, "Heil! and holi ay be þi name," a late-fourteenth-century acrostic on this prayer.

1   *thorgth worde consaywyng.* Geometer, a seventh-century Greek commentator, writes: "By the word *behold,* he denotes rapidity and actual presence, implying that with the utterance of the word the conception is accomplished" (*CA,* Luke 1:30–33). The iconographic tradition symbolizes the conception with the dove (representing the Holy Spirit) speaking into Mary's ear.

8   *sokour.* MS: *sokou;* the leaf is trimmed at the edge of the word. Heuser's emendation.

15   *see sterre.* See note to §9, line 1.

17   *lesse and more.* All humankind, regardless of class.

19   *profycy.* See 2 Kings (2 Samuel) 7:13–16 and Isaias 9:6–7.

21   *the Trinité pyghth hys owen place.* Mary is often described as "chamber of the Trinity"; compare, for example, §88, line 2. The image of her womb enclosing Father, Son, and Holy Spirit is common in medieval visual art (see, for example, Plate C). On the Trinity, see §66, note to line 36. It is worth noting that the singular *hys* is used with *Trinité* here, emphasizing the idea of the three in one.

22   *doe. Do* is commonly used in Middle English as a sign of causative aspect; thus "bring" or "cause for us."

24   *to be.* Added in margin.

26   *ley in stalle.* See Luke 2:7.

33   The beginnings of the Latin words are cut off on fol. 92b, which begins with this line.

34   *honowereth.* MS: *honowre thet.* Heuser's emendation.

36   *ne maye.* "May not [help]"; i.e., where I lack the capacity to help myself. Mary is often called upon as mediatrix; see poems below.

44   *manyfolde*. The initial letter has been obliterated.

49   *swote*. MS: *swete*, emended for rhyme.

50   *Fruyt . . . byhote to come oute offe Jesses rote*. See §8, note to line 17.

63   *that soe with man hathe wrowghth*. The phrase is difficult to gloss. It may refer to Jesus' actions toward man, or *with man* may mean "in human likeness"; the word *wroughth*, in any case, suggests a double meaning: God acts, does, or creates [himself] both *with* and *as* man.

§12

Hayle, glorious lady and hevenly quene. By John Lydgate. *Index* no. 1045. MS: Trinity College Cambridge 601 (R.3.21), fol. 274a–b (1461–83, Suffolk). Also in Longleat 30, fol. 25a; and Huntington HM 142 (formerly Bement), fols. 21a–22b. Edition of Trinity MS: MacCracken, EETS e.s. 107, pp. 280–82.

The poem is prefaced with the following inscription: *"His sequitur Salutacio Angelica per dictum dompnum Iohannem Lydegate translata"* [Here follows the Salutation of the Angel translated by the aforementioned master John Lydgate]. It is a meditation on the joys of Mary (in this case, the Immaculate Conception, the Annunciation, the Nativity, the Purification, the Resurrection, the Ascension, and the Assumption). The poem is found in a miscellany of English poetry, containing devotional prayers and instructions, as well as several poems by Lydgate. The Latin lines appear in red in the Cambridge MS.

2   *cage*. A place of security. Mary is commonly depicted as dwelling (or being) in a cloister or enclosed place.

6   *Cuius honore tu nobis fave*. "By which honor (i.e., the honor of the holy conception) grant us favor (or protect us)."

24   *Ave Maria, gracia plena*. See Luke 1:28.

32   *Gracia plena, dominus tecum*. See Luke 1:28.

35–36   *And yet thow madyst thy purificacion, / To puryfy oure sowles*. The virgin birth meant that Mary had no need of purification. Bede writes that although Mary was exempt according to the Jewish law, she willingly underwent the ritual in order "that we might be loosed from the bonds of the law" (*CA*, Luke 2:22–24). See Jacobus de Voragine's *Golden Legend* on the Feast of the Purification, 1:143–51.

40   *Dominus tecum, benedicta tu.* See Luke 1:28.

48   *Benedicta tu in mulieribus.* See Luke 1:28 and Luke 1:42.

56   *Et benedictus fructus ventris tui.* See Luke 1:42.

§13

I syng of a myden. Index no. 1367. MS: BL Sloane 2593, fol. 10b (fifteenth century). Editions: CS, no. 54; B15, no. 81; A. H. Bullen, *Carols and Poems* (London: J. C. Nimmo, 1886), pp. 4–5; W. W. Greg, "I Sing of a Maiden that is Makeless," *Modern Philology* 7 (1909), 166; Rickert, p. 6; Cecil, p. 30; Auden and Pearson, p. 29; Chambers, p. 91; Sir Arthur Quiller-Couch, *The Oxford Book of English Verse, 1250–1900* (Oxford: Clarendon Press, 1901), pp. 34–35; Segar, p. 59; John Jacob Niles, *The Anglo-American Carol Study Book* (New York: G. Schirmer, 1948), p. 27; Mason, p. 175; Speirs, pp. 67–68; Manning, *PMLA* 75 (see below), 8; Davies, no. 66; Stevick, no. 54; Silverstein, no. 79; LH, no. 181; Gray, *Selection*, no. 6; Burrow, p. 301; Dunn and Byrnes, p. 515; Manning, *Wisdom and Number*, p. 159; Reiss, p. 158; Wilhelm, no. 284.

This is one of the most famous of the Marian lyrics, set exquisitely to music in Benjamin Britten's *Ceremony of Carols*.

The following essays on "I Sing of a Maiden," all excerpted in LH (pp. 325–49), offer a variety of readings of the poem: Thomas Jemielty, "'I Sing of a Maiden': God's Courting of Mary" in *Concerning Poetry* 2 (Bellingham: Western Washington State College, 1969), 53–71; Stephen Manning, "'I Syng of a Myden,'" *PMLA* 75 (1960), 8–12; D. G. Halliburton, "The Myden Makeles," *Papers on Language and Literature* 4 (1968), 115–20; Leo Spitzer, "*Explication de Texte* Applied to Three Great Middle English Poems," *Archivum Linguisticum* 3 (1951), 1–22 and 137–56. See also George Kane, *Middle English Literature* (London: Methuen, 1951), pp. 161–65; and Speirs, pp. 67–69; Davies, pp. 14–19; Weber, pp. 55–60; Douglas Gray, "Typology in Some Medieval English Religious Lyrics," *Typology and English Medieval Literature*, ed. Hugh T. Keenan (New York: AMS, 1992), pp. 275–88.

Greg's article discusses the relationship between this poem and §16. Manning suggests that the poet has adapted the earlier six-stanza poem to five stanzas to correspond to the five joys and the five letters in the name *Maria* (LH 226).

1   *I syng of a myden.* MS: *I syng A of a myde* (with line over *e* to indicate *n*).

1–4   Compare §16, lines 3–4.

2   *makeles.* Without a mate or husband; also and/or without an equal or peer; and, without spot — immaculate. Compare lines 17–18.

4   *che ches.* This might be seen as an unusual interpretation of the dynamics of the event; it is *God* who chooses Mary (compare §3, line 51 and §11, line 21). But several commentators, notably Bernard, discuss the importance of her willingness, which amounts to *her* choosing. The phrase also evokes the chivalric circumstances of a knight approaching his lady to seek her favor in, as Jemielty puts it, "what is to be a most far-reaching love affair" (LH, p. 330).

5   *stylle.* The word connotes gentleness, absence of commotion or violence, and silence. Jemielty interprets it as suggesting God's "reverential hesitation" (LH, p. 329).

7   *dew in Aprylle.* This is a common image in the liturgy, recalling Gideon's fleece. See §8, note to line 26, and compare Deuteronomy 32:2 and Isaias 45:8. Jemielty comments that the April dew marks a season of rebirth: it is the beginning of the medieval year and the beginning of the "new year of salvation in Mary's womb" (the Annunciation is celebrated on March 25, nine months before Christmas).

8   *gras.* Manning interprets the grass as a symbol of humility (LH, p. 334).

12   *flour.* Mary is often compared to a flower, a symbol of purity; compare, for example, the burden to §26. See also Canticles 2:1–2: "I am the flower of the field, and the lily of the valleys. As the lily among thorns, so is my love among the daughters."

16   *spray.* Compare Isaias 11:1: Mary as flower, or branch, growing from the root of Jesse. In this poem, the image completes an ascending motion from *gras* (line 8) to *flour* (line 12) to *spray* (line 16), a counter-motion of Mary's yearning (choosing) to the falling of the dew (God's loving motion) upon the mother's place (line 6), her bower, (line 10), and her supine body itself (line 14).

17–20   Compare §16, lines 19–20.

§14

At a spryng wel under a thorn. Index no. 420. MS: Magdalen College Oxford 60, fol. 214a (fourteenth or fifteenth century). The MS is a collection of exempla. Editions: Coxe, p. 37; B14, no. 130; Speirs, p. 64; Mason, p. 149; Greene, *Selection*, no. 55; Davies, no. 114; Dronke, p. 69 (with commentary); Silverstein, no. 49; LH, no. 192.

This poem appears in a Latin exemplum, *de confessione* ("on confession"), in which the poem's symbols are interpreted. It is a story of a nobleman turned poor, who is ashamed to come to court to receive grace. Gray discusses the poem's kinship to medieval romance (*Themes,* pp. 92–93). Peter Dronke's note on the poem merits inclusion here: "It was at a fountain, beside a thornbush, that, according to some of the early Christian apocryphal writings, the angel's annunciation to Mary took place. This is the moment of the incarnation, the 'bote of bale' for all mankind. It is to a fountain, too, that girls in the *romances* and dance-songs of medieval Europe often come to meet, or dream about, their beloved. The poet is aware of both associations: impalpably he makes the bridge that joins the omnitemporal moment to the particular one. The annunciation took place 'a little while ago'; but still a maiden is standing at that fountain, rapt in the fullness of love. It is at once the Virgin, whose true love can absorb all human love, and any girl made beautiful by loving. The image is left unbroken, hence enigmatic: this girl opens the gate of poetic imagination behind which 'heavenly things are joined to earthly ones, divine to human'" (p. 70). See also Wenzel, *Preachers*, pp. 231–33.

1   *spryng wel.* Gray and Coxe read *sprynge wel.* In the *Protevangelium* account of the Annunciation, Gabriel greets Mary at a well. In the exemplum, the *spryng wel* is identified with the wound in Christ's side. Compare §82, and see also *The Shewings of Julian of Norwich,* ed. Georgia Ronan Crampton (Kalamazoo: Medieval Institute Publications, 1994), p. 55.

            thorn. See note to §20, line 1.

2   *bote of bale.* David Fowler writes that this phrase often refers to a lady's acceptance of her lover's plea — ultimately sexual union — but here we learn that though she has consented to his desire, she is yet a maid (*The Bible in Middle English Literature* [Seattle: University of Washington Press, 1984], p. 55).

§15

Blissid be that lady bryght. Index no. 998, *Goddys Sonne is borne.* (The *Index* lists carols by first line of first verse rather than by refrain.) MS: Bodl. 29734 (Eng. Poet e.1), fols. 52b–53a (mid-fifteenth century). Editions: Wright, *Songs* (Percy Society), pp. 82–83; CS, no. 73; *EEC*, no. 44; Rickert, p. 41; Davies, no. 124 (burden and first three stanzas).

This carol uses the events of Christ's birth as occasions for praising his mother, each stanza concluding with an image of Mary. The poet's artistic sense is evident from his love of word-play and his use of a modified bob-and-wheel stanza form.

The burden and first stanza emphasize the doctrine of the virgin birth. In similar fashion the poet notes the powerful lord/humble servant paradox of Christ's incarnation in lines 20 and 29–30. It may be that stanzas 4 and 5 were added later. Stanzas 1–3 are unified in shape, and Davies prints only these. Stanzas 4–5 deviate from the unified metrical pattern of 1–3. Furthermore, Luke is the source for the first three stanzas; the fourth and fifth draw on Matthew instead.

3   *Withouten peyne.* This reflects a belief in Mary's sinlessness; since pain in childbirth was, according to Genesis 3:16, woman's punishment for Eve's sin, then Mary's sinless state would allow her to give birth without pain. The gradual for the Sarum mass "In honour of the glorious Virgin, on behalf of women labouring with child" begins "Behold a virgin hath conceived, and without pain hath borne to us a son, whose name was called Jesus" (Warren, Part 2, p. 162). The related notion of Mary's immaculate conception was the subject of much debate throughout church history and was widely taught by medieval Franciscans, but was not formally proclaimed as dogma by the Roman Catholic Church until 1854. On the Immaculate Conception, see Warner, ch. 16.

8   *prophycy.* Isaias 7:14: "Behold a virgin shall conceive, and bear a son, and his name shall be called Emmanuel."

9   *With ay.* An exclamation: With wonder, joy, assent, surprise, reverence, O!, Oh!

23   *Two sons togyther.* Greene: "This figure probably results from the combination in the writer's mind of the 'sol de stella' of the 'Laetabundus' prose and the favourite 'sun through glass' simile for Mary's conception of Jesus" (*EEC*, p. 353). See notes to §17, especially to lines 18–20.

26   *light.* See MED *lighten*, v.2.4.a.(a): "Of Christ: (a) to descend (into the Virgin Mary); ~ in (into, on, upon, within); (b) to be incarnate." There may also be a pun on *lighten*, "to shine." Some apocryphal accounts associate a bright light with the birth of Jesus: In the *Protevangelium*, 19:2, a cloud fills the cave until the child is born, "And immediately the cloud disappeared from the cave, and a great light appeared in the cave, so that our eyes could not bear it" (Schneemelcher, p. 434); and in *Pseudo-Matthew* 13, Mary gives birth in a cave "in which there was never any light, but always darkness, because it could not receive the light of day. And when the blessed Mary had entered it, it began to become all light with brightness, as if it had been the sixth hour of the day [i.e., noon]; divine light so illumined the cave, that light did not fail there by day or night, as long as the blessed Mary was there" (Cowper, pp. 50–51).

30   *assis stall.* According to Luke (2:7 and 2:16), Mary lays the newborn Jesus in a manger.

32–38   *The sheperdes . . . to man is dyte.* Luke 2:8–14.

38   *dyte.* The verb *dighten* has a number of appropriate meanings here: to prepare, to arrange, to command, to predetermine, to bring about, to give, to perform, to ordain, to proclaim; also *diten*, to sing, declare, compose; indict.

41–49   *Thre kynges . . . to hys modere Mary.* Matthew 2:1–12.

§16

Nu this fules singet and maket hure blisse. Index no. 2366. MS: Trinity College Cambridge 323 (B.14.39), fol. 81b (thirteenth century). Editions: W. W. Greg, "I Sing of a Maiden that is Makeless," *Modern Philology* 7 (see above, §13), 166–67; B13, no. 31; Stevick, no. 10. Selected criticism: Woolf, p. 143; Weber pp. 48–55 (discussing structure and imagery, and defending the poem against Spitzer's and Greg's description of it as "mediocre" and "not very remarkable").

§13 quotes lines 4–5 and 10–20 of this poem (see note to §13).

Initial rubric: *Exemplum de beata virgine et gaudiis eius* [Exemplum of the blessed virgin and her joys]. The MS is a collection of Dominican sermons.

1   *and.* MS: *hand.*

4   *king.* MS: *kind* (Brown's emendation).

        halle. As in line 1, the scribe has a tendency toward aspiration of words beginning with vowels. See also *hut* for "out" in line 8.

6   *of Gesses more.* See §8, note to line 17.

9–11   From the *Ave Maria*; see notes to §11.

15   *Hu.* MS: *thu* (Brown's emendation).

15–16   *He saide . . . y nout iuis.* Luke 1:34. Compare §2, line 10.

16   A word is erased after *ymone.*

20   *he.* MS: *the.*

§17

Alleluya! Now wel may we merthis make. Index no. 2377. MS: Bodl. 3340 (Arch. Selden B.26), fol. 10a (fifteenth century, southern dialect, with music). Other MSS: Bridgewater Corporation Muniments 123 (written on the back of a parchment indenture dated 1471, though carol may be a later addition); BL Addit. 5665 (Ritson), fols. 36b–37a, with music, burden, and stanzas 1–3 (sixteenth century). Editions of Arch. Selden B.26: Stainer and Stainer, 2:109; Padelford, p. 91; Stevens, *Mediaeval Carols*, p. 14; Robbins, *Early English Christmas Carols*, no. 5. Editions of Bridgewater: *EEC*, no. 14; Greene, *Selection,* no. 7. Editions of Ritson: Fehr, *Archiv* 106, 273; Rickert p. 177; Stevens p. 94.

This carol is one of many adaptations of the *Laetabundus* sequence attributed to Bernard of Clairvaux; for the Latin text and other translations, see *EEC*, pp. xcviii–civ. See also §20. (On the development of the prose in medieval liturgy and on Bernard's text, see Greene, *Selection*, pp. 37–38.)

1   Initial *A* rubricated.

3   *manhode.* Bridgewater: *mankynd.*

4   *Only for our synnes sake*. Bridgewater: *Of a mayden withoutyne make*.

          synnes. MS: *synes*. So emended by all.

5   *Gaudeamus*. Bridgewater MS. Selden: *Alleluya. Chorus*.

6   *kynge of kynges*. See 1 Timothy 6:15 and Apocalypse 17:14 and 19:16.

11   *y seide*. Bridgewater: *as y sayd*; Ritson: *as prophesye sayde*.

18–20   The light-through-glass simile is common in medieval Latin and vernacular theological writings on the Virgin birth. Compare §15, line 23; §50, line 13; and *Index* no. 1471 (fifteenth century), "In Bedleem in that fair cete": "As the sunne schynyth thorw the glas / So Jhesu in his modyr was." Arthur S. Napier has compiled several more examples in *History of the Holy Rood-tree*, EETS o.s. 103 (London: Kegan Paul, 1894), pp. 81–83.

20   *withoute wem*. The image of Mary as "spotless" comes from her association with the bride in Canticles 4:7: "Thou art all fair, O my love, and there is not a spot in thee." See also note to §15, line 3, and compare §16, line 16, and §2, line 10.

§18

Mary so myelde of hert and myende. By James Ryman. *Index* no. 2122. MS: Cambridge University Ee.1.12, fol. 76a–b (1492). Editions: Zupitza, *Archiv* 89, 275–76; *EEC*, no. 54.

1   *myelde*. The MED suggests several appropriate connotations for the word — merciful, forgiving, kind, gracious, benevolent, friendly, humble, and gentle — and mentions specifically its frequent association with Mary's name (*milde*, adj.2.c). The poem addresses Mary's mildness rather than her purity, perhaps echoing Bernard of Clairvaux's insistence that Mary's humility, her desire to do God's will, was far more significant than her virginity (Homily 1, p. 9).

7   Here and at the beginning of each successive stanza, Mary's name is written in large, bold letters.

26   *heven quere*. The choir of heaven could mean "among the elect," or it could refer to the chancel itself.

§19

My Fader above, beholdying thy mekenesse. Possibly by John Lydgate. *Index* no. 2238. MS: BL Harley 2251, fol. 78a (between 1464 and 1483). Edition: Henry Noble MacCracken, *John Lydgate: The Minor Poems*, p. 235. On the MS, see E. P. Hammond, "Two British Museum MSS," *Anglia* 28 (1905), 19, and Derek Pearsall, *John Lydgate* (Charlottesville: University Press of Virginia, 1970), p. 74.

MacCracken attributes this poem, which is apparently an early and incomplete effort, to Lydgate with the note: "A charming ballade to the Virgin, which I admit 'atwixen hope and dred'" (p. xiii).

1   *My.* Initial M rubricated.

8   *who.* MS: *whan.* MacCracken's emendation.

10   *Thow.* MS: *that.* MacCracken's emendation.

18   *rosis fyve.* Lydgate makes a similar association between roses and Christ's five wounds in his poem "As a Mydsomer Rose," contrasting fading midsummer roses and the mortal glories they symbolize with the lasting glory of Christ, "whos five woundys prent in your hert a rose" (*John Lydgate: Poems*, ed. John Norton-Smith [Oxford: Clarendon Press, 1966], p. 24). George Ferguson mentions the ancient Roman association of the rose with victory; in Christian symbolism, the rose symbolizes martyrdom as well as heavenly joy (*Signs and Symbols*, pp. 37–38).

§20

Ther is no rose of swych vertu. Index no. 3536. MS: Trinity College Cambridge 1230 (O.3.58) recto, no. 13, with music. This mid-fifteenth century MS contains thirteen carols; Rickert notes that part of the MS is attributed to John Dunstable of Henry VII's chapel. Editions: J. A. Fuller-Maitland, *English Carols of the Fifteenth Century, From a MS. Roll in the Library of Trinity College, Cambridge* (London: The Leadenhall Press, 1891), pp. 26–27, with music; CS, no. 52; *EEC*, no. 173; Stevens, pp. 10–11 (rpt. in *Tidings True: Carols Selected from Volume 4 of Musica Britannica* [New York: Galaxy Music, n.d.], p. 9); Greene, *Selection,* no. 46; Sisam, *Oxford,* no. 169; Rickert, p. 8; Segar, p. 65; Robbins, *Early English Christmas Carols,* no. 23 (with music); Oliver, p. 82; Gray, *Themes,* pp. 88–90, with commentary; Gray, *Selection,* no. 12; Terry, p. 56; Stevens, *There is No Rose of Such Virtue,* Fayrfax Series no.

16 (London: Stainer and Bell, 1951); Manning, p. 155, with music; Oliver, pp. 82–83, with music; Bullett, p. 5, with music; E. Routley, *The English Carols* (London: H. Jenkins, 1958), p. 29, with music.

This end of the roll is barely readable. Where necessary, I supply readings from Gray's transcription.

The Latin lines concluding the first three stanzas are from the *Laetabundus* prose attributed to Bernard of Clairvaux (see note to §17).

1	*Ther is no rose of swych vertu.* I.e., there is no other like Mary. Oliver notes "a sensuous-theological pun on 'vertu' as 'strength or fragrance' [or quality] and 'virtue' in the modern sense [of goodness]" (p. 82).

The image of Mary as the unparalleled *rosa sine spina* (rose without thorn) derives from Ecclesiasticus 24:18: "I [Wisdom] was exalted like a palm tree in Cades, and as a rose plant in Jericho." In Genesis 3:18, the thorn is associated with sin; thus to be without thorn is to be without sin. The fourth sequence for the Daily Mass of St. Mary (Sarum) begins "*Eterni numinis mater et filia diuini luminis lucerna preuia nostrique germinis rosa primaria sine contagio*" (Legg, p. 495, line 22): "Hail, holy parent, rose / On which thorn never grows" (Warren, Part 2, p. 87). See also *DBT*, "Rose Without a Thorn" (James P. Forrest).

Initial *T* and *is no* are no longer visible in MS.

3   *Ther is no rose of.* No longer visible in MS.

6–10   *For in this rose . . . personys thre.* On the image of Mary as chamber of the Trinity, see §11, line 21 and note, and see Plate C. For the related concept of God contained in the small space of Mary's womb, compare §8, lines 50–52.

10   *That he is God.* CS reads *There be o* (i.e., "one") *God*; Rickert and Fuller-Maitland follow this reading. Robbins and Gray follow Greene. The MS is no longer legible.

11   *Pari forma.* Fuller-Maitland reads *pares forma.* The MS is no longer legible.

15   *Leve.* The *L* is obliterated by a stain in the MS.

§21

Holy moder, that bere Cryst. Attributed to William Herebert. *Index* no. 1232. MS: BL Addit. 46919, fol. 207b (Herebert's commonplace book, early fourteenth century, Southwest Midlands). Editions: B14, no. 19; LH, no. 186; W. F. Bryan and Germaine Dempster, eds., *Sources and Analogues of Chaucer's Canterbury Tales* (New York: Humanities Press, 1958), p. 469; Reimer, pp. 122–23.

This is a paraphrasing of the Latin antiphon *Alma redemptoris mater* (Mother of the Redeemer), used especially from Advent through Candlemas (February 2). Herebert includes with this text a marginal note in Latin, briefly summarizing a popular legend, best known today through Chaucer's The Prioress' Tale, in which a child slain by Jews continues to sing this hymn after his death. The Latin hymn is as follows:

> Alma redemptoris mater, quae pervia coeli
> Porta manes et stella maris, succure cadenti
> Surgere qui curat: populo tu quae genuisti
> Natura mirante tuum sanctum genitorem
> Virgo prius ac posterius, Gabrielis ab ore
> Sumens illud Ave, peccatorum miserere.
>   (Daniel 2:318)

"Alma redemptoris mater, etc" appears above the first line. Herebert's name appears in the margin.

3   *gat of hevene blisse.* See note to §4, line 9.

5   *sterre of se.* See §9, note to line 1. The eleventh-century Latin source borrows freely from the older *Ave maris stella.*

7   *holy.* Written above the line to replace *oune.*

§22

Syng we, syng we. Index no. 1230, *Holy maydyn blyssid þou be.* MS: BL Sloane 2593, fol. 25a (c. 1450). Five stanzas also appear in Bodl. 3340 (Arch. Selden B.26), fol. 10b (c. 1450). Editions of Sloane: Wright, *Songs* (Warton Club), pp. 71–72; Fehr, *Archiv* 109 (1902), 64–65; Rickert, p. 18. Editions of Arch. Selden: Stainer and Stainer, 2:110; Stevens, *Mediaeval Carols*, p. 14. Editions of both: Padelford, *Anglia* 36, 91–92; *EEC*, no. 185.

Notes

This poem is a *tour de force* in rhyme — thirty lines in a single rhyme sound.

7–14   These two stanzas are transposed in Arch. Selden.

9   *chosyn.* Arch. Selden: *cosyn.*

19   *solumné.* MS reads *solūte.* Fehr expands to *solunte*, Greene to *solumte.*

15–26   These stanzas are omitted in Arch. Selden. In their place is a single stanza which reads:

>Lo, this curteys kynge of degré
>Wole be thy sone with solempnité;
>Mylde Mary, this ys thy fee;
>*Regina celi, letare.*

21   *rede.* Several meanings of *reden* might apply here: to proclaim, to tell, or to teach; to read (we read of the three Kings); or to counsel (we counsel you to rejoice, queen of heaven).

§23

Lullay, myn lykyng. Index no. 1351. MS: BL Sloane 2593, fol. 32a–b (mid-fifteenth century). Editions: Wright, *Songs* (Warton Club), p. 94; CS, no. 69; Fehr, *Archiv* 107 (1901), 49; *EEC*, no. 143; Bullett, p. 7 (without burden); Greene, *Selection*, no. 40; Percy Dearmer, R. Vaughan Williams, and Martin Shaw, *The Oxford Book of Carols* (London: Oxford University Press, 1928), no. 182 (setting by Gustav Holst); Davies, no. 77; Gray, *Selection*, no. 13; *EEC* no 143; Rickert, p. 66; H. C. Beeching, ed., *A Book of Christmas Verse,* second ed. (London: H. Milford, Oxford University Press, 1926), p. 10; Segar, p. 66; E. Sayre, ed., *A Christmas Book; 50 Carols from the 14th to the 17th Centuries* (New York: C. N. Potter, 1966), p. 125.

4   The margin reads *lull myn*, indicating the repetition of the burden.

6   See note to §17, line 6; see also Deuteronomy 10:17 and Psalm 135:3 (RSV 136:3).

The margin reads *lullay.*

12   *makyn chere.* I.e., Grant blessing to those who participate in the carol by dancing and singing.

§24

Ler to loven as I love thee. Index no. 1847. MS: National Library of Scotland Advocates 18.7.21, fol. 126a (Grimestone's commonplace book, 1372). A shorter version appears in BL Harley 7322, fol. 135b (c. 1375). Edition of Advocates: B14, no. 75. Editions of Harley: Furnivall, EETS o.s. 15, p. 255; Sisam, *Fourteenth Century*, pp. 167–68; Sisam, *Oxford*, no. 87.

The arrangement of stanzas in the Advocates MS raises questions about whether the first stanza is, in fact, part of this poem: lines 7–30 appear at the top of the left column, followed by another poem; lines 1–6 appear at the top of the right column and are linked to the rest with a line of red dots. Wenzel defends the present order, noting that the poem is quoted in the context of a sermon in Harley 7322 (*Preachers*, pp. 167–68). See below for notes on the Harley version. See also Edward Wilson, *A Descriptive Index of the English Lyrics in John of Grimestone's Preaching Book, Medium Aevum* Monographs n.s. 2 (Oxford: Basil Blackwell, 1973), p. 55.

1–6   In Harley, the newborn Jesus addresses Mary in these lines. At the end of the stanza, the Harley scribe inserts a Latin directive: *Et Regina mater sua nichil habuit unde posset eum induere; ideo dixit sibi* [And the queen his mother had nothing with which to clothe him; therefore she said to him].

3   *thei.* Harley: *ich.*

4   *michil wo.* Harley: *much colde and wo.*

5   *suete.* Harley: *wel.*

8   *thu list nou.* Harley: *list thou.*

10   *thi credel is als a bere.* The image foreshadows Jesus' death and contrasts the painless birth with the suffering he will endure later for the sake of humankind (see lines 20–24).

12   *mai I.* Harley: *ich mai.*

14–16   Harley reads as follows: *Thou ich nabbe clout ne cloth / The on for to folde / The on to folde ne to wrappe / For ich nabbe clout ne lappe.* The second line disrupts the stanzaic pattern and is probably a scribal error.

Notes

17   *Therfore ley thi fet.* Harley: *Bote ley thou thi fet.*

18   *kepe.* Harley: *wite.*

§25

Lullay, lullay, la, lullay. Index no. 352: *Als I lay upon a nith.* MS: National Library of Scotland Advocates 18.7.21, fols. 3b–4b (Grimestone's commonplace book, 1372). Fragments (early stanzas) of this text appear in three fifteenth-century MSS: St. John's College Cambridge 259, fol. 4a–b (stanzas 1–9, late fifteenth century); BL Harley 2330, fol. 120a (stanzas 1–5 copied onto the end of a fifteenth-century MS); and Cambridge University Addit. 5943, fol. 169a (first stanza only, fifteenth century). Editions of Advocates: B14, no. 56; *EEC*, no. 149; Davies, no. 38 (some stanzas). Robbins prints the text of Cambridge Addit. 5943, with music, in *Early English Christmas Carols*, no. 27.

This lyric combines elements of dialogue, carol, dream vision, and lament, as Jesus sings the refrain and teaches Mary the part of the song she does not know. Davies identifies the poem as one of the earliest examples of a lullaby to Jesus (p. 40). Compare §29, which is from the same MS.

9   *dede.* MS: *de.* Brown, Davies emend so. Greene gives *ded.*

11   In margin: *iesu.*

23   In margin: *Maria.*

55–58   *The sepperdis . . . In time of thi birthe.* Luke 2:8–20.

57   *ther.* MS: *tht.* So emended by Brown, Greene, and Davies.

63   In margin: *Christus loquitur.*

67–70   Luke 2:21.

68   In Genesis 17:10–14, Abraham receives the covenant of circumcision from God.

69   *Kot sal I ben with a ston.* Jesus is circumcised to fulfill Jewish law. Christian commentators observe that in this ritual Jesus sheds his first drop of blood for man-

199

kind, thus anticipating the Crucifixion and Resurrection. On the further significance of this circumcision, see *CA*, commentary on Luke 2:21, in which Epiphanius notes that the circumcision proved "the reality of His flesh" against the Manichaean heretical belief that Jesus was not truly human.

71–74   Matthew 2:1–12. The Church celebrates the visit of the Magi on Epiphany, twelve days after Christmas.

75–78   Luke 2:22–40.

79–82   Luke 2:41–50.

84   *suerve*. MS: *sterue*. Brown's emendation. However, *sterve* could be the correct reading, as if Jesus is assuring Mary that he will not abandon her.

91–94   Matthew 3:13–17; Mark 1:9–11; Luke 3:21–22.

95–98   *I sal ben tempted . . . But I sal betre withstonde*. Matthew 4:1–11; Mark 1:12–13; Luke 4:1–13. The reference to Adam comes from Genesis 3.

99–102   *Disciples I sal gadere . . . to teche*. Matthew 4:18–22; Mark 1:16–20, 3:13–19, 6:7; Luke 5:1–11, 9:2; John 1:35–51.

105–06   *That most partiye . . . Sal wiln maken me king*. John 6:15.

107   In margin: *Maria*.

111   In margin: *iesus*.

119   *The sarpe swerde of Simeon*. Luke 2:34–35: "And Simeon blessed them, and said to Mary his mother, 'Behold, this child is destined for the fall and for the rise of many in Israel, and for a sign that shall be contradicted. And thy own soul a sword shall pierce, that the thoughts of many hearts may be revealed.'"

123–24   *Samfuly for I sal deyye . . . on the rode*. Matthew 27:32–56; Mark 15:21–41; Luke 23:26–49; John 19:17–39.

127   In margin: *Maria*.

131   In margin: *iesu.*

132   *liven I sal ageyne.* Matthew 28 ff; Mark 16 ff; Luke 24 ff; John 20 ff.

133   *in thi kinde.* I.e., Mary has given him her flesh, and that flesh will be redeemed.

135–36 *To my Fader . . . to hevene.* Luke 24:50–53; Acts 2.

137   *The Holigost I sal thee sende.* John 23:21–22.

138   *sondes sevene.* The Douay translation from the Vulgate identifies the seven gifts as wisdom, understanding, counsel, fortitude, knowledge, godliness, and the fear of the Lord (Isaias 11:2–3).

139–42 *I sal thee taken . . . have I caste.* In the absence of any evidence regarding Mary's death or burial, belief in her bodily assumption into heaven developed in the fifth century. See Introduction, pp. 25–26.

149   *Yolisday.* The setting suggests that the speaker's "longing" is fulfilled by the birth of Jesus.

§26

Modyr, whyt os lyly flowr. Index no. 361. MS: Bodl. 29734 (Eng. Poet e.1), fol. 34a–b (fifteenth century). The first twenty lines also appear in BL Sloane 2593, fols. 16b–17a (fifteenth century). Editions of English Poet: Wright, *Songs* (Percy Society), pp. 50–51; *EEC*, no. 145. Edition of Sloane: Wright, *Songs* (Warton Club), pp. 48–49. Composite text: CS p. 141; Rickert p. 68.

1   *lyly flowr.* The lily symbolizes Mary's purity.

2   Word canceled before *langour* in MS.

3   *up.* Sloane: *me.*

        a. Sloane: *on.*

5   *That.* Sloane: *che.*

6   *swet*. Sloane: *dere*.

7   *held*. Sloane: *tok al*.

8   *hyr lovely*. Sloane: *that maydyn*.

9   *And therof swetly he toke a nappe*. So emended by Greene. The MS, which Wright follows, reads *an appe*. Sloane: *& tok therof a ryght god nap*.

11   *gen he*. Sloane: *than he gan*.

12   *For this mylke*. I.e., for humankind.

13   *kynd*. The word has several theological implications here. It could mean station, duty, or inheritance; it also implies that it is Jesus' destiny, purpose, or intention to die for humanity's sake.

14   *paramowr*. Sloane: *myn paramour*. Rickert reads *par amour*, glossing the phrase "for love's sake."

15   *The maydyn*. Sloane: *That mayde*.

       gen. Sloane: *be gan*.

17   Sloane: *That here sone that is oure kynge*.

18   *shed*. Sloane: *schred*.

       blod. MS: *b*.

19   *Modyr, thi wepyng*. Sloane: *Your wepyng moder*.

20   *thu haddys be*. Sloane: *ye wern for*.

21   *Do awey*. Sloane: *dowey*.

22   *Thy*. Sloane: *Your*.

       lessyth. MS: *lsyth*. Greene's emendation.

       langowr. MS: *lango*. Greene's emendation.

26   *for.* Greene supplies the word from Wright; it is not visible in the present binding.

§27

Lullay, my fader, lullay, my brother. Index no. 4242.5. MS: Stanbrook Abbey 3, fol. 241a (early fifteenth century). Editions: N. R. Ker, "Middle English Verses and a Latin Letter in a Manuscript at Stanbrook Abbey," *Medium Aevum* 34 (1965), 233; *EEC*, no. 144.1.

Ker writes that the poem appears in five stanzas, "with a refrain after each stanza set out in the margin. They are written below Morton's note about his purchases and are separated from it by doodles and brief notes in Latin" (pp. 232–33). Greene notes that "the burden appears to have been written at a time different from that of the writing of the stanzas."

11   *And.* Canceled at beginning of line.

      fader. MS: *fadrer.* Greene's emendation. So also at lines 15 and 19.

13   *on.* MS: *in.* Greene's emendation.

18   *Myn owyn dyre sone, lullay.* MS: *Myn owyn &c.*

21   *myn herte perschyth in tweye.* Perhaps an allusion to Simeon's prophecy in Luke 2:34–35.

§28

I passud thoru a garden grene. Attributed to John Hawghton. *Index* no. 378. MS: National Library of Scotland Advocates 19.3.1 (formerly Jac. V.7.27), fols. 94b–95b (c. 1430). The poem also appears in BL Sloane 2593, fol. 18b (c. 1450). Brown describes the differences between the two MSS in B15, pp. 317–18; the Advocates arrangement of stanzas is the more logical, and the Sloane version sacrifices some alliteration. Editions of Advocates: W. B. D. D. Turnbull, *The Visions of Tundale, Together with Metrical Moralizations and Other Fragments of Early Poetry; Hitherto Inedited* (Edinburgh: Stevenson, 1843), pp. 157–59; B15, no. 78; Stevick, no. 60. Editions of Sloane: Fehr, *Archiv* 109, 58; Wright, *Songs* (Warton Club), pp. 53–55; Rickert, p. 174.

| 2 | *a herbere made full newe.* The newly-made garden might represent the world, given new life through the birth of a savior. |

| 4 | *tree.* The word is difficult to decipher in the MS; Brown reads *treo.* |

| 5 | *Theryn.* Brown reads *thereyn.* |
| | *mayden.* Turnbull reads *maydon.* |

| 6 | *sest.* Brown's emendation. MS: *sesest.* |

| 8 | *Verbum caro factum est.* John 1:14. The *CA* contains extensive discussion of this concept, focused primarily on answering charges that Jesus was not human. St. Augustine writes: "As our word becomes the bodily voice, by its assumption of that voice, as a means of developing itself externally; so the Word of God was made flesh, by assuming flesh, as a means of manifesting Itself to the world" (*De Trinitate,* as quoted in *CA,* John 1:14). A note in MS BL Additional 37049, fol. 26b, indicates that Pope Clement I granted a pardon of three years and forty days to anyone who "devoutly hers or says Sant John Gospell, that ys to say, 'In principio erat verbum;' and then to the end whenne 'Verbum caro factum est' is sayd" (fol. 26b). |

The refrain is popular in carols: see *EEC* nos. 23B, 35B, 38, and 39. Its presence in a secular drinking song (from Bodl. 2240, fol. 25a, printed in Robbins, *Secular Lyrics,* second ed. [Oxford: Clarendon Press, 1955], no. 10) suggests its familiarity:

Verbum caro factum est	
Et habitavit in nobis.	*dwelt among us*
Fetys bel chere,	
Drynk to thi fere,	
Verse le bavere,	*pass around the drink*
And synge nouwell!	

| 18 | *song.* Omitted in this MS; Brown supplies from Sloane. |

| 20 | *Gloria in excelsis Deo.* Luke 2:14. See also *DBT,* "Gloria," for a discussion of this element of the liturgy. |

| 26 | *abovun*: Turnbull reads *aboun.* |

| 27 | *pece.* Turnbull reads *that.* |

30   *betwene to best*. According to Luke 2:7, Mary gives birth to Jesus and places him in a manger. Tradition adds the two beasts, generally supposed to be an ox and an ass, from Isaias 1:3, quoted in the apocryphal *Pseudo-Matthew*: "Mary went out of the cave and, entering a stable, put the child in the manger, and an ox and an ass adored him. Then was fulfilled that which was said by Isaiah the prophet, 'The ox knows his owner, and the ass his master's crib'" (Elliott, *The Apocryphal New Testament*, p. 94).

     best. Turnbull reads *bestes*.

31   *Sche*. Turnbull reads *scho*.

34   *three*. Possibly, as Brown reads, *threo*.

     commely. Turnbull reads *comely*.

     crone. Turnbull reads *gone*.

35   *spod*. Perhaps *sped*, as Brown suggests.

     speke. Turnbull reads *spoke*.

37   *home*. Turnbull reads *hom*.

     con rone. Turnbull reads *com rene*.

38   *We*. Turnbull reads *Wo*.

41   *we seo God becomun yn mannus flech*. Turnbull reads *wose God be comm in mannis flesh*. The kings translate the carol's Latin refrain.

42   *That bote hasse broght of all oure bale*. Compare §14, line 2.

     bale. Turnbull reads *bele*.

43   *Awey oure synnus*. Turnbull reads *Away owre synnis*.

45   *Sche*. Turnbull reads *Scho*.

45   *sothly.* Turnbull reads *sothty.*

47   *Foll.* Turnbull reads *Full.*

49   *prences.* Turnbull reads *princes.*

55   *sange.* Turnbull reads *sung.*

§29

Als I lay upon a nith / I lokede upon a stronde. Index no. 353. MS: Advocates Library 18.7.21, fols. 5b–6a (Grimestone's commonplace book, 1372). A garbled copy of lines 1–44 also survives, with music, in Bodl. 2240 (Arch. Selden B.26), fol. 18a–b. In Selden, the scribe has copied stanzas arranged horizontally as if they were arranged vertically: 1, 2, 7, 3, 8, 4, 9, 5, 10, 6. Editions of Advocates: B14, no. 58; LH, no. 198; Silverstein, no. 41. Editions of Selden: Padelford, pp. 102–04; Stainer and Stainer, vol. 1, plates lxvii and lxviii (facsimiles); vol. 2, pp. 130–31 (transcription, with music); Stevens, p. 112; J. Copley, *Seven English Songs and Carols of the Fifteenth Century* (Texts and Monographs VI, University of Leeds, 1940), pp. 14–15 (with music). Weber prints Brown's edition and discusses the poem's structure on pp. 61–86, commenting on the transformation of Mary's limited perspective by means of her child.

2   Selden: *For soth y sawe a semely syȝt*

3   *mayden.* Selden: *berde so.*

4   *hadde in.* Selden: *bare on.*

5   *Hire loking.* Possibly "To look upon her."

7   *sorwe sikerli.* Selden: *care & sorwe.*

8   *mithte.* Selden: *may.*

9   Selden: *y behelde that swete wyght.*

11–12   I.e., if Mary is not a virgin, then a terrible deception has been practiced on the world. Joseph responds to this fear of "misdeed" in lines 37–44. In Matthew 1:19–25 Joseph assumes the worst of Mary and "being a just man, and not wishing to expose her to reproach, was minded to put her away privately" until an angel comes to him in a dream and assures him that all is well. But it is the *Protevangelium* (chs. 13–14) and the *Gospel of Pseudo-Matthew* (chs. 10–11) which provide material for cycle plays, such as the N-Town "Joseph's Doubt" (*The N-Town Play, Cotton MS Vespasian D.8*, ed. Stephen Spector, vol. 1, EETS s.s. 11 [Oxford: Oxford University Press, 1991], pp. 123–30).

13   *sergant.* Selden: *seruant.*

14   *That sadli seide his sawe.* Selden: *that seide al in his sawe.*

      seide his sawe. According to the OED, a "saw" is a speech, a story, or a wise saying. The word also might suggest a catechism, prayers, holy wisdom, or the law.

17   *on hevede.* Selden: *al on his hede.*

19   *He herde wel.* Selden: *She herde ful wel.*

23   *An I dede so.* Selden: *And so y dyde.*

25–28 In Selden, these lines follow lines 17–20 of the present text, and read as follows:

       and saide she was alone
       maide and moder ycore   *chosen*
       and withoute wem of man   *taint*
       a childe she hadde ybore.

29–30 Selden reads: *They that y unworthy be, / she is mary myn owne wyf.*

32   *I love.* Selden: *& yit y love.*

33   *wiste I.* Selden: *y wiste.*

35   *thee.* MS: *the.* The word could be read as a definite article, but see Selden: *ʒow.*

36   *I not.* Advocates: *In wot.* Silverstein's emendation. Luria and Hoffman emend to *I ne wot.* In Selden the line reads *y note in whoche wyse.*

37   *to.* Selden: *unto.*

38   *wolde no thing misdo.* Selden: *wolde not mysdoo.*

39–40   *I wot et wel iwisse / For I have founden et so.* Selden: *that y wyst ful wel ywys / for ofte y haue yfounde hit soo.*

52   *Emanuel.* The name (from Isaias 7:12 and Matthew 1:23) means "God with us."

61–64   In the Advocates MS, these lines appear at the bottom of the next page, following a separate lullaby in a different rhyme scheme.

§30

Ecce quod natura. By James Ryman. *Index* no. 488. MS: Cambridge University Ee.1.12., fols. 23a–24a (late fifteenth century). Editions: Zupitza, *Archiv* 89 (1892), 185–86, notes in *Archiv* 93 (1894), 383–90; *EEC*, no. 66, Greene, *Selection*, no. 14.

The burden is from a *cantio* or *cantilena* (a sacred Latin piece; see Greene, *EEC*, p. cx) which appears in Arch. Selden B. 26 and in Bodl. Ashmole 1393, fol. 69 (printed with music in Stainer and Stainer, 2:63–64). In the Cambridge MS, this carol is followed by a similar one using the same burden and beginning: "Bothe younge and olde, take hede of this" (*Index* no. 546; *EEC*, no. 65).

3–4   Compare a line in the lyric which follows this one in the MS: "The cours of nature chaunged is."

3–7   These lines paraphrase the Latin burden.

7–8   See note to §8, line 26.

9–10   Numbers 17:6–11. See the *Biblia Pauperum* leaf for the Nativity (Plate A in this volume).

11–14   Isaias 7:14.

15–16   Isaias 11:1–2.

19–23   Matthew 1:23.

23–24   *to us is borne a chielde; / A sonne is yeven to us.* Isaias 9:6.

27   *stone cutte of the hille.* In Daniel 2:34–35, King Nabuchodonosor dreams of "a stone cut out of a mountain without hands"; after destroying a statue which represents his divided kingdom, the stone becomes a great mountain. Daniel interprets the mountain as the kingdom of God; thus the stone itself represents the Messiah, and its divine creation parallels the miracle of Jesus' birth.

31   *Prince of Peas.* Isaias 9:6.

35–38   Greene, following R. W. Southern, explains that though this simile is not found in any "acknowledged work" of St. Anselm, it is a common simile in the "School of Anselm" (*EEC* p. 365; see also R. W. Southern, "St. Anselm and His English Pupils," *Medieval and Renaissance Studies* 1 [1943], 10).

§31

Quhat dollour persit our ladyis hert. Index no. 3904. MS: BL Arundel 285, fol. 141b (late fifteenth or early sixteenth century). Editions: Karl Brunner, "Mittelenglischen Marien-stunden," *Englische Studien* 70 (1935), 106–09; B15, no. 94; J. A. W. Bennett, *Devotional Pieces in Verse and Prose, from MS. Arundel 285 and MS. Harleian 6919,* STS third series no. 23 (Edinburgh: William Blackwood and Sons, 1949), pp. 234–36.

      houris. The Breviary contains the liturgies of the Divine Office, including the canonical hours (consisting of psalms, antiphons, and hymns) to be recited daily. The hours include prime (usually around 6 a.m., the "first hour"), terce (the "third hour," or 9 a.m.), sext (noon), none (mid-afternoon, around 3 p.m.), evensong (around 6 p.m.), and compline (around 9 p.m.). The poem is an adaptation of the "Hours of the Cross" form, unusual for its focus on Mary; for additional examples of the form see B14, nos. 30, 34, and 55; and B15, no. 93. In the MS, this rubric and the hours heading each stanza appear centered, in red.

1   *persit.* A good example of affective piety. Through empathy, Mary (and thus the poet/meditator) is experiencing the Crucifixion in her heart. The line also recalls Simeon's prophecy; see note to §25, line 119.

3   *Annas.* After Jesus is arrested in the Garden of Gethsemane, he is taken to the high priest Caiaphas for questioning. According to the account in John 18:12–13, Jesus

is first taken to Caiaphas' father-in-law, Annas. Annas and Caiaphas appear regularly as characters in medieval dramas. (See also Matthew 26:57–75; Mark 14:53–65; Luke 22:54.)

4   *fals witnes agane him.* See Mark 14:55–59.

5   *Pilotis place.* Jesus' trial takes place before Pilate, governor of Judea. See Matthew 27:2, 11–26; Mark 15:1–15; Luke 23:1–5 and 13–25; John 18:28–40.

9   *Crucify him!* Matthew 27:23; Mark 15:13–14; Luke 23:21–23; John 19:6 and 15.

10   *quhit coit and purpour claith.* His torturers mock Jesus as "King of the Jews" with a purple cloak (the color of royalty) and a crown of thorns (line 12). See Matthew 27:27–31; Mark 15:16–20; John 19:1–5. They also cast lots (play quoits) for his garments (Matthew 27:35; Mark 15:24; Luke 23:34; John 19:23–24).

11   *Thai scurgit him.* John 19:1–16; Mark 15:15.

13   *nalit on a tre.* Accounts of Jesus' Crucifixion are given in Matthew 27:35; Mark 15:24; Luke 23:33; John 19:17–18.

14   *For drink thai gaif him bitter gall.* Matthew 27:34 (fulfilling the prophecy of Psalm 69:21).

16   *The erd trimblit, and cragis begouth to fall.* The earthquake, recorded in Matthew 27:51–54, comes at the moment of Jesus' death. (Mark 15:28 and Luke 23:45 also indicate that the curtain of the temple is torn in two at the moment of his death.)

17   *he commendit his moder to Sanct Johnne.* John 19:25–27. Compare §37.

19   *The sone tynt licht fra the sext till none.* Luke 23:44–45: "It was now about the sixth hour, and there was darkness over the whole land until the ninth hour. And the sun was darkened, and the curtain of the temple was torn in the middle." See also Matthew 27:45; Mark 15:33–41; John 19:28–37.

20   *His passioun betuix God and ws maid peace.* I.e., Jesus paid for the sins of humankind with his death. In his account of the Passion, Jacobus de Voragine cites St. Augustine on humanity's debt of sin: "Eve borrowed sin from the devil and wrote a bill and provided a surety, and the interest on the debt was heaped upon posterity.

She borrowed sin from the devil when, going against God's command, she consented to his wicked order or suggestion. She wrote the bill when she reached out her hand to the forbidden apple. She gave a surety when she made Adam consent to the sin. And so the interest on the debt of sin became posterity's burden" (*The Golden Legend*, 1:210). Christ's death redeems, or pays for, the debt of sin. §59 echoes this idea: "Marie, out of synne help thu me, / And out of dette, for charité" (lines 7–8).

20   *ws.* Brunner reads this as an abbreviation and expands to *world.*

21   *his syd oppinnit with a speir.* John 19:34: "but one of the soldiers opened his side with a lance, and immediately there came out blood and water."

25–27   The account of Jesus' burial is given in Matthew 27:57–66; Mark 15:42–47; Luke 23:50–56; and John 19:38–42.

28   *allane.* MS: *all.* Bennett and Brown complete the rhyme with *allane.* On the tradition that Mary alone remained faithful through the events of the Crucifixion, see the *Fasciculus Morum*, p. 619.

29   *mercy.* A word is crossed out with red ink before this word.

At the close of the piece, the MS reads: *Heir endis the exercicioun for Setterday and begynnis the exercicioun for Sonday.* The poem is a devotional "exercise" for Holy Week meditation.

§32

Jesu Cristes milde moder. Index no. 1697. MS: BL Arundel 248, fols. 154b–55a, with music (thirteenth century). Editions: Martin Jacoby, *Vier Mittelenglische Geistliche Gedichte aus dem 13. Jahrhundert* (Berlin: Bernstein, 1890), p. 42; B13, no. 47. The music, an early example of English polyphony, appears in Woolridge, p. 308, and in Gustave Reese, *Music in the Middle Ages,* (New York: Norton, 1940) p. 389. Commentary: Weber, pp. 139–45.

The poem is a paraphrase of the sequence *Stabat juxta Christi crucem* (printed in B13, p. 8), but the music (which supplies a different melody and descant for each verse) appears to be unique to this MS. For another example of that tradition, see B13, no. 4 (MS Bodl. 9995, opening stanzas missing).

8   *neverre.* Jacoby transcribes *nevere.*

           no. Added above line.

10   *The brithe day went into nith.* For literal interpretation, see §31, note to line 19. But
           the death of Jesus, his mother's "heart's light" (line 11), also brings a figurative
           darkness. John's gospel emphasizes imagery of light and darkness; see, for example,
           John 1:1–9, 12:46, and 13:35–36.

11   *thin.* MS: *hin.* Brown's emendation.

18   The story of Simeon's blessing and prophecy at the purification of the infant Jesus
           is recorded in Luke 2:22–35. He represents the old heritage waiting patiently for this
           ecstatic and excruciating moment.

20   After Jesus dies on the cross, a soldier pierces his side with a spear (John 19:34).

27   *the.* Added above line.

           wel crossed out after *herte.*

31   *yielde.* MS: *þielde.* Brown emends the *þ* to *ʒ.*

35–36   *That thu . . . withelde thar biforn.* Perhaps an allusion to Mary and Joseph's flight
           into Egypt with the infant Jesus; see Matthew 2:13–23.

40   MS: *nu the þiolden,* with *s* added above the line. Brown emends to *the's ʒiolden,*
           "you have yielded."

40–42   *Nu thes thiolden . . . quite and fre.* Now she knows the pain other women experience
           in labor. On the traditional belief that Mary suffered no pain in giving birth to Jesus,
           see note to §15, line 3.

43–48   These lines recall imagery of lines 10–11: darkness is restored to light, literally and
           figuratively, as morning follows night and the sun/son (line 47) rises on Easter
           morning. For the accounts of Jesus' resurrection, see Matthew 28, Mark 16, Luke 24,
           and John 20.

46   *wende.* MS: *wen.* Brown emends to *wende;* Jacoby emends to *wenten.*

Notes

50   See 1 Peter 3:18–20.

         aros. MS: *tharos.* Brown's emendation.

51   *he.* MS: *the.* As in §3, "Gabriel, fram evene kingh," I follow Brown's reading of *h*
         for initial *Þ* in the Arundel MS. So also at lines 52 and 55.

         Thur the hole ston he glod. The line suggests a double sense: the miracle of Jesus'
         passing through a solid (whole) tombstone, but also perhaps a parturition metaphor
         as Jesus passes through the passageway (hole) of the tomb and death into life.

63   *yvel.* The sense seems to be "affliction" as well as "sin." The comment is on the
         human condition under sin and death which the Resurrection and Mary's experience
         have so eloquently addressed.

65   Word erased at beginning of line.

66   *wit his.* MS: *wit þis.*

<h2 style="text-align:center">§33</h2>

Stond wel, Moder, under rode. Index no. 3211. MS: BL Royal 12.E.1, fols. 193a–94b, with
music (early fourteenth century, East Midlands). Other MSS: BL Harley 2253, fol. 79a (early
fourteenth century); Trinity Dublin 301, fol. 194 (early fourteenth century, North/Midlands).
The first 54 lines also appear in Bodl. 1687 (Digby 86), fol. 127a–b (c. 1275, West Midlands).
Lines 1–28 appear, with the Latin sequence set to music, in St. John's College Cambridge 111,
fol. 106b (thirteenth century, Southeast); and the first stanza appears as a sermon quotation in
BL Royal 8.F.2, fol. 180a (c. 1300). Editions of Royal 12.E.1: B13, no. 49b; Sisam, *Oxford*,
no. 56 (incomplete). Editions of Harley: Wright, *Specimens*, pp. 80–83; Böddekker, pp.
205–08; Wülcker, 1:46–48; Bruce Dickins and R. M. Wilson, *Early Middle English Texts*
(Cambridge: Bowes and Bowes, 1951), pp. 129–30; Brook, no. 20; Davies, no. 24; LH, no.
226; DH, no. 11. Editions of Digby: B13, no. 49a; Varnhagen, "Eine Marienklage," *Anglia* 2
(1879), 253–54; Furnivall, EETS o.s. 117, pp. 763–65; Kaiser, p. 260, Stevick, no. 19.
Editions of St. John's Cambridge: B13, pp. 203–04. Edition of Royal 8: B13, p. 204.

Like §32, this poem is based on the *Stabat juxta Christi crucem* sequence which appears in the
York Missal, c. 1390. Its music is adapted from the Latin hymn and uses the same meter, but
the Latin source is not a dialogue. Crowne writes that this poem "was called by Wright 'Stabat

Mater,' and was said by Böddekker to be unmistakably related to that poem. In reality, there is nothing in common between the Latin classic and this English *Tenson* or *Debate*, except the subject, the introductory words, and the metrical form" (p. 311); furthermore, "the 'Stabat Mater,' so popular throughout the Middle Ages, does not seem to have made a great impression in England. It influenced no extant Middle English poem, and, though found in late MSS., was not used in the office of the English Church." (Julian, p. 1082, supports this.)

The Royal MS represents a separate tradition from the other MSS. The Royal poet addresses Mary in an intimate tone absent in the other versions (the Harley version addresses Mary directly only once) and continues to address Mary where the other texts shift the focus to Christ (see notes below). In these stanzas, Royal translates its Latin source more closely than do the other MSS.

The earliest extant version of the poem is Digby (c. 1275). This version contains several unique variants, noted below, and ends at line 54. The Cambridge MS agrees with Royal on most variants, and probably shares a common source. Harley changes the order of stanzas. On the MSS, sources, variants, and music, see DH, pp. 153–60.

Wenzel discusses the various contexts in which this poem occurs and speculates on its origins (*Preachers*, pp. 48–53). For a theological analysis of the dialogue, see Weber, pp. 125–45. Weber discusses the poem as a counterpart to the dialogue in §25, "Als I lay upon a nith."

2   *child.* Harley: *sone.*

3   *Blythe, Moder.* Digby: *Moder, blithe.*

         mittu. Cambridge: *mai thu.*

4   *quu may.* Harley: *hou should y.* Digby: *hou may ich.*

5   *Hi se thin honden.* Digby: *and thine honde.*

7   *Moder, do wey.* Cambridge: *Do wai moder.*

8   *Hi thole this ded for mannes thinge.* Digby: *Ich tholie deth for monnes kuinde.* Harley: *y thole deth for monkynde.* Cambridge: *I thole this ded for mankende.* Only Royal gives a rhyming line.

9   *For owen gilte tholi non.* Digby: *Vor mine guiltes ne tholie non.* Harley: *For my gult thole y non.*

13   *reu upon thi bern.* Digby: *do wei thine teres.* Harley: *thou rewe al of thi bern.* Cambridge: *rewen of thi barne.*

14   *wasse.* Digby: *wip*; Cambridge: *vipe.*

17   *blodi flodes hernen.* Digby: *blodi woundes herne.* Harley: *blody stremes erne.* Cambridge: *blod on flod erne.*

18   *thin herte to min fet.* Digby: *thin herte to thi fot.*

22   *swngen.* Cambridge: *suingen;* Harley: *byswngen*; Digby: *iswonge.*

23   *Thi brest, thin hond, thi fot thur-stungen.* Digby: *Thine honde, thine fet, thi bodi istounge.* Harley: *Fet ant honden thourhout stongen.* Cambridge: *brest and hend ond fet thurtet sting.*

24   *selli.* Harley, Digby: *wonder.*

25   *if y dar.* Harley: *now y shal.* Cambridge: *wel I may.*

26   *Yif y ne deye.* Cambridge: *bot i deie.*

26–27   Compare John 16:7, in which Jesus explains to his disciples, "But I speak the truth to you; it is expedient for you that I depart. For if I do not go, the Advocate will not come to you; but if I go, I will send him to you."

27   *thole this ded.* Harley omits *this*. Cambridge: *tholie det.*

28   *thu best me so minde.* Digby: *thou me bihest so milde.* Harley: *thou art so meke ant mynde.*

29   *With me nout; it is mi kinde.* Digby: *Icomen hit is of monnes kuinde.* Harley: *Ne wyt me naht; hit is my kynde.*

30   *for thee.* Digby: *sike and.* Harley: *for this.*

31–36   Harley inserts this stanza after line 12 in the present text.

34   *to rede.* Digby: *the stounde.*

35   *pined.* Harley: *pyneth*; Digby: *pinen.*

        to dede. Digby: *to the grounde.*

37   *Moder, mitarst thi mith leren.* Digby: *Swete moder, nou thou fondest.* Harley: *moder nou thou might wel leren.*

38   *Wat pine tholen that childre beren.* Digby: *Of mi pine ther thou stondest.* Harley: *Whet sorewe haveth that children beren.*

39   *Wat sorwe haven that child forgon.* Digby: *Withhoute mi pine nere no mon.* Harley: *Whet sorewe hit is with childe gon.*

40   *Sune.* Harley gives *Sorewe*, which breaks the pattern of "Mother"/ "Son" addresses.

41   *the.* Omitted in Harley.

43   *reu of moder kare.* Digby: *of moder thus I fare.*

44   *Nu thu wost of moder fare.* Digby: *Nou thou wost wimmanes kare.* Harley: *For nou thou wost of moder fare.*

44–45   See note to §32, lines 40–42.

45   *Thou thu be clene mayden man.* Digby: *Thou art clene mayden on.*

50   *y fare.* Digby: *I go.* Harley: *y shal.*

51   *The thridde day y rise upon.* Digby: *I tholie this for thine sake.*

52   *y wyle withe funden.* Digby: *Iwis I wille founde.*

53   *Y deye ywis of thine wnden.* Digby: *I deye almost, I falle to grounde.* Harley gives *for* in place of Royal's *of.*

54   The Digby MS ends with this line.

        reuful. Digby: *serwful*; Harley: *soreweful.*

55 *thi*. Harley: *hire*. In the Royal MS, the speaker addresses Mary directly and personally (see also note to line 58).

56 *The*. Harley: *Hire*.

57 *Wen*. Omitted in Harley.

58 *Moder*. Harley: *Levedy*. Only in this line does the Harley speaker address Mary directly, and less intimately than in the Royal version.

59 *Bisech ure God, ure sinnes lesse*. Harley: *Bysech thi sone of sunnes lisse*.

61 *quen of hevene*. Harley: *ful of blysse*.

62 *Bring us ut of helle levene*. Harley: *Let us never hevene misse*.

63 *dere*. Harley: *suete*.

64–66 *Moder . . . Led us into hevene lith*. While the speaker in Royal continues to address Mary, Harley reads *Louerd, for that ilke blod / That thou sheddest on the rod, / Thou bryng us into hevene lyth*. Trinity follows Harley.

§34

Suete sone, reu on me. *Index* no. 3245. MS: National Library of Scotland Advocates 18.7.21, fol. 120a (Grimestone's commonplace book, 1372). Editions: B14, no. 64; LH, no. 225. Commentary: Weber, pp. 117–21.

The MS inscription above the poem reads: "*Beda. Audi cum Maria quae dixit.*" Brown notes a general similarity between this poem and a meditation on Christ's Passion sometimes attributed to Bede (B14, p. 266; sermon in PL 94, col. 568).

3 *honges*. MS: *honge*; Brown's emendation.

7 *tholen*. The word suggests both "endure" and "outlive."

10 *deth*. MS: *detȝ*.

§35

The angell sayde to thee that the fruyt off thi body sulde be blyssyde. Index no 427.5: *At his burth thow hurdist angell syng.* MS: Worcester Cathedral F.10, fol. 25a (early fifteenth century). Also in Balliol College Oxford 149 (262.D.3), fol. 12b (late fourteenth century). Both are sermon collections. In each MS, this poem and the next appear in a Latin sermon for Good Friday. Editions of Worcester: John Kestell Floyer, ed., rev. Sidney G. Hamilton, *Catalogue of Manuscripts Preserved in the Chapter Library of Worcester Cathedral* (Oxford: James Parker and Co., 1906), pp. 5–7; William H. Hulme, review of Floyer and Hamilton, *JEGP* 8 (1909), 292; Owst, p. 541. Balliol: Coxe, p. 46, lines 3–6.

Floyer speculates that this English fragment might be part of a Passion play. It is introduced in the Worcester MS by the following: "A, blyssedful mayden and modyr! This is a wonderful change: the angell behette the that Kryst walde be thi sonne and dwel wyt the and now he takys the a new son and gosse fro the."

1   *The angell sayde to thee . . . .* In Balliol, a line precedes this one: *O blesful mayden and moder thys his a wondirful thaunge / The angel bihete the . . . .*

6   *despyte.* Balliol: *spit.*

7   *thow wantyd womanes wo.* I.e., did not suffer the pains of childbirth (see note to §15, line 3).

8   *wel.* Omitted in Balliol.

11   *to.* Balliol: *at.* So also at line 12.

12   *bitter gall.* See Matthew 27:32.

13   *thou founde hym in the mydyl off the doctors in the temple.* When Jesus was twelve years old, his parents found him conversing with the teachers in the temple. See Luke 2:42–52.

§36

A Son! tak hede to me. Index no. 14. MS: Worcester Cathedral F.10, fol. 25a. Also in Balliol College Oxford 149 (262.D.3), fols. 12b–13a. Editions of Worcester: Floyer and Hamilton (see notes to §35 above), p. 6; William H. Hulme, review of Floyer and Hamilton, *JEGP* 8 (1909), 292; Owst, p. 542; B14, no. 128; Stevick, no. 45.

Brown (B14, p. 285) notes that while the lines are ascribed to Chrysostom, they are not found in Chrysostom's works, but instead appear to be from the *Liber de Passione Christi et Doloribus et Planctibus Matris Eius*, "doubtfully" attributed to St. Bernard, the text of which is found in PL 182, cols. 1134–42. A Middle English metrical translation of that work occurs in the *Cursor Mundi*, Part 4, ed. Richard Morris, EETS o.s. 66 (London: Oxford University Press, 1876): see the extensive dialogue between Jesus and Mary in the assumption section, lines 20217–20682. G. Kribel prints both English and Latin texts in "Studien zu Richard Rolle de Hampole," *Englische Studien* 8 (1885), 84–114. The *Liber de Passione Christi* also appears to be the source for §41.

2   *set me uppe wyt thee on i crosse.* Balliol: *set me with the opon thi crosse.*

3   *thus hense go.* Balliol: *hennys thus go.*

4   *wo.* Balliol: *endeles wo.*

6   *ever was god.* Balliol: *were ever godliche.*

10   *hyt.* Balliol: *this.*

         the. Balliol: *thus.*

11   *in thoghte.* Balliol: *in thi thoughe.*

14   *Jone, thi kosyne, sall be thi sone.* See §37, note to lines 1–2.

§37

Womman, Jon I take to thee. Index no. 162: *Allas wo sal myn herte slaken.* MS: National Library of Scotland Advocates 18.7.21, fol. 121b (Grimestone's commonplace book, 1372). Edition: R. H. Robbins, "The Earliest Carols and the Franciscans," *Modern Language Notes* 53 (1938), 244.

1–2   John 19:25–27: "Now there were standing by the cross of Jesus his mother and his mother's sister, Mary of Cleophas, and Mary Magdalene. When Jesus, therefore, saw his mother and the disciple standing by, whom he loved, he said to his mother, 'Woman, behold, thy son.' Then he said to the disciple, 'Behold, thy mother.' And from that hour the disciple took her into his home."

5   *forwaken*. Robbins' reading of MS. Perhaps a scribal error for *forsaken*? Mary has kept vigil fastidiously to the point of exhaustion; thus, she is *for*-waken. Or perhaps the sense is simply that she is exhausted by sleeplessness.

<h2 style="text-align:center">§38</h2>

Nou goth sonne under wod. Possibly by St. Edmund of Abingdon. *Index* no. 2320. MS: Bodl. 3462 (Arch. Selden *supra* 74), fol. 55b, col. 2 (late thirteenth century). This poem appears in St. Edmund's *Speculum ecclesie* (composed in the early thirteenth century), which survives in more than forty French, English, and Latin MSS. For a more complete listing of MSS and editions, consult the *Index* and *Supplement*. Editions of this French MS: B13, no. 1; Sisam, *Oxford*, no. 269; Bennett and Smithers, second ed. (1968), p. 129; Davies, no. 6; Stevick, no. 4; LH, no. 190; Wilhelm, no. 269. Editions of Bodl. 1621 (Digby 20), fol 155a: B13, p. 166; J. E. Wells, *First Supplement to A Manual of the Writings in Middle English, 1050–1400* (New Haven: Connecticut Academy of Arts and Sciences, 1923), p. 988. Editions of Cambridge University Ii. 6.40: Henry Wolcott Robbins, "An English Version of St. Edmund's *Speculum*, Ascribed to Richard Rolle," *PMLA* 40 (1925), 250. Edition of BL Royal 7.A.1: Helen P. Forshaw, ed. *Edmund of Abingdon: Speculum Religiosorum and Speculum Ecclesie* (London: Oxford University Press, 1973), p. 93.

Criticism: John L. Cutler, "Nou Goth Sonne Vnder Wod," *Explicator* 4 (1945), item 7; George Kane, *Middle English Literature* (London: Methuen, 1951), p. 140; C. G. Thayer, *Explicator* 11 (1953), item 25; Manning, pp. 80–84 (on spatial and temporal movement in the poem); W. B. Lockwood. "A Note on the Middle English 'Sunset on Calvary,'" *Zeitschrift fur Anglistik und Amerikanistik* 9 (1961), 410–12; Stevick, "The Criticism of Middle English Lyrics," *Modern Philology* 64 (1966), 115; Dronke, pp. 64–65; Peck, pp. 461–68.

In the MS, the poem follows an account of Jesus' giving Mary to John. In several MSS, the poem is preceded by a reference to Canticles 1:5 (RSV Song of Solomon 1:6): "Do not consider me that I am brown, because the sun hath altered my colour." In Digby (a French MS), the poem is introduced by two biblical passages (given here in the Douay translation): Ruth 1:20, "But she said to them: Call me not Noemi (that is, beautiful), but call me Mara (that is, bitter), for the Almighty hath quite filled me with bitterness," and Canticles 1:15, "Behold thou art fair, my beloved, and comely."

1   *sonne*. As Reiss (pp. 15–17) observes, the pun on son/sun suggests a solar eclipse.

2   *rode*. Peck observes a pun, where the meaning of *rode* shifts from "countenance" to "cross" as the sun is eclipsed at the Crucifixion and the sense shifts from love conventions in praise of a woman to the speaker's anguish for the mother and son at the Crucifixion (p. 467).

§39

Sodenly afraide, half waking, half slepyng. Index no. 4189: *With favoure in hir face ferr passyng my reason.* MS: Manchester Rylands Library 18932 (Latin 395), fol. 120a–b (late fifteenth century). Also in Trinity College Cambridge 1450 (O.9.38), fols. 63b–64a (late fifteenth century). Editions of Rylands MS: Joseph Haslewood, *Censura Literaria* 10 (1809),186–87; B15, no. 9; Sisam, *Oxford,* no. 227; *EEC,* no. 161; Stevick, no. 86; Reiss, pp. 145–46 (commentary, pp. 146–50). Editions of Trinity: F. J. Furnivall, *Hymns to the Virgin and Christ,* pp. 126–27; CS, no. 79; Segar, pp. 61–62.

A much longer poem with the same refrain, "Who can not wepe com lerne att me," which survives in the fifteenth-century MS Harl. 2274, fols. 35a–46b, tells the story of Mary's life from birth to Assumption. It is edited by Robert Max Garrett in "De Arte Lacrimandi," *Anglia* 32 (1909), 270–94. The line also recalls the *Liber de Passione Christi et Doloribus et Planctibus Matris Eius* (see note to §36), in which Bernard appeals to Mary to teach him to relate her feelings so he may share them: "Ladi, the teres, that thou ther gef, / Graunte me summe! he seide tho" (G. Kribel, "Studien zu Richard Rolle de Hampole," *Englische Studien* 8 [1885], 91, lines 135–36).

1–2 Sisam's punctuation and gloss suggest that the *speaker* is "Sodenly afraide . . . and gretly dismayde" to discover the weeping woman. Reiss acknowledges that the participles may refer to Mary or to the speaker and, implicitly, to the reader (Reiss, p. 146).

11   *at*. Trinity: *of.*

13   *with wordys shortly*. Trinity: *schortly with wordys.*

14   *Lo*. Omitted in Trinity.

     thee. Greene reads *the.*

16 Trinity: *Jesus so my sone ys bobbed.*

18 "To weep," notes Reiss, "is to have contrition, and contrition is the first step toward salvation. To weep is also to go beyond words, to let action be acknowledgment, and to go beyond *reason*" (p. 147).

19 *the.* Trinity: *thys.*

    she seid to me. Trinity: *seyng to the.*

20 *may lerne at thee.* Trinity: *com lern at me.*

22 *Jewlye.* Trinity: *fuly* ("foully").

23 *me.* Omitted in Trinity.

24 *lygh.* Omitted in Trinity.

25 *Ever.* Greene reads *Evu* in MS, emends and expands to *Ever.* Brown reads *ever* in MS and emends to *Ay.*

26 *soon.* MS: *soone.*

28 *thee.* Trinity: *these.*

30 *said.* Trinity: *and seyd.*

32 *In sownyng.* Trinity: *And swonyng.*

35 *So.* Trinity: *how.*

37 *was.* Trinity: *ys.*

38 *word.* Trinity: *wordys.*

§40

Thou synfull man of resoun that walkest here up and downe. *Index* no. 3692. MS: Bodl. 6777 (Ashmole 189), fol. 109a (fifteenth century). Edition: B15, no. 8.

This poem combines the *Planctus Mariae* tradition with that of Christ's admonitions from the cross. The opening lines seem at first to be spoken by Jesus (compare *Index* no. 497, "Beholde me, I pray the," and *Index* no. 2150, "Men rent me on rode," both printed by Gray in *Selection*, nos. 27 and 28). The confusion emphasizes Mary's empathy for her son's suffering; we are to "learn to weep" with her as she has learned to weep with her son. Mary appeals first to the least selfish instincts of the listener, to pity for a stranger. She then moves progressively closer to the sinner's own heart, from appealing to feelings for a mother and child relationship (with which, perhaps, the listener can sympathize), then to Christ, who suffers for the sake of the listener, and finally to the most selfish instinct, to the sinful listener's own well-being. But the poem is not simply a call for pity. From inward examination, the listener is directed to move outward again, finding comfort and support in Christ and Mary. Thus the poem offers a model for meditation on the Passion, for understanding both the personal and the universal significance of the events.

4   *chased.* The verb employs connotations of hunting as well as dismissal and expulsion, all of which are metaphors laden with appropriate typology contingent on Mary's dismal situation.

5   *swerd.* See note to §25, line 119.

9   The visual image projected here, that of the Pietà, focuses dramatic attention on the darkest moment of Mary's agony as she, guided by faith and love alone, exemplifies the power of blind faith as she would have others "lerne to wepe wyth me" (lines 7 and 14).

21   *come dwell wyth me.* The refrain (lines 7 and 14) changes from an invitation to "lerne" to an invitation to "dwell," thus marking the progress of the plot as the exemplum addresses humankind's errant yearning for stability.

§41

Why have ye no reuthe on my child? Index no. 4159. MS: National Library of Scotland Advocates 18.7.21, fol. 24a (Grimestone's commonplace book, 1372). Editions: B14, no. 60; Davies, no. 44; Gray, *Selection,* no. 22, LH, no. 223. Commentary: Weber, pp. 110–17.

The MS attributes these verse to "B"; Brown notes that the verses are based on St. Bernard's *Liber de Passione Christi et Doloridus et Planctibus Matris Eius*. See note to §36.

2   *murning.* MS: *murnig.*

§42

Of alle women that ever were borne. Index no. 2619. MS: Cambridge University Ff.5.48, fols. 73a–74b (fifteenth century). Also in Cambridge University Ff.2.38, fol. 55b and Manchester Chetham Library 8009, fol. 119b. Edition based on Chetham MS: B15, no. 7; Wright and Halliwell, 2:213–15. Editions of Ff.2.38: Wright, *The Chester Plays* (London: Shakespeare Society, 1847), 2:207–09; Davies, no. 112. Edition of Chetham: Max Förster, "Kleinere Mittelenglische Texte," *Anglia* 42 (1918), 167–72.

Compare *Index* no. 1447, which prefaces a similar monologue with a *chanson d'aventure* setting in which the poet observes the vision while kneeling in church (printed in Helen Sandison, *The "Chanson d'aventure" in Middle English* [Bryn Mawr: Bryn Mawr College, 1913], pp. 104–09; and in Rose Cords, "Fünf me. Gedichte aus den Hss. Rawlinson Poetry 36 und Rawlinson C. 86," *Archiv* 135 [1916], 300–02).

4   *kne.* Chetham, Cambridge Ff.2.38: *skyrte.*

10   *dose.* Chetham: *settist.*Cambridge Ff.2.38: *castyst.*

11   *ble.* "Appearance" is perhaps too neutral a gloss; "skin color," "youthful glow," "cheerful vitality" would perhaps come closer to the effect.

18   *dose.* Chetham: *doth.* Cambridge Ff.2.38: *dere.*

19   *with gret solas.* Chetham, Cambridge Ff.2.38: *gret ioy thou mas.*

28   *gret gap is.* Chetham: *many gappis.*

34   *stroke.* The mother uses "stroke" in the sense of caress or playful cuff, but there is a pun on the more violent strokes (blows, slashes) Mary's son has received on the cross.

36   *layke.* Cambridge Ff.2.38: *laghe.*

38   *speyre.* Chetham, Cambridge Ff.2.38: *sere.*

43   *Ye fele ther fete, so fete are thay.* MS: *He fele therfor fittys or day.* Emended by Brown from Chetham and Cambridge Ff.2.38.

45   *any hande.* Chetham, Cambridge Ff.2.38: *my hand.*

49   *town.* MS: *towm.* Brown's emendation.

63   *be holdyne.* Chetham: *were holdyn.* Cambridge Ff.2.38: *were wele holden.*

81–82   *I may no more / For drede of deth reherse his payne.* Here, as in Bernard's dialogue, Mary's suffering is so intense that she fears she may die if she continues to tell about it.

§43

O litel whyle lesteneth to me. Index no. 2481. MS: BL Royal 18.A.10, fol. 126b (early fifteenth century). A longer text, lacking opening stanzas, *Index* no. 2718, occurs in Bodl. 3938 (Eng. Poet a.1, the Vernon MS), fol. 315b, and in BL Addit. 22283 (Simeon), fol. 124b. Edition of Royal: Morris, *Legends of the Holy Rood, Symbols of the Passion and Cross-Poems*, EETS o.s. 46 (London: N. Trübner, 1871), pp. 197–209. Editions of Vernon: Morris, EETS o.s. 46, pp. 131–49; F. J. Furnivall, EETS o.s. 117, pp. 612–26; Susanna Greer Fein, ed., *Moral Love Songs and Laments* (Kalamazoo: Medieval Institute Publications, 1998), pp. 87–160.

Indented lines indicate a change of speaker.

1–13   Vernon omits this stanza. *Apocrifum* (line 12) is "a writing or statement of doubtful authorship or authenticity" (OED), though the root of the term simply designates a "hidden meaning." The Royal scribe is perhaps aware of Wycliffite attitudes toward fiction; he is careful to label the story spurious in order not to mislead his audience, yet he believes the use of fiction in the service of truth and teaching is justified. Compare lines 343–55, also omitted from Vernon.

10   *expouned.* To "expound" is to set forth, present, interpret, translate, paraphrase, render, comment upon, or gloss.

11   *bryght.* The luminosity of the example connotes moral resonance. See MED adj.4.

14   In margin: *Maria.*

20–21   Vernon reverses these lines.

24   *fle.* Probably a form of *flen,* "to flay" (MED v.2). Vernon reads *fleo,* which could either be a form of *flen* or of *flouen,* "to flow."

26   *Tre.* Vernon: *Cros.*

32   *gode.* Vernon: *fayre.*

34   *unfyled.* MS: *unfyle.* Morris emends for rhyme and sense.

35–38   *Child . . . werkis wylde.* Mary briefly addresses her son as he hangs on the cross.

37–38   *As grete thevys that were gramed, / That. . . .* Vernon: *Grete Iewes* [Jews] *thus were gramed / And. . . .*

40–43   Vernon: *In mournyng I may melte / Mi fruit that is so holi halwed / In a feeld is fouled and falwed /With grete Jewes he is galwed / And dyeth for Monnes gelte.*

48   *deep.* Vernon: *deth,* which may be a preferable reading.

50   *breyde.* The MED suggests the following meanings: attack, blow, affliction, torment, deceptive act, or insult (see *breid,* n.1 and n.2). In any case, the sense is that the Cross acts intentionally to harm Jesus.

51   *stont in stroke and stryfe.* Vernon: *stont nou in a strong stryf.*

53–56   Here Vernon uses the lines found at lines 40–43 of Royal.

55   *briddes.* The word *brid* can refer to a young bird, a baby, or a child (MED *brid*, 3.a),
       or it can be used as a term of endearment (*brid*, 3.b). The *brid* metaphor here and in
       lines 66, 85, 110, and 120 may be glossed as "bird," suggesting painfully the
       unnatural nesting place for this one of God's creatures (see note to lines 100–05); but
       it also suggests "bride" in the sense of spouse or virginal loved one, to whom Mary
       is so devoted, in which case the blood is virtually a sign of rape. See OED *bride*,
       sb.2.

56   *Droppynge as dewe on ryssche.* Perhaps an allusion to Proverbs 19:12, which
       compares the cheerfulness of a king to dew upon the grass; thus a suggestion that
       Christ's suffering is a blessing. But Mary does not realize this yet. Dew is often a
       biblical symbol of blessing.

57   *The jugement have thei joyned.* Vernon: *Thorw Jugement thou art enjoynet.*

61   *twyned.* Vernon: *teynet.*

62   *fenne.* Thieves lurk in fens, where hiding is easy. The metaphor does not suit well the
       image of Golgotha as a hill, but it works superbly with the notion that truth is hidden
       amidst the muck.

63   *feet.* Vernon: *limes.*

66   *brid.* Vernon: *fruit.*

67   *this tree.* Vernon: *a theoves tre.*

69   *hert now hath a wounde.* Vernon: *holi herte hath wounde.*

81   *The goode hangeth among the wikke.* This might be read as a gloss on *Apocrifum*
       (lines 12 and 347), that fictive statement in which the message (the good, the
       connotation) is obscured by the fictive (wicked, the literal, with its criminal
       designations) — a sense Mary, in her grief, seems not yet to have allowed.

83   *Cros.* Vernon: *Tre.*

85   *bridde.* Vernon: *fruit.*

86   *fruyt.* Vernon: *flour.*

86   *falle.* MS: *fall.*

88   *eysell and galle.* Though this alludes to the soldiers who offered the thirsting Jesus vinegar (Luke 23:36) or gall (Matthew 27:42), Mary seems more concerned with the figurative bitterness of Jesus' suffering.

89   *white rose.* A symbol of purity, often used to describe Mary herself as well as Jesus.

90   *floryssched.* Vernon: *fostred* (fostered).

96   *hys leir.* Vernon: *the eyr.*

96–99   Mary juxtaposes her confining of the infant Jesus by binding him in the cradle with swaddling clothes so that his hands be not hurt with the Cross' binding him to its frame. There may be a pun on *wynde* in line 99, implying a kind of aery winding sheet binding his nakedness which harms rather than protects his hands in a wild, irresponsible way.

100–05 *Fowles formen her nest . . . My sones hed hath reste none.* Compare Jesus' words in Matthew 8:20: "The foxes have holes and the birds of the air nests: but the son of man hath nowhere to lay his head."

101   *Foxes.* Vernon: *Wolves.*

103   *holdeth.* Vernon: *leoneth.*

        thornes. See John 19:2.

105   *My sones.* Vernon: *Godes.*

107   *the panne.* Vernon: *his flesch.*

108   *Thys.* Vernon: *His.*

112   *Hys faire feet.* Vernon: *Mi fruites feet.*

113   *putte.* Vernon: *pulte* (thrust out).

114   *Hys feet to kys.* Vernon gives a full line: *To cusse his feet, Soth thing hit is.*

122   In margin: *sta crux.*

124   *palme.* The palm leaf is a symbol of victory, glory, or reward.

125   *of.* Vernon: *thorw.*

126   *Thy trye fruyt I to-tere.* Vernon: *Thi feire fruit on me ginneth tere.*

128   *as thou mayst here.* Vernon: *that lay in lure.*

132   *waltereth.* Vernon: *swelte.*

137   *fruit.* Vernon: *son.*

138   *tyndes towe.* Vernon: *teone inouh.*

139   *body . . . ny the tharmes.* Vernon: *flesch . . . with dethes tharmes.*

140   *swemely swow. Swemely* is a form of *swimble,* meaning "a swaying motion"; OED cites Harley *CT,* The Knight's Tale, lines 1126–27: "Then ran a swymbul and a swough, / As though a storm shodde bresten every bough."

141   *armes.* Vernon: *swarmes.*

143   *goode.* Vernon: *leove.*

144–47 *Isayas spak . . . .* See Isaias 25:8.

147   Vernon inserts a stanza not found in Royal:

>   The stipre that is under the vyne set   support
>   May not bringe forth the grape;
>   Theih the fruit on me beo knet,
>   His scharpe schour have I not schape:
>   Til grapes to the presse beo set
>   Ther renneth no red wyn in rape;
>   Nevere presse pressed bet,
>   I presse wyn for kniht and knape   servant
>   Upon a blodi brinke
>   I presse a grape, with strok and stryf,

The rede wyn renneth ryf:
In Samaritane God gaf a wyf
That leof licour to drynke.   *precious*

148   *dothe thee alegge.* Vernon: *doth the to alegge.*

151   *beest of horde.* Vernon: *of godes hord.*

153   *The bak.* Vernon: *His bodi.*

155   *one.* Vernon: *of.*

161   *hys figour.* Vernon: *in his figour.*

161–62   *And Moyses fourmed . . . noon other beest.* See Exodus 12 on the rites of Passover,
          which specify that an unblemished lamb be eaten, with no bone broken.

163   *He sacred so oure savyour.* Vernon: *Schulde be sacred ur saveour.*

165   *in honour.* Vernon: *chargeour.*

167   *creatour.* Vernon: *saveour.*

168   *Hys flessche fedeth.* Vernon: *He fedeth bothe.*

172   *Whan flessche and veynes.* Vernon: *Til feet and hondes.*

174   *this resoun rad.* Vernon: *in rule hath rad.*

175   The line in Vernon reads *We schulde ete ur lomb in sour vergeous.*

176   *saws.* Vernon: *vergeous.*

178   *fende.* Vernon: *devel.*

184   *take.* Vernon: *cake.*

185   *devyll.* Vernon: *feond.*

187   *is schewed with a scryne.* Vernon: *scheweth be a shrine.*

187–99 *Whan pardoun is schewed with a scryne . . . . Your boke was bounde in blode.*
        Christ's body is compared to a sign declaring pardon, his body the board, his blood
        the ink with which the decree is written. Compare §60, line 23 and note.

189   *blyne.* Vernon: *be lyne.*

190   *me.* Vernon: *men.*

191   *My.* Vernon: *Ur.*

195   *rede in hys rode.* Vernon: *red upon the rood.* Although the intended meaning for
        rode here is probably "countenance" (MED *rode,* n.1), there are several possible
        puns, both on *rede* (read, counseled) and *rode,* as "redness," or "cross" (as the
        Vernon reading suggests), or "reckoning," or "account" (MED *rode,* n.4); or, given
        Jesus' mount at the Crucifixion (n.5), perhaps even on *rode* as "journey" (n.3).

196   *Youre.* Vernon: *Ur.*

        boke. Vernon: *brede.*

199   Vernon adds two stanzas (16 and 17 in Morris, p. 138, and Fein, pp. 112–13) after
        this line; their content is repeated elsewhere in the poem.

202   *good scheperde.* John 10:11, 14.

207   *draf.* Chaff, waste; both a thrashing/judgment metaphor as well as a term of rhetoric,
        where the good reader separates the hidden sense from the literal to arrive at the
        nourishing fruit.

210   *bande.* MS: *hande.*

215–18 *Thus seyde Poule . . . Thei bete a lambe withoute lothe.* Possibly a reference to
        1 Corinthians 5:7, which simply says, "for Christ, our passover, has been sacrificed."
        Christ is thus compared to the lamb sacrificed at the Passover feast.

216   *fikell Jewes, withoute othe.* Vernon: *feolle Jewes, with false othe.*

222   *mylk.* Vernon: *eny.*

225   *brisseden.* Vernon: *wolden ha broken.*

        Vernon inserts a stanza here (19 in Morris and in Fein); again, the sense is redundant.

232   *The Cros seyde.* Vernon: *Ladi.*

234   *Sithe.* Vernon: *Til.*

235   *yelde hys goost with voys.* Matthew 27:50; Mark 19:30.

236   *Men chose me a relyk choys.* Vernon: *I was chose a relik chois.*

249–51 Compare Jesus' final words according to John 19:30: "It is consummated"; note also his prayer during the Last Supper: "I have glorified thee on earth; I have accomplished the work that thou hast given me to do" (John 17:4).

252   The Vernon MS inserts a somewhat redundant stanza here, followed by the lines found at lines 200–12 in Royal. Vernon then inserts nine stanzas in which Mary describes three Jews who were sorrowful after witnessing Jesus' Crucifixion; and if the Jews were sorrowful, she says, then it behove Mary to grieve with the sorrow of both mother and father. Mary then describes the cosmic disorder that followed Jesus' death: planets going out of orbit and birds falling out of their flight.

255   *faunt.* MS: *faint.*

256   *schelde of scrifte.* I.e., no man had the protection of confession. Old Testament law required confession and restitution; Leviticus 5:5 specifies the sacrifice of a lamb, commonly interpreted as an anticipation of Christ's sacrifice, the ultimate "shield."

257   *lyoun raumpaunt.* The lion is sometimes identified with the devil through Psalm 90:13 (RSV 91:13): "Thou shalt walk upon the asp and the basilisk: and thou shalt trample under foot the lion and the dragon." The passage is interpreted as referring to Christ defeating Satan (variously represented by each of the creatures named).

272   *Hys.* MS: *Hy.*

278   *Nichodemus.* See John 3:3 ff.

299   *God.* Vernon: *Jhesu.*

311   *Truyt and treget.* Compare line 41.

313   *hys.* MS: *hy.*

        flessch trewe. Vernon: *fleschly trene.* The Vernon scribe describes Mary as a tree branch, alluding to the tree of Jesse (see note to §8, line 17) and, of course, drawing a parallel between Mary and the Cross.

314   *lele and newe.* Vernon: *leothi and lene.*

315–16 *It is right the Rode to Eve helpe schewe, / Man, woman, and chylde.* Because Eve sinned by means of the tree that bore forbidden fruit, it is fitting that a tree should play some part in Eve's redemption. See note to §9, line 8. In Vernon, this sense is lost: *Hit is riht the Roode helpe to arene / Wrecches that wratthe thi chylde.*

321–24 These lines are missing in the MS; they have been supplied from the Vernon MS (pp. 147–48 in Morris).

331   *sorwe to seighe.* Vernon: *wo to wite.*

332   *As he had see in scharp schour.* Vernon: *He saih himself that harde stour.*

333   *Cristes.* Vernon: *Godes.*

        rune. Slandered, as in oaths sworn by "Goddes armes." See Chaucer's The Pardoner's Tale with its admonition against such swearing:

> Hir othes been so grete and so dampnable
> That it is grisly for to heere hem swere.
> Oure blissed Lordes body they totere —
> Hem thoughte that Jewes rent hym noght ynough. (lines 472–75)

But "sweryng is a thyng abhominable" (line 631), the Pardoner declares and warns that if you swear "By Goddes armes, if thou falsly pleye, / This daggere shal thurgh-out thyn herte go" (lines 654–55).

336   *This tale florrissched with a faire flour.* "Flourish" suggests rhetorical embellishment as well as a pun on "flourishing" and "flowering."

343–55   Not found in Vernon.

348   *In swich a lay dar thee naght dere.* This may be read in several ways: *daren* (or *durren*) may mean "to dare" (or "to risk"), "to fear," or "to lurk." So the line might be read "In such a poem fear you no harm" or "In such a poem you risk no harm."

352   *lombe.* I gloss as "lamb" (compare line 234), which suggests both a member of the Christian flock (MED *lomb*, n.2), and a gentle or kind person. However, Morris glosses the word as "? clerk" (possibly thinking of "loom" as an "implement or tool" [OED sb.1, 1.a]).

363–64   *roode . . . rede . . . rede.* Compare the word-play in line 195 (see note, above).

§44

Upon my ryght syde y me leye. Index no. 3844. MS: BL Harley 541, fol. 228b (late fifteenth century). Editions: B15, no. 127; *Gentleman's Magazine* 69 (1799), 33; John Brand, *Observations on the Popular Antiquities of Great Britain*, rev. Sir Henry Ellis (London: Henry G. Bohn, 1855), 3:131.

1   *me.* So MS. Brand transcribes as *may.*

8   *frwte.* So MS. Brand reads *freute.*

8–9   *Owre Lorde is the frwte . . . Blessed be the blossome that sprange.* An allusion to the tree of Jesse; see §8, note to line 17.

§45

M and A and R and I. Index no. 1650. MS: BL Sloane 2593, fol. 24b (fifteenth century). Also in Bodl. 29734 (Eng. Poet e.1), fol. 25a. Editions of Sloane: *EEC,* no. 180B; Wright, *Songs* (Warton Club), 69–70; Fehr, *Archiv* 109, 64; Rickert, p. 7. Editions of Eng. Poet: Wright, *Songs* (Percy Society), p. 31; Greene *EEC*, no. 180a; Greene, *Selection,* no. 48; Davies, no. 74.

Notes

For additional examples of carols on initial letters, see *EEC* nos. 83 and 139.

1   *M and A and R and I.* Bodleian: *Of M, A, R, I.*

3   *It wern fowre letterys of purposy.* Bodleian: *Of thes iiii letters purpose I.*

5–6   *Tho wern letteris of Mary / Of hom al our joye sprong.* Bodleian: *Thei betokyn mayd Mary; / All owr joy of hyr it sprong.*

6   The Bodleian MS inserts a stanza after this line:

>   Withoughten wem of hyr body,
>   M and A, R and I,
>   Of hyr was borne a Kyng truly
>   The Jewys dedyn to deth with wrong.

9   *bryte.* The MED suggests "radiant," "morally pure," and "untarnished." Bodleian: *bar* ("bare").

13   *with here ey.* Bodleian: *ful bytterly.*

14   *alwey the blod folwyd among.* The image of Mary's weeping tears of blood and water recalls John 19:34, where water and blood flow from the wound in Jesus' side after his death. Compare §46, line 17. In the *Liber de Passione Christi et Doloribus*, Mary is so overcome by sorrow that she weeps tears of blood (see note to §36, and Kribel, pp. 88–89). Bodleian: *And terys of blod ever among.*

15–18   Not found in Bodleian.

§46

Mary myelde made grete mone. By James Ryman. *Index* no. 3944. MS: Cambridge University Ee.1.12, fol. 77a (late fifteenth century). Editions: Zupitza, *Archiv* 89 (1892), 277–78; *EEC*, no. 159.

3   *fals Judas.* See Matthew 26:14–15; Mark 14:10; Luke 22:3–6.

7   *Cayphas and An.* See §31, note to line 3.

235

17   *watre and bloode.* See §45, note to line 14.

22   *alone.* Omitted in MS.

§47

I syke when y singe. Index no. 1365. MS: BL Harley 2253, fol. 80a (West Midlands, early fourteenth century). Also in Bodl. 1603 (Digby 2), fol. 6a (late thirteenth century). Editions of Harley: Wright, *Specimens*, pp. 85–87; Böddekker, pp. 210–12; Cook, *Reader*, pp. 455–57; Kaiser, p. 293; Davies, no. 22; Brook, no. 22; LH, no. 228. Editions of Digby: Furnivall, *Archiv* 97 p. 308; Furnivall, *Minor Poems of the Vernon Manuscript*, vol. 2 (EETS o.s. 117), p. 753; B13, no. 64; Sisam, *Oxford*, no. 18.

1   *when.* Digby: *al wan.*

5   *Ant.* Digby: *hi* (I).

9   *stille ant mete.* A formula rich in connotations. *Stille:* silently, gently, perpetually; *mete:* fittingly, appropriately, copiously, equitably.

9–10   Digby: *Marie, milde and sute / thu haf merci of me.*

10   *reweth.* Brook suggests an impersonal construction: "Mary, it grieves thee."

13   *from uch toune.* Digby: *wyt hute the tune.*

15   *is.* Digby: *was.*

15–20   The poet creates an image for the reader to contemplate; such imagistic devices characterize poetry of Mary at the Cross and parallel iconographic representation in medieval art and drama, which is likewise directed toward the eye as preceptor for meditation.

16   *His.* The Cross'. Personification of the cross is common in medieval poetry, the most famous example being the Anglo-Saxon *Dream of the Rood.* Compare §43.

        aren. Digby: *werin al.*

Notes

19   *Marie stont hire one.* Digby: *Mari hir selfe al hon.*

20   *Ant seith "Weylaway!"* Digby: *Hir songe was wayle.*

21   *thee.* Digby: *him.*

22   *eyghen bryhte.* Digby: *hey and herte.*

31–50   These two stanzas are transposed in Digby.

38   *Johan. John* with *a* above line.

41   The introspective conclusion completes the contemplative journey that began with Mary as companion and model, in empathy, and ends with the opening of the dreamer's (viewer's) heart and the awakening into a redemptive mood.

48–50   *smerte . . . gon.* Brook reads these as infinitives depending on *y se* in line 45.

§48

Maiden and moder, cum and se. Index no. 2036. MS: National Library of Scotland Advocates 18.7.21, fol. 121a, col. 2 (Grimestone's commonplace book, 1372). Editions: B14, no. 67; *EEC*, no. 157D; Edward Bliss Reed, *Christmas Carols Printed in the Sixteenth Century* (Cambridge: Harvard University Press, 1932), p. 82. The poem forms the basis for a later carol; see *EEC* nos. 157a–c (*Index* nos. 1219, 1211, and 3575); *EEC* no. 158 is similar.

1–8   In the carol found in BL Sloane 2593 (*EEC* 157c), these lines are attributed to John.

21   *falle.* The sense seems to be "fallen," in opposition to the notion of the "risen" flesh of the Resurrection.

§49

Com, my swete, com, my flour. Not in *Index.* MS: Bodl. 17680 (Gough Eccl. Top. 4), fol. 128b (c. 1425). The verses occur in John Mirk's sermon *De Assumpcione Beate Marie* as dialogue in his narrative of the Assumption. Editions: T. Erbe, *Mirk's Festial*, EETS e.s. 96 (London:

Kegan Paul, 1905), p. 224; Sisam, *Oxford*, no. 143 (first quatrain). Woolf quotes the verses in her discussion of Assumption lyrics (p. 299).

2   *culver.* The term of endearment suggests associations with the Immaculate Conception, for which the dove is a common symbol, and perhaps also of the Holy Ghost, by whom Mary conceived.

boure. See note to §56, line 15.

6   *to thyn.* See note to §55, line 4.

§50

The infinite power essenciall. Index no. 3391. MS: BL Addit. 20059, fols. 99a–100a (this is a fifteenth-century addition to an older MS). Editions: B15, no. 38; Davies, no. 104.

8   *Ecce virgo, radix Jesse.* See Isaias 11:1 and §8, note to line 17. This phrase occurs in a Sarum antiphon for the None hour (text in Dreves and Blume, 10:107, no. 141, 31).

9   *Tota pulcra.* Canticles 4:7: "Thou art all fair, my love, and there is not a spot in thee."

to the lillé like. The lily symbolizes purity. See Canticles (RSV Song of Solomon) 2:2. The *Fasciculus morum* compares the lily to virginity. It smells sweet and pleasing when it is fresh and unbroken, but when it has been "crushed and broken by lust, it has a terrible stench" (pp. 704–05). See also Levi D'Ancona, p. 64.

10   *saphures.* The *North Midland Lapidary* describes several properties that make the sapphire's association with Mary appropriate: it is said to have powers to give physical and emotional comfort, to heal sickness and injury, and to free prisoners. The sapphire is the color of heaven; "He yt lokes appon a saphir, he most have in mynd ye joy of heven and most be in gret hope" (Joan Evans and Mary S. Serjeantson, *English Mediaeval Lapidaries*, EETS o.s. 190 [London: Oxford University Press, 1933], p. 43).

13   *clerer . . . then the cristall.* The *London Lapidary* provides a suggestive description of the crystal's property: "This stone conceiveth wele the fire atte the sonne-beem, and catcheth and brennyth" (Evans and Serjeantson, p. 37). Compare §86, line 8.

17   *Oleum effusum.* Canticles 1:2 (RSV Song of Solomon 1:3).

       medsyne. Compare the hymn *"Santa Maria, porta coeli,"* line 15: *Medicina infirmorum* (Mone, p. 505).

21   *Phebus.* The sun god of classical mythology, who here yields his glory to Mary.

       abdominacioun. MS: *abhominacioun*, which clashes with the sense of line 23. Brown's emendation.

26–27 *Trones and dominaciones . . . Angells, archangells.* Four of the nine orders of angels (see note to §51, line 2) who honor Mary; note also *seraphynnes* at line 46.

27   *dubbit.* Two meanings are appropriate here and at line 51: I. "to invest with a dignity or title," or II.4: "to dress, clothe, array, adorn" (MED *dub)*.

31   *Columba mea.* See §49, note to line 2.

38   *the pellicane of perpetueté.* The pelican is a common and fitting symbol for Christ because "according to legend, the pelican, which has the greatest love of all creatures for its offspring, pierces its breast to feed them with its own blood" (Ferguson, p. 23).

41   *spectable.* "worthy of regard, excellent, virtuous" (MED).

45   *incontynent.* The word is used here as an adverb meaning "straightway, forthwith, at once, immediately, without delay" (OED).

46   *seraphynnes.* See Isaias 6:2 and 6:6.

52   *Trone of the Trinité.* Compare §11, note to line 21.

§51

Hayle, luminary and benigne lanterne. By John Lydgate. *Index* no. 1056. MS: Trinity College Cambridge 601 (R.3.21), fol. 162a–b and again at fol. 233a (mid-fifteenth century, Suffolk). Also in BL Harley 2251, fols. 34b–35a. Edition of Trinity: MacCracken, pp. 291–92.

2   *holy ordres nyne.* The orders of angels. Pseudo-Dionysius the Areopagite (c. 500) described nine orders in his *Celestial Hierarchy*: seraphim, cherubim, thrones,

dominations, powers, authorities, principalities, archangels, and angels. The terms come from Romans 8:38; Ephesians 1:21, 3:10; Colossians 1:16; and from 1 Peter 3:22.

5   *Eclypsyd.* Harley: *ay clypsed.*

27   *Tetragramaton.* The four letters of the Hebrew name of God, a name believed too sacred to utter.

31   *So lyst the Holygost in thee hys wynges wrappe.* "So yearned the Holy Ghost to wrap you in his wings," or perhaps "So desired the Holy Ghost to wrap his wings in you."

§52

Lefdy blisful, of muchel might. Index no. 1832. MS: Merton College Oxford 248, fol. 148b, col. 2 (fourteenth century). Editions: B14, no. 38; Silverstein, no. 36.

This is a translation of the second half of the hymn *Quem terra pontus aethera* (Daniel 1:144, and Connelly, no. 95), sometimes ascribed to Venantius Fortunatus, and often included in medieval breviaries for Marian feasts. The stanzas translated here often appear independently as *O gloriosa domina excelsa* (Mone, 2:129–30; Connelly, no. 95, lines 21–32).

5–6   *Thet thet Eve us hadde bynome . . . thy sone.* See note to §9, line 8.

8   *Thorw . . . thorwgeth.* As the prepositional system of modern English is taking shape during the Middle English period, pleonasm is not uncommon.

9   *kynges gate.* See note to §4, line 9.

§53

Haill, quene of hevin and steren of blis. Index no. 1077. MS: BL Arundel 285, fols. 196b–97a. (late fifteenth century). The poem appears among a group of several Marian pieces. Editions: B15, no. 21; Bennett, STS third series 23, p. 298: Davies, no. 179.

2   *thi sone thi Fader is.* Compare §60, lines 1–6. The phrase *Parens et puella* in §83, line 4, likewise suggests "mother and daughter."

5   *fontane.* See Canticles 4:12–15 and Psalm 35:10 (RSV 36:9): "For with thee is the fountain of life; and in thy light we shall see light."

§54

I pray thee, lady, the moder of Crist. Index no. 1340. MS: Bodl. 11755 (Rawlinson B.408), fol. 6a (c. 1450). Editions: Andrew Clark, *The English Register of Godstow Nunnery*, EETS o.s. 129 (London: Kegan Paul, 1905), p. 11; Patterson, no. 19; B15, no. 43.

3   *John Baptist.* John the Baptist, a cousin of Jesus (see Luke 1:39–56), is the prophet who foretells Christ's coming (Matthew 3:11–12; Luke 3:15–18; Mark 1:7–8).

6   *participacioun.* Augustine argued that while humankind does not have the capacity to know God, in grace and moments of faith, or what he termed "divine illumination," they can participate in God's presence. On this process, see Boethius' *Consolation of Philosophy*, Book III.

§55

Sancta Maria, ora pro nobis / O moder mylde, mayde undefylde. By James Ryman. *Index* no. 2527, *O moder mylde mayde undefylde.* MS: Cambridge University Ee.1.12, fol. 5a (1492). Editions: Zupitza, *Archiv* 89 (1892), 327, notes *Archiv* 97(1896), 143–44; *EEC*, no. 220; Stevick, no. 90.

This piece appears with six others (see next item) employing the *Ora pro nobis* refrain; Ryman's experiments with the form involve repetition and variation of the phrases in this one.

4   *hys.* Those Christ has chosen — the elect.

7   *trace.* A theological term indicative of the idea of the creator marked in the effects of his creation. St. Bonaventure, for example, in the second chapter of *The Mind's Road to God*, explores "the reflection of God in His traces in the sensible world." God is contemplated in the "mirror of sensible things . . . not only *through* them, as by His traces, but also *in* them, in so far as He is in them by essence, potency, and presence" (trans. George Boas [Indianapolis: The Liberal Arts Library Press, 1953], pp. 14–21).

§56

Sancta Maria, ora pro nobis / O tryclyn of the Trinité. By James Ryman. *Index* no. 2575. MS: Cambridge University Ee.1.12, fol. 6a (c. 1492). Editions: Zupitza, *Archiv* 89 (1892), 329–30, notes *Archiv* 97 (1896), 145; *EEC*, no. 224.

2   *tryclyn.* According to the OED, a triclinium is "a dining-room with three couches" or "a couch, running round three sides of a table, on which to recline at meals; a table-couch." The image, then, is an elaboration on the image of Mary as "chamber of the Trinity."

10   *emperesse of helle.* An epithet from the Office of the Blessed Virgin Mary in the Prymer: "Marie queene of hevene; lady of the word: empresse of helle" (Maskell, 2:78). The implication is that Mary is beyond the power of Satan and his hordes. Her dominion exceeds theirs, which makes her intercession all the more potent. Compare §43, line 294; §69, line 2, and §85, line 20.

15   *chast bowre.* Mary's womb. Compare §11, lines 5 and 53; §13, line 10; and §49, line 2.

§57

Sainte Marie, virgine. Attributed to St. Godric. *Index* no. 2988. MS: BL Royal 5.F.7, fol. 85a (with music) (=A; early fourteenth century). The poem is found in several other MSS: Bodl. 970 (Laud Misc. 413), fol. 39b (=B; first stanza only, early thirteenth century); BL Harley 153, fol. 26a (=C; late sixteenth century); Cambridge University Mm.4.28, fol. 149a (=D; c. 1200); BL Harley 322, fol. 74b (=E); Bodl. 21781 (Douce 207), fol. 125b (=F; c. 1300); BL Cotton Otho B.5, Part 2, fol. 32b (=G; mid-fourteenth century); Corpus Christi College Cambridge 26, p. 259 (=H; thirteenth century); BL Cotton Nero D.5, fol. 150b (=I; thirteenth century); BL Harley 1620, fol. 172a (=J); Lambeth 51, cap. cliiii (=K; early thirteenth century); and Bodl. 3886 (Fairfax 6), fol. 185 (=L; fourteenth century); Paris Bibliothèque Mazarine 1716, fol. 207b (=M, late thirteenth century). Editions: MSS A–L and composite text: Zupitza, "Cantus Beati Godrici," *Englische Studien* 11 (1888), 415–21. Editions of Royal 5.F.7: Joseph Ritson, *Bibliographia Poetica* (London: C. Roworth for G. W. Nicol, 1802), pp. 1–4; J. W. Rankin, "The Hymns of St. Godric," *PMLA* 38 (1923), 700; Joseph Hall, *Selections from Early Middle English Literature, 1130–1250* (Oxford: Clarendon Press, 1920), 1:5. Editions of Harley 322: Ritson, pp. 1–4. Editions of Bodl. 21781: Joseph Stevenson, *Libellus de Vita et Miraculis S. Godrici, Heremitae de Finchale*, Surtees Society 20 (London: J. B. Nichols, 1847), 119; R. M. Wilson, *The Lost Literature of Medieval England*, second ed. (London: Methuen, 1970), pp.

Notes

159–60; Henry G. Hewlett, *The Flowers of History, by Roger of Wendover*, vol. 1, Rolls Series 84 (London: Longman, 1886), 73. Edition of Corpus Christi 26: Davies, no. 1. Edition of Cotton Otho: Hewlett, p. 73. Edition of Cambridge 4.28: Brown, *Register* 1:199. Composite text: Patterson, no. 58. Edition of Paris: Alexandra Barratt, "The Lyrics of St Godric: A New Manuscript," *Notes and Queries* 32 (1985), 439–45.

On the textual history of the piece, particularly the garbled transmission of texts through linguistic and orthographical confusion, see Barratt's article, cited above.

1   *virgine.* F, H, I, J: *clane virgine.* G: *clene virgine.*

2   *Jhesu.* F: *Crist.*

3   *Onfo.* C: *un fo.* E: *on fong.* M: *on sang.* Barratt suggests that M has been garbled by "at least one scribe, and possibly also a translator, to whom Middle English was a foreign language" (p. 443).

          schild. C: *child.* F: *sciso.*

          help. Omitted in H, I, J.

          Godric. According to the history by Reginald of Durham in which this poem appears, Godric, a hermit who died in 1170, learned this song from the Virgin Mary herself when she appeared to him in a vision. She promised that she would come to him whenever he sang it.

4   *heghilich.* B: *eghhtlech.* F, G: *heali.* H: *hoeali.* I: *hali.* J: *halili.*

          with. MS: *thith.* F, H, I, J: *widh.* G: *thidh.* M: *piz.*

5   *Cristes bur.* The allusion is to Mary's womb, Christ's dwelling place, his home on earth. M: *tristes bur.*

5–8   Omitted in B, C, D, E.

6   *clenhad.* J: *cleuad.*

7   *Dilie.* F: *Delivere.* Rankin bases his gloss, "destroy," on the Latin texts of the poem. The OED gives "blot out, erase." But the MED gives *dilie* as a form of *delen,* to

separate or divide. Perhaps the sense is "remove"; Godric wants to be emptied of sin, filled with Mary's goodness, so that he might, like her, be a "bower" or vessel for Christ.

rix. F: *regne.*

8 *winne.* G: *wunne.* H, I, J: *thinine.* F: *blisse. Winne* is a particularly evocative term since it connotes the heavenly bliss that Godric yearns for, but might also hint at the struggle (OE *winn*, labor, struggle, contention).

 with the selfd God. Literally, "with the very God." G, H, I, J: *widh self god.* F: *wit thiself god. Self(d)* is used here as an intensifying pronoun; see MED *self*, 1.b.

§58

Ave maris stella. Index no. 454. MS: BL Sloane 2593, fol. 27a (c. 1450). Editions: Wright, *Songs* (Warton Club), pp. 77–78; Fehr, *Archiv* 109 (1902), 66; CS p. 209; B15, no. 18; Rickert p. 8.

This prayer is inspired by the Latin hymn *Ave maris stella* (see note to §9), the source of the four titles with which the poet here addresses Mary.

5 *Gabriel.* See Luke 1:26–38.

5–6 In the MS, these lines precede lines 3–4; the two couplets are marked for transposition.

9 *withoutyn dedly synne.* See §75, note to line 4.

10 *Forty dayis of pardoun.* A reference to the Church's practice of granting partial indulgences (remission of sins) for prescribed acts of penance.

§59

Marie moder, wel thee be. Index no. 2119. MS: Bodl. 15834 (Rawlinson liturg. g.2), fols. 4b–6a (late fourteenth century). Editions: B14, no. 122; Stevick, no. 46. The verses occur in the *Speculum Christiani* (a late-fourteenth-century instructional work, probably by an English Franciscan), which survives in more than thirty MSS, as well as separately in more than fifteen

MSS (see *Index* and *Supplement* for complete listing). Editions of BL Harley 6580, fol. 35b, Lansdowne 344, fol. 36b, and Lambeth 559, fol. 19a: Gustaf Holmstedt, *Speculum Christiani,* EETS o.s. 182 (London: Oxford University Press, 1933; rpt. Kraus, 1971), pp. 160–69. Edition of St. Cuthbert's College 28: T. E. Bridgett, *Our Lady's Dowry* (third ed., London, 1890), p. 34. Edition of Bodl. 6922 (Ashmole 61), fol. 22b (late fifteenth century): Rossell Hope Robbins, "Private Prayers in Middle English Verse," *Studies in Philology* 36 (1939), 468–69. Edition of Cambridge University Ff.5.48, fols. 74b–75b (a late variant): Wright and Halliwell, 2:212–13. Editions of BL Harley 2382, fol. 86b; Thomas Warton, *History of English Poetry*, 4 vols. (1774–81; rpt. New York: Johnson Reprint Corp., 1968), 3.153; Patterson, no. 60. Edition of BL Addit. 39574, fol. 58a: Mabel Day, *The Wheatley Manuscript*, EETS o.s. 155 (London: Oxford University Press, 1921), pp. 74–75. Edition of Chetham Library 8009, fol. 121a: Max Förster, "Kleinere Mittelenglische Texte," *Anglia* 42 (1918), 172–75.

Patterson comments: "This prayer to Mary shows no influence of the *chanson d'amour*, but seems rather to belong to the more commonplace poetry that succeeded the *chansons* in the fifteenth century in France. The stylistic trick of *Anaphora* [the repetition of initial words], so prominent in this poem, was very popular in French poetry of the time. Though this poem in its general origin owes much to late French poetry, there can be little doubt that in this instance the anaphora has been ultimately influenced chiefly by the Litany, and this fact in turn suggests that perhaps the constant use of the Litany in the Middle Ages has much to do with the widespread popularity of this mannerism" (p. 193).

8   *out of dette, for charité.* See note to §31, line 20.

31   *wrathe.* One of the seven deadly sins; or, perhaps, God's wrath. In either case, the speaker is praying for the souls of enemies as well as friends.

46   *Schrift and hosel at myn endyng day.* I.e., the last rites administered to the dying. Confession and absolution are required before partaking of Holy Communion.

§60

Thou wommon boute vere. Possibly by William Herebert. *Index* no. 3700. MS: BL Addit. 46919, fols. 206b–07a (early fourteenth century, Southwest Midlands). Editions: Wright and Halliwell, 2:227–28; B14, no. 16; Kaiser, p. 287; LH, no. 184; Davies, no. 28; Helen Gardner, ed., *The Faber Book of Religious Verse* (London: Faber, 1972), pp. 34–35; Reimer pp. 118–19.

Friar William Herebert's name appears in the margin of this text, and Reimer speculates that the piece may be an original composition. The MS contains many emendations that appear to be authorial. Brown compares the opening stanzas to the hymn *Virgo gaude speciosa,* for which he prints partial lyrics (B14, p. 248).

7   *suster and moder.* MS: *suster and my moder,* with *my* marked for deletion. The prominent back vowels (*sunne* for *sin, monne* for man) are characteristic of the southern dialect.

7–12   These lines appear in the bottom margin, with a line indicating their insertion after line 6.

8   *thy sone my brother.* MS: *thy sone is my brother,* with *is* marked for deletion.

10   *Whoso.* MS: *Who so,* with *so* possibly marked for deletion (one dot under the word; usually there are two).

12   *vor to. For to* commonly functions as the stem in fourteenth-century infinitive constructions.

18   *My robe he haveth opon.* Christ's taking of human form makes him representative of and sympathetic to the human condition. Compare *Piers Plowman* B.18.22–23, in which Christ jousts in Piers' armor: "This Iesus of his gentries wol Iust in Piers armes, / In his helm and in his haubergeon, *humana natura*" (ed. George Kane and E. Talbot Donaldson [London: Athlone Press, 1975]). Davies, p. 319, notes additional biblical and medieval references to Christ's robe.

23   *love the chartre wrot.* On the metaphor of Christ's crucified body as a legal charter of salvation, see Mary Carol Spalding, *The Middle English Charters of Christ* (Bryn Mawr: Bryn Mawr College, 1914). Compare §43, lines 187–99.

24   MS: *And the enke orn* with *And* marked for deletion.

32   *help at the noede.* MS: *help me at the noede,* with *me* marked for deletion.

42   In the MS, the word *Amen* appears at the end of this line; lines 43–48 appear in the bottom margin, marked for insertion.

46   *Suster, boe ther.* Reimer interprets marks in the MS to indicate a transposition: *Ther, Suster, boe.*

46   *Suster.* The *r* is written above the line.

§61

Marie, yow quen. Index no. 2125. MS: BL Harley 2316, fol. 26a (late fourteenth century). Editions: Halliwell and Wright, *Reliquiae Antiquae*, 2:120; Patterson, no. 59.

Patterson notes: "These ejaculatory verses to Mary seem to have been well known. A variant is found as an inlaid stanza to Mary in the Vernon MS. of the long poem on the passion of Jesus, beginning, *Swete Jhesu, now wol I synge.*" Those lines read:

> Marie ladi, Mooder briht, —
> Thou darst, thou wolt, thou art of miht, —
> Myn herte love, my lyf, my liht,
> Thou prey for me bothe day & niht.
>   (Furnivall, EETS o.s. 117, p. 454)

§62

Levedie, ic thonke thee. Index no. 1836. MS: Trinity College Cambridge 323 (B.14.39), fol. 42b (thirteenth century). Editions: B13, no. 27; LH, no. 183; Sisam, *Oxford*, no. 29; Davies, no. 11.

11   *herdie.* Sisam emends to *erndie,* from ME *ernden,* "to intercede."

16   *deyen.* MS: *dethen.* Brown's emendation to suit the rhyme.

§63

Blessed beo thu, lavedi, ful of hovene blisse. Index no. 1407. MS: BL Egerton 613, fol. 2a–b (thirteenth century). Also in BL Harley 2253 (see §64). Editions: Mätzner, p. 54; Böddekker, 457–59; Wright and Halliwell, 1:102–03; Morris, EETS o.s. 49, pp. 195–96; Patterson, no. 65; B13, no. 55.

This follows §83, "Of on that is so fayr," in the same hand.

21   *hore.* Morris identifies this as a form of *or(e)* (MED n.2), which means "mercy," "pardon," "forgiveness," "compassion," "pity," "favor," "grace."

27   *wende.* MS: *thende.* So emended by all editors.

§64

Blessed be thou, levedy, ful of heovene blisse. Index no. 1407. MS: BL Harley 2253, fol. 81a–b (early fourteenth century). Also in BL Egerton 613 (see §63). Editions: Böddekker, pp. 216–17; Wright, *Specimens*, pp. 93–94; Brook, no. 26; LH, no. 189.

3   *Preyghe.* MS: *prereyghe.* Brook's emendation.

29   *of mylse thou art well.* Written over erasure.

30   *fleysh ant fell.* "Flesh and skin." A common phrase in Middle English, meaning "the whole substance of the body" (see OED *flesh*, sb.I.1.c; and OED *fell*, sb.1.2: "said of the human skin, rarely of the skin covering an organ of the body").

36   *worldes.* The first letter is written over erased *oþ.*

§65

Mary, modur of grace, we cry to thee. Index no. 2114. MS: Gonville and Caius College Cambridge 71/38, fol. 17b (c. 1400). A translation of a prayer which appears in Anselm's *Admonitio morienti* (PL 158, col. 687), this poem appears in the *Fasciculus morum* I, ix, "*Quibus est humiliandum,*" in ten MSS. Edition of Caius 71: Rossell Hope Robbins, "Popular Prayers in Middle English Verse," *Modern Philology* 36 (1939), 345. Edition of Bodl. 12514 (Rawlinson C.670), fol. 15b: Silverstein, no. 52. Edition of Rawlinson C.670: Woolf, p. 120. Edition of Canterbury Cathedral Lit. D.14: *Fasciculus morum*, pp. 72–73.

3   *Put. Wyte* in Rawlinson.

7–8   The lines are transposed in Rawlinson.

10   The omission of the subject (here "I") is common in Middle English syntax.

Notes

§66

Hayl Mari, / Hic am sori. Index no. 1066. MS: Bodl. 1603 (Digby 2), fol. 6b (late thirteenth century). Editions: F. J. Furnivall, *Archiv* 97 (1896), 311; F. J. Furnivall, *Minor Poems*, p. 755; Patterson, no. 29; B13, no. 65; Sisam, *Oxford*, no. 19.

9   *In worde, in worke, in thoith foli.* Compare the lines of confession from the Ordinary of the Mass: "I have sinned exceedingly in thought, word, and deed" (Warren, *Sarum Missal*, Part 1, p. 21).

10–11   *her mi bon. / Mi bon thu her.* Each stanza of this poem is linked to the next with a repeated phrase (concatenation), a technique common to French secular lyrics, particularly the *chanson d'aventure.* The speaker's plea for the lady's pity also echoes secular conventions.

14   *her.* MS: *her lefdi der*, with *lefdi der* marked for deletion.

15   *fer.* Sisam glosses as "in health." It could also mean "fearful."

17   *Ne let me noth ler that thu ber.* Sisam's gloss is "Do not deny me the countenance you bear."

20   *Forto.* MS: *fort.* Furnivall's emendation.

36   *Trinité.* The idea of God as three persons in one being — Father, Son, and Holy Spirit — is central to Christian theology. The Athanasian Creed elaborates on the doctrine.

44   *drupe and dar.* MED *daren*, v.2.c.113, cites the *Promptorium parvulorum*: "Darynn or drowpyn or prively to be hydde," which suggests a common alliterative phrase meaning "to slink or hide or remain motionless." Thus, in lines 46–48, the speaker compares himself at Judgment Day to a hare freezing motionless as the hounds close in. Though he cries out to Mary now in his terror (line 15), at Judgment he would be silent as Christ enduring the fiend's blows.

49   Furnivall emends to read *haf ned[e þan &] þare.*

50   The MS line concludes with *&c*, suggesting that the text may be incomplete.

§67

On hire is al mi lif ilong. Index no. 2687. MS: BL Cotton Caligula A.9, fol. 246b (thirteenth century). Also in Jesus College Oxford 29, Part 2, fol. 180b (lines 1–31, thirteenth century); Trinity College Cambridge 323 (B.14.39), fol. 81b, incomplete due to misbinding (thirteenth century); and BL Royal 2.F.8, fol. 1b (late thirteenth century). Editions of Cotton Caligula: Morris, EETS o.s. 49, pp. 158–62; Wright, *Religious Songs*, Percy Society 11 (London: T. Richards, 1844), pp. 65–66; B13, no. 32B; Patterson, no. 31. Edition of Trinity: CS, p. 94; B13 no. 32A; Stevick, no. 12. Edition of Jesus College: Morris, EETS o.s. 49, p. 159–63. Edition of Royal: B13, no. 32C.

3   *ther among.* Singling out Mary as the one most praiseworthy among women is commonplace. She is one among ten thousand; compare Chaucer's use of the Marian epithet in praise of the good fair White in *The Book of the Duchess*, lines 972 and 818–19.

4   *Heo.* Trinity: *Thad.* Royal: *That.*

6   *Heo.* Trinity, Royal: *Ant.*

8   *Ich . . . mi.* Trinity: *We . . . ur.*

10   *Thah we.* MS: *thah the.* Brown's emendation. Trinity: *Than we.* Royal: *Then we.* It is conceivable that *Thah the* is the right reading, however, and the subject (we) understood: "though we have done wrong to you (Mary)." The shift to second person (*the*) would thus anticipate the next stanza.

11   *Thu art.* Trinity: *Ho is.* Trinity gives *Ho* for *Thu* at lines 13 and 14 as well. The Trinity scribe evidently wished to maintain an objective tone by employing third person until midway in the stanza, where Mary is juxtaposed with Eve.

11–20   Here the tone shifts to a more personal level as the speaker begins to address Mary directly. The Trinity scribe maintains use of the third person until midway through the stanza. (In Trinity this stanza occurs after line 40 in the present text.)

14   *geve.* Royal: *broht.*

             weole. The word suggests "satisfaction," "opulence," "worthiness," "status," or "opportunities."

Notes

14   *and.* Omitted in Royal.

         wunne. MS: *thunne.* Brown's emendation.

16   *woht.* Jesus College: *wo.*

18   *Bisih to me.* Trinity: *Thu do us merci.*

19   *ich.* Trinity: *we.*

21–30   In Royal and Trinity, this stanza follows the first.

22   Omitted in Jesus College.

23   *lif we schule forgo.* Trinity: *blisse ic mot forgon.* Royal gives *blisse* for *lif.*

         we. MS: *the.* Brown's emendation.

24   *Ne of thunche hit us so sore.* Trinity: *Nofthingit me so sore.*

25   *This world nis butent ure ifo.* Trinity: *This worldis blis nis wrd a slo.* Royal: *Thes worldes blysse nys wrt a slo.*

26   *thenche hirne at go.* Trinity: *wille henne gon.*

         hirne. Jesus College: *hire.*

26–28   These lines are omitted in Trinity.

27   *do bi.* Trinity: *lernin.*

28   *This lives blisse nis wurth a slo.* See note to line 25. Royal: *Thes world nys bote hure yfoh.*

         lives. Trinity: *worldis.*

         slo. The sloe is the small, sour fruit of a blackthorn tree.

29   *Ich bidde, God, thin ore.* Royal: *Levedy, thyn horee.*

34   *prude and feire wede.* Trinity: *hevir* [ever] *fayre wedin.* Royal: *Heyte and fayre ywede.*

35   *dweole.* Trinity: *nout.* The MED provides several applicable meanings for *dwele*: "a wandering course," "trickery," "false belief; heresy," or "delusion."

36   *ich thenche sunne fleo.* Trinity: *we sulin* [should] *ur sunnis flen.* Royal: *yg wlle hem flee.*

37   *And alle mine sot dede.* Trinity: *And ure sothede.* Royal: *And lete my sothede.*

38   *Ich bidde hire to me biseo.* Trinity: *We biddirt hire us to seo.* Royal: *Hy bydde hyre thet ys so fre.*

39   *And helpe me and rede.* Trinity: *Thad con wissin and redin.* Royal: *Helpen hus and rede.*

40   *That is so freo.* Royal: *Wel hit may be.*

43   *Awrec thee nu on me, levedi.* Trinity: *Thu do me merci, lavedi brit.* Royal: *Bysy to me, suete levedy.* The literal sense in Cotton Caligula is "avenge yourself now on me, lady."

44   *fecche.* Trinity: *wecche.* Royal: *dregche.*

45–46   *Do nim thee wreche . . . / Other let me.* Trinity: *Yif me thi love . . . / Let me.* Royal: *To nyme bote . . . / And let me.*

47   *That no feond me ne drecche.* Trinity: *Thad fendes me ne letten* (release). Royal: *Here deed me hynne veyge.*

49   *Of this world.* Trinity: *Of my lif.* Royal: *That lyves.*

§68

Worsshipful maiden to the world, Marie. By Thomas Hoccleve. *Index* no. 4233. MS: Huntington HM 744, fol. 33b (1422–26). Edition: Frederick J. Furnivall and I. Gollancz, eds., *Hoccleve's Works: The Minor Poems*, EETS e.s. 61 and 73 (1892 and 1925; rpt. as one volume, Oxford: Oxford University Press, 1970), pp. 283–85.

26   *Thou sparyng and thow preyynge.* In the MS, "*s. deus*" appears above *sparyng*; "*s. domina*" appears above *preyynge*. The *s* is an abbreviation for *scilicet*, "that is to say."

35   *Satisfaccioun* is the reward of penance; see Chaucer's The Parson's Tale with its progress from "Contricioun of herte" to "Confession of Mouthe" to "Satisfaccioun" (*CT* X[I]107), or the fruit of the tree of charity being defined as satisfaction (*CT* X[I]113). But humankind's lot is often said to be a state of perpetual anxiety, and here the speaker worries that his penance has been inadequate. See Boethius' *Consolation of Philosophy* and such lyrics as "In the vale of resteles mynde" (*Index* no. 1463; Stevick, no. 50).

§69

Hayl, oure patron and lady of erthe. Index no. 1073. MS: BL Addit. 37049, fols. 29b–30a (fifteenth century). Editions: Karl Brunner, "Kirchenlieder aus dem 15.Jahrhundert," *Anglia* 61 (1937), 140; B15, no. 26; LH, no. 182. MS facsimile: James Hogg, ed. *An Illustrated Yorkshire Carthusian Religious Miscellany, British Library London Additional MS. 37049, Vol. 3: The Illustrations, Analecta Cartusiana* 95 (Salzburg: Universität Salzburg, 1981), pp. 38–39.

In the MS, the poem is preceded by a picture in which Mary sits holding the infant Christ. She holds a scepter; Jesus holds an orb in one hand and raises the other hand in a gesture of benediction. A monk kneels before them, saying, "O suete lady, mayden mylde, pray for me to Jesu thi childe." Mary says, "I am redy for all to pray, that my son wil luf god verray."

The poem is an expanded translation of the antiphon *Salve Regina* (Connelly, no. 33; Julian, 2:991). In the MS, the abbreviated Latin words appear in red to the left of the English text.

1   *Salve.* The Latin words correspond to the first words of each English line.

2   *emprys of helle.* See note to §56, line 10.

3   *ferth.* The word may be a derivation of the Scottish *firth*, estuary, suggesting Mary's function as contributor to mercy; or it may be a form of the Northern *frith*, preserve, wood, or hunting-ground, presenting an image of Mary as a "place" where mercy may be found.

4   *secunde welle.* The first is the well of Jacob, where Jesus meets the woman of Samaria and tells her about the "living water" of everlasting life (John 4:1–30).

7   *et spes nostra.* The MS reads *mea*, but the English text translates the Latin *nostra* from the hymn.

16   *for.* Added above the line.

17   *payne.* The word *rayne* is blotted out before *payne*.

25   *Illos tuos misericordes oculos*: abbreviated in MS.

34   *luf.* Brown reads *lust*.

39   *joyful.* In margin, to replace canceled *gentyl*.

§70

Mayden moder milde. Index no. 2039. MS: BL Harley 2253, fol. 83a (West Midlands, early fourteenth century). Editions: Wright, *Specimens*, pp. 97–98; Böddekker, pp. 220–22; Wülcker, 1:49–50; CS, no. 49; B13, no. 87; Brook, no. 28; LH, no. 191; Silverstein, no. 28.

1–8   Brook calls attention to the similarity of the short prayer which concludes Dan Michel's version of the *Ayenbite of Inwit* (MS Arundel 57, fol. 96b): "Mayde and moder mylde, uor loue of þine childe, þet is god an man, Me þet am zuo wylde uram zenne þou me ssylde ase ich þe bydde can. Amen."

12   *Ly soverein creatour.* One of the mysteries of Mary is that she gave birth to her creator, the author of the universe. But *creatour* might also be translated as "creature" or "created thing," which sometimes is spelled *creatur* as well as *creature* in Old French.

25   *stou.* Possibly *ston*, as Brown reads; Brook also admits *ston* (stony ground) as a possible reading.

31   *ferede.* Brook argues that "the syntax of the line demands the transitive sense 'to cause fear to': 'He caused fear in every living creature.'"

§71

Mary, for thine joys fyve. Index no. 2099. MSS: BL Royal 8.F.6, fol. 21a; Lincoln Cathedral 91 (Thornton), fol. 177b (mid-fifteenth century). The verses appear as a prayer tag in both MSS. They also appear with paintings of the Life of the Blessed Virgin Mary on the chancel wall of Broughton Church, Oxon (noted in Robbins and Cutler, *Supplement*). Editions: Rossell Hope Robbins, "Popular Prayers in Middle English Verse," *Modern Philology* 36 (1939), 348; Brown, *Register*, 1:362. Edition of Lincoln: Reginald M. Woolley, *Catalogue of the Manuscripts of Lincoln Cathedral Chapter Library* (London: H. Milford, 1927), p. 54; Carl Horstmann, *Yorkshire Writers: Richard Rolle of Hampole* (New York: Macmillan, 1895), p. 377.

1   *joys fyve.* Usually the Annunciation, the Nativity, the Resurrection, the Ascension, and the Assumption. But compare §77 and §74, in which the five joys are the Annunciation, the Nativity, Epiphany, the Resurrection, and the Assumption. And §73 combines both traditions to commemorate *six* joys.

1–2   Lincoln MS: *Lady, for thy joyes fyve / Wisse me the waye of rightwys liffe. Amen.*

§72

Be glad, of al maydens flourre. Index no. 465. (Final quatrain: *Index* no. 1833.5.) MS: Huntington HM 127, fol. 53a–b (fifteenth century). Editions: B15, no. 34; LH, no. 187.

A song of the seven heavenly joys, not to be confused with the five earthly joys. These joys are all conditions of being: Mary is celebrated as queen of great honor, spouse of God, vessel of virtue, mediatrix, comforter, Mother of Christ, and flower of womanhood. Brown indicates that the seven heavenly joys do not appear in pre-fifteenth-century poetry. The poem is introduced in the MS as follows:

> Hit is yfounde and ywrite that oure lady apered to Seint Thomas of Caunterbury and badde him and taught him to worschipe here for the seven joyes durable and everelastinge that sche hath now in hevene as wel as he deede now for the five temperal joyes that sche hadde on erthe the which beth passed and these beth the seven that folweth.

19   *Jesu.* MS: *ihū*.

§73

Heyle be thou, ladye so bryght. Index no. 1027. MS: Cambridge University Ii.6.43, fol. 88a–b or 90a–b (fifteenth century). Edition: B14, no. 92.

The poem is structured according to the joys of Mary; see note to §71, line 1.

1–3   These lines are indented in the MS, leaving space for an unfinished initial rubric.

4   *swotyst.* Most lovely, fairest, sweetest; a figurative term often used to describe Christ as well as Mary. (Compare 2 Corinthians 2:15: "For we are the fragrance of Christ for God," an allusion to the incense of triumphal procession or sacrifice.) See also MED *sōt(e)*, 1.a. The poet's desire to engage all the senses in meditation is reinforced by the use of *fonde*, which may mean "taste," in line 7.

27   *Holy Thursdaye.* After the Last Supper, Jesus was betrayed and captured on Holy Thursday; see notes to §31.

32–33   *thou wentyst wysse / To blys.* A reference to the Assumption; see note to §77, lines 50–51.

§74

Haile be thu, Mari maiden bright. Index no. 1029. Göttingen University Theol. 107, fol. 169a (early fourteenth century, Northern). The poem occurs only in this MS of the *Cursor Mundi*, in a group of prayers at the end of the MS. Editions: Richard Morris, *Cursor Mundi*, Part 5, EETS o.s. 68 (London, 1878; rpt. London: Richard Clay, 1966), lines 25619–83; Carl Horstmann, "Ein Beitrag zu Celestin," *Anglia* 1 (1878), 391; B14, no. 31; Sisam, *Oxford*, no. 82.

6   *Mi.* Morris supplies the missing initial letter.

9   *levedi.* MS: *leved.* Brown's emendation.

13   *fra hevene toure.* MS: *fra heve.* Brown's emendation.

17   *broght.* MS: *brogh.* Morris' emendation.

21   *The.* Initial letter missing in MS. Morris' emendation. So also at lines 26 and 41.

22   *Als sun schines thoru the glas.* See note to §17, lines 18–20.

30   *Mir, reclis, and gold red.* Jacobus de Voragine suggests that "these three gifts corresponded to Christ's royal power, divine majesty, and human mortality" (*Golden Legend* 1: 83).

32   *The reclis fel til his goddhed.* Incense, *reclis*, is sometimes used in the Mass to symbolize the ascendance of prayer or the spirit to God.

33   *Mir to man that sal be dede.* Myrrh is a balsam gum used in embalming, so the gift signifies Jesus' mortality.

35   *Levedi.* MS: *Levid.* Brown's emendation.

42   Compare John 7:36.

§75

Heyl be thou, Marie, milde quene of hevene. Index no. 1030. MS: St. John's College Cambridge 256, pp. 269–70 (early fourteenth century). Also in Bodl. 3938 (Eng. Poet a.1, the Vernon MS), fol. 115b (c. 1385); BL Royal 17.A.27, fol. 81a (early fifteenth century); Lambeth 559, fol. 15b (fourteenth century). Edition of St. John's: B14, no. 26. Editions of Vernon: Carl Horstmann, *The Minor Poems of the Vernon MS,* vol. 1, EETS o.s. 98 (London: Kegan Paul, 1892), pp. 30–32; Patterson, pp. 149–51.

3   *mene.* Vernon: *make.*

4   *sennes sevene.* The seven deadly sins are pride, envy, wrath, sloth, avarice, gluttony, and lechery. See Chaucer's The Parson's Tale and Gower's *Confessio Amantis.* See also M. W. Bloomfield, *The Seven Deadly Sins: An Introduction to the History of a Religious Concept, with Special Reference to Medieval English Literature* (East Lansing: Michigan State College Press, 1952), and Siegfried Wenzel, "The Seven Deadly Sins: Some Problems of Research," *Speculum* 43 (1968), 1–22.

5   The Latin lines appear in red.

6   *Heil.* Vernon, Royal: *Ladi.*

7   *thou haddest wan Crist the aungel sende.* Vernon: *thou were inne whon god his angel dude sende.*

8   *bodi.* Inserted above line.

        wende. Vernon: *lende.*

9   *Thou bring me out of sinne and schuld me fram the fende.* Vernon: *Thou bringe me to that blisse that is withouten ende.*

11   *withouten eni drede.* Vernon: *therof have I no drede.*

13   *in bok.* Omitted in Vernon and Royal.

14   *that joie.* Vernon: *the love of him.*

15   Vernon inserts an additional stanza after this line:

                Sete ladi thou rewe on me and mak myn herte clene,
                Bring us out of sunne that doth us traye and tene,
                Wo hit us byginneth in werkes as we han sene,
                Schild us from the peynes ther non may other mene.

22–23   The lines are transposed in Vernon.

23   *woundes five.* Jesus received five wounds on the cross: two in his hands, two in his feet, and one in his side.

24   *Thou help me out of senne.* Vernon: *Get me hevene blisse.*

27   *thiself lete.* Vernon: *for thi son thu lete.*

28–29   Royal: *Thow give me grace in erthe my sines to bete / and that I may in heven sitte before thi fet.*

32   *and redi.* Vernon: *in saumple.*

Notes

34   *me . . . save me at the nede.* Vernon: *us . . . schild us from mis dede.*

36   *flour of alle.* Vernon: *Seinte Marie.*

38   *Thou be in stude and stalle ther I draue to ded.* Vernon: *Thou help me at myn ende whon I drawe to the dede.*

          stude and stalle. Stude is a form of *stode,* or stable, suggesting that Mary will be present at the final moments of the speaker's imprisonment in his mortal, bestial state. But MED also cites uses of *stude* to indicate a) a state of mental perplexity, and b) a place or room in which to read, write, or study. *Stalle* might then allude to a meditational compartment or carrel, in which case the phrase could refer to the speaker's final moments of spiritual contemplation.

41–50   These stanzas are transposed in Royal.

43   *to hevene.* Vernon: *in to his riche.*

          is evere inne. Vernon: *schal never blynne.*

46   *Marie.* Vernon: *Ladi.* So also at line 51.

52   *Now I thee biseche.* Vernon: *Love of alle blisse.*

58   *Thou helpe me.* Vernon: *Thou gif me miht and grace.*

59   *withoute ende.* Vernon: *ever newe.*

          nyght. Corrected in MS above canceled *lyght.*

64   *And geve me grace in erthe my sinnes to reue sare.* Vernon: *And send me hosul and schrift ar I hethene fare.*

66–70   Omitted in Vernon and Royal.

§76

Levedy, for thare blisse. Index no. 1833. MS: Jesus College Oxford 29, fol. 181a–b (late thirteenth century). Editions: Morris, EETS o.s. 49, pp. 87–88; Patterson, no. 68; B13, no. 41.

The MS introduces the poem: *Her bigynneth the vif Blyssen of ure levedi seynte Marie.*

6   *Sunnen.* MS: *sūmen.* Brown's emendation.

12   *That scop thee and alle thing.* Compare the Sarum Office of the Blessed Virgin Mary, Evensong *capitulum:* "Blessid art thou virgyn marie, that hast born the lord maker of the world; thou hast getyn hym that made thee" (Maskell, 2:61); and Matins, responsory after second lesson: "Blessid art thou maide marie, that baar the lord maker of the world: thou hast engendrid him that made thee, and thou dwellist mayde with outen ende" (Maskell, 2:11).

18   *gled and blithe.* MS: *blithe and gled,* marked for transposition.

25   *Munt of Olyvete.* According to the account in Acts 1:6–12, after Jesus' ascension into heaven, his disciples returned from the Mount of Olives and gathered in the upper room; Mary was part of this group.

§77

Ase y me rod this ender day. Index no. 359. MS: BL Harley 2253, fol. 81b (West Midlands, early fourteenth century). Editions: Wright, *Specimens,* pp. 94–96; Böddekker, pp. 218–19; Wülcker, 1:48–49; B14, no. 11; Brook, no. 27; Davies, no. 20; LH, no. 194, Stevick, no. 33; Dunn and Byrnes, pp. 205–07; Cook, pp. 462–64; Otto Funke, *A Middle English Reader,* third ed. (Berne: A. Francke, 1966), pp. 49–51. Selected criticism: William McClellan, "Radical Theology or Parody in a Marian Lyric of Ms Harley 2253," *Voices in Translation: The Authority of "Olde Bookes" in Medieval Literature; Essays in Honor of Helaine Newstead,* ed. Deborah M. Sinnreich-Levi and Gale Sigal (New York: AMS, 1992), pp. 157–68.

1   *Ase y me rod.* A conventional opening for the *chanson d'aventure. Index* no. 360, "Now spryngeth the spray" (Stevick, no. 25, Davies, no. 19) shows the form's secular origins.

7   *suete ant fre.* Written over an erasure.

23   Stevick suggests emending to *If that you leste* (if it please you) or *If that ye leste* (If you will listen) for rhyme and meter.

25   *wymman.* Brook's and Brown's emendation. MS: *wynman.*

33   *on thoro lay.* Brook rejects Böddekker's reading of *þore,* emended to *þorwe* and glossed as "crib," as "phonologically unlikely." He concurs with Sister Mary Immaculate ("A Note on 'A Song of the Five Joys,'" *Modern Language Notes* 55 [1940], 249–54) that Brown's glossing of the phrase as "according to due law" or "in due form" is "theologically inappropriate," and agrees with her reading of *lay* as "light." He comments: "This explanation seems the most satisfactory in view of v. 35 and the passages quoted by Sister Mary Immaculate from sermons on the Nativity which stress the miraculous brilliance of the star; for example, St. Bernard says 'Nox enim ut dies illuminata est' (Migne, P.L. 183, col. 126)" (p. 86).

34   *brohte us lyhtnesse.* Brown calls attention to the line "*Et erranti populo lucem protulist*" ("And to a wandering people you proffered light") in *Primum fuit gaudium,* a Latin hymn of the five joys (p. 246).

35   *The ster.* MS: *þest,* followed by *i* above the line. Brook writes: "Brown's reading *þe ster* fits the sense much better than Böddekker's reading *þestri,* but the latter is probably the reading of the manuscript, since the hook used to represent *er* in this manuscript is much rounder than the short vertical stroke used here. It is therefore necessary to regard the reading *þe ster* as an emendation" (p. 86).

44 ff.   *On Estermorewe . . . .* Accounts of Jesus' resurrection occur in Matthew 28, Mark 16, Luke 24, and John 20.

50–51   *When hire body to hevene cam, / The soule to the body nam.* The legend of Mary's bodily assumption into heaven appeared first in fourth-century apocryphal writings. Jacobus de Voragine discusses several versions of the story in *The Golden Legend*; see 2:77–97. Some medieval mystery cycles incorporate the story; see, for example, "The Assumption of Mary" (based on the *Golden Legend*) in *The N-Town Play, Cotton MS Vespasian D.8*, vol. 1, ed. Stephen Spector (EETS s.s. 11 [Oxford: Oxford University Press, 1991], pp. 387–409), where Jesus receives Mary's soul in heaven, then returns to earth to place it again in her uncorrupted body. The two then re-ascend incarnate into heaven among choirs of singing angels.

§78

Nou skrinketh rose ant lylie flour. Index no. 2359. MS: BL Harley 2253, fol. 80a (West Midlands, early fourteenth century). Editions: Wright, *Specimens*, p. 87; Böddekker, pp. 212 ff.; CS, no. 48; Patterson, no. 33; B14, no. 10; Brook, no. 23; Stevick, no. 31; Silverstein, no. 27, with commentary; Davies, no. 14; LH, no. 193; Sisam, *Oxford*, no. 51; Kaiser, pp. 288–89 (50 lines); Segar (part), no. 26.

The rose and the lily, traditional symbols of Mary, are here seen literally as earthly and transient; but they remind the speaker of the rose and lily who restores rather than withers, the life-giving Mary.

1   *skrinketh.* MS: *skrnketh.* Brook's emendation. Brown emends to *skrynketh.*

7   *fleysh.* The *h* is crossed with a horizontal stroke which, Brook suggests, may indicate a final *e*.

13   *folie.* Brook comments: "*folie* in Old French often means 'illicit love', and this may be the meaning here, cf. *Handlyng Synne.* vv. 12393 ff."(p. 85).

29   *We.* MS: *whe.* Brown and Brook emend.

30   *medicine.* Patterson calls attention to a line from the antiphon for Evensong: "Such a deeth underȝede the medicyn of liif" (Maskell, 2:64).

41   *his.* Sisam emends to *hir.*

51   *dude is body.* The sense might be "placed his body" instead of "died [with] his body," the implication being that Jesus as God took human form and put that body on the tree for "oure sunnes."

55–59 This is the MS reading. Brown rearranges the lines to fit the pattern of the previous stanzas:

> Thah thou be whyt and bryth on ble
> Thou thench on Godes shoures
> . . . .
> Falewen shule thy floures.
> Jesu have merci of us
> That al this world honoures.

Brook notes Brown's transposition, but comments: "there are other examples of differences of structure between the last stanza of a lyric and the other stanzas . . . and it is not necessary to assume that a line has been lost. As it stands in the manuscript v. 58 does not rhyme with any other line in the stanza, but the emendation of *us* to *me* restores the rhyme."

56   *bryth*. Brook emends to *bryht*.

58   *us*. CS and Sisam emend to *me*.

§79

In a tabernacle of a toure. Index no. 1460. MS: Bodl. 21896 (Douce 322), fols. 8b–9b (c. 1400). Other MSS: Bodl. 6943 (Ashmole 59), fol. 66a (mid-fifteenth century); Bodl. 11951 (Rawlinson C.86), fol. 69b (late fifteenth century); Bodl. 21652 (Douce 78), fol. 1b (late fifteenth century); BL Harley 1706, fol. 9b (fifteenth century); BL Addit. 37049, fol. 25b (first 11 stanzas, with illustration of Mary holding infant Christ in "tabernacle" and monk praying before them: "O Maria the flowre of virgyns clere in al oure nede oure prayer thou here") (early fifteenth century); Lambeth 853, p. 4 (8 stanzas, c. 1430); Manchester Rylands Library 18932 (Latin 395), fol. 138a (stanza 11 only, late fifteenth century); Paris Bibl. Nat. Anglais 41 (Supplément Français 819), fol. 3b (10 stanzas). Editions of Douce 322: B14, no. 132; H. S. Bennett, *Quia Amore Langueo*, with engravings by Eric Gill (London: Faber and Faber, 1937); Davies, no. 62; Stevick, no. 49; Gray, *Selection*, no. 61; Silverstein, no. 50; LH, no. 196. Editions of Addit. 37049: Bennett. Editions of Lambeth 853: F. J. Furnivall, EETS o.s. 15, pp. 177–79; *Quia Amore Langueo* (London: Carridoc Press, 1902); Philip Warner, "Quia Amore Langueo and Richard de Castre's Prayer to Jesus," *Medici Society Memorabilia* 3 (1915), 9–32; Bennett. Edition of Bibl. Nat. Anglais: S. Segawa, *The Paris Version of Quia Amore Langueo* (N.p.: Kanazawa, 1934).

Of this poem, Silverstein comments: "Mary, at once man's mother and sister, treats of love in a family tie made intense by its figurative complexity . . . which yet permits her to voice the reason for her complaint — man's flight from God — movingly as a son's neglect of a woman's yearning devotion" (p. 72). But Rosemary Woolf criticizes the "curiosity" of the use of the Canticles imagery to refer to Mary's love for humankind rather than for Christ, arguing that "the language of love-longing is not fitting to a loving mother" (302). She says: "It was customary in both devotion and literature to transfer to the Virgin what was said of Christ: this poem is an example of such a transference not succeeding" (p. 302). Compare, however, line 95, "Take me for thy wyfe and lerne to synge," with *Pearl* XIII–XIV, in which Pearl, citing

Apocalypse 14:1–5, explains that she is one of Christ's many virgin brides; marriage is, in *Pearl* and in this poem, a metaphor for spiritual devotion. For a similar poem, a *chanson d'aventure* in which Christ is the speaker, see *Index* no. 1463 (Stevick, no. 50).

1   A *tabernacle* is "a canopied niche or recess in a wall or pillar, to contain an image" (OED *tabernacle*, sb.4.b). Ashmole: *tourret.*

2   *musyng on the mone.* Typological readings provide associations between the moon and Mary; see Canticles 6:9: "Who is she that cometh forth as the morning rising, fair as the moon . . ." and the vision in Apocalypse 12:1 of a figure often associated with Mary, "a woman clothed with the sun, and the moon was under her feet." The associations could be extended: if Christ is the sun, Mary is the moon, which "sends out its light without itself losing any of its brightness, just as Mary gave birth to her Child without forfeiting her virginity. It is smaller and weaker than the sun, but as a morning star it can announce the advent of the great light, just as Mary announces Jesus" (Hirn, pp. 322–23).

3   *crouned.* Ashmole: *comly.*

4   *Apered in gostly syght ful sone.* Rawlinson: *I saw wittande high in a trone.* Lambeth: *Me thouȝte y siȝ sittinge in trone.*

8   *Quia amore langueo.* See Canticles 2:5 and 5:8.

11   *I am hys moder — I can none other.* Douce 78 and Rawlinson: *Y am his mediatrice and his modur.*

14   *Though.* Brown emends to *Through.*

15   Rawlinson and Ashmole read *me*, which Stevick adopts.

     ryse. See MED *risen*, 5.c: "to rise to a higher or more perfect moral or spiritual state; arise after a moral or spiritual fall." Compare *Cursor Mundi*, line 25745: "Bot quen we fall, ai mai we ris, For es na man sa gret mai sin . . . that he ne his merci has in hij."

18   *I love, I loke.* Rawlinson: *And busy I loke.*

21   *soule.* Rawlinson: *sonne.*

23   *my son forgave.* Rawlinson, Ashmole, Lambeth: *I forgave.*

25–40   These two stanzas are reversed in Paris and Lambeth MSS.

30   *thow stelest me fro.* In Canticles, the bride repeatedly seeks the groom but never secures him for long, as he steals away while she sleeps.

31   *Sewe:* MS: *shewe.* Brown, Gray, and Stevick emend.

        Sewe to me, synner, I thee pray. Rawlinson: *Shew to me love sonne I the pray.*

34   *nedeth hit but.* Addit. 37049: *nedys it none;* Douce 78: *nedithe hit man.*

41–48   Omitted from Paris and Lambeth MSS.

50   *Mankynde ys bette for hys trespasse.* Paris and Lambeth: *Hys body was beten for this trespas.* Stevick emends to *My child is beten for thy trespas.*

53–55   Paris and Lambeth MSS: *My son is thi fader, thi* [Paris: *his*] *modur y was / He sucked my pappe, he lufd the so / He dyed for the, my hert thou has.* The shift in point of address from *Thow* (sinner) to *Thow* (Jesus) in lines 53–54 is awkward, but it effectively dramatizes Mary's role as intercessor as she first addresses humankind and then Jesus. Addit. and Rawlinson give *thy moder* for *hys moder;* Addit. gives *thow has* for *he has.*

57   The Lambeth text ends with a stanza not found in Douce 322:

        My sone deede for thi love,   *died*
        His herte was persid with a spere
        To bringe thi soule to hevene above,
        For thi love so diede he here.
        Therfor thou must be to me moost dere,
        Sithen my sone loved thee so;
        Thou praiest to me nevere but y thee here,   *hear*
          Quia amore langueo.

62   *Why shulde I flee thee?* Douce 78, Rawlinson, Ashmole: *Why schuldest thou fle?*

        soo. MS: *loo.* Brown's emendation.

63   *I helpe*. Ashmole: *thy helpe*, which Stevick adopts.

65–72   Davies notes: "Paris MS. omits this and the last stanza but includes the intermediate stanzas in reverse order. B.L. MS. has a different version of this and the next stanza and omits the last."

70   *were me fro*. Ashmole: *were foo*.

76   *he ys myne hosprynge*. Compare §60, lines 7 ff.

79   *For hym had I thys worshippyng*. I.e., Mary's prominence — and her influence — result from what she has done for the sake of humankind.

86   *me helpe*. Douce 322: *mercy*.

87   *kepe*. Douce 322: *helpe*.

90   *thus*. MS reads *thys*; Brown and Gray emend.

92   *wynge*. Although Mary is never represented with wings, her robes function as shelter as a bird's wings might to her chicks. She is sometimes depicted as *Mater Misericordia*, with her mantle spread open to shelter Christians (see, for example, Plate C in this volume). John V. Fleming discusses this tradition in light of a thirteenth-century legend of a Cistercian monk who goes to heaven and sees none of his brothers; Mary opens her mantle and reveals a host of them, held close ("The Summoner's Prologue: An Iconographic Adjustment," *Chaucer Review* 2 [1967], 95–107).

94   *Thys heritage ys tayled; sone, come therto*. Davies glosses: "This inheritance is for yourself and your heirs — come quickly into it."

95   *wyfe*. Douce 78: *modure*.

§80

Upon a lady my love ys lente. *Index* no. 3836. MS: BL Cotton Caligula A.2, fol. 91a (early fifteenth century). Editions: Wright and Halliwell, 2:255–56; Wülcker, 2:7; B15, no. 48; LH, no. 188.

Notes

This poem exemplifies the dedicated lover trope that is often brought into Marian lyrics. The first six stanzas declare the lover's erotic commitment to his beloved in all its exclusive intensity: she is the stabilizing force in his life, and his love for her dominates his desire, his heart, his strength, his vows. She is worthy of his complete devotion, gentle and meek, ready to serve, and attentive, and courteous. Mary is never named; her identity is only hinted at in her mothering (line 15) and in the range of her service (not just for a man, but for women and children too, line 19). She is revealed only in the last stanza as the supreme mediatrix between human needs and desires and God, through whom eroticism is transmuted to *charyté* (line 29).

11   *vowes*. MS: *vowe*. Brown emends for the sake of rhyme.

14   *well*. The speaker puns on *well* and *weál*: the lady in love poems is often the lover's *well* — his place of drink, nurture, and sustenance. She is also his *weal* — his sense of abundance, prosperity, being, wealth, and domain.

17   *nyght*. MS: *nygh*.

§81

Maiden in the mor lay. Index no. 2037.5. MS: Bodl. 13679 (Rawlinson D.913), item 1b (early fourteenth century). Editions: R. L. Greene, "The Maid of the Moor in the *Red Book of Ossory*," *Speculum* 27 (1952), 504; Heuser, "Fragmente von Unbekanntenn Spielmannsliedern des 14.Jahrhunderts, aus MS. Rawl. D. 913," *Anglia* 30 (1907), 175; Sisam, *Fourteenth Century*, no. 188; R. H. Robbins, *Secular Lyrics*, no. 18; Auden and Pearson, 1:26; Kaiser, p. 471; Hughes and Abraham, p. 119; Speirs, p. 62; Davies, no. 33; Stevick, no. 38; Reiss, p. 98; Wilhelm, no. 277.

D. W. Robertson, Jr., reads this as a Marian poem ("Historical Criticism" in *English Institute Essays 1950*, ed. Alan S. Downer [New York: Columbia University Press, 1951] pp. 26–27); his interpretations are indicated in the notes below. R. J. Schoeck (*TLS*, June 8, 1951, 357), concurred with Robertson. This reading has been opposed by a number of critics, however, most notably E. Talbot Donaldson (who, however, allows that medieval audiences might have thought of Mary, "the paramount innocent maiden," in connection with the poem) in "Patristic Exegesis in the Criticism of Medieval Literature," *Critical Approaches to Medieval Literature*, ed. Dorothy Bethurum (New York: Columbia University Press, 1960), pp. 21–24. E. M. W. Tillyard argued instead that the maiden might be Mary Magdalene or Mary of Egypt (*TLS*, May 11, 1951, p. 293; see also David Fowler *A Literary History of the Popular Ballad* [Durham: Duke University Press, 1968], pp. 113–14). Others believe the poem has no

Christian significance at all. When Greene found the opening line as an incipit indicating the tune for a Latin hymn (*Peperit virgo,* a Marian roundel, for which Greene prints the full text) in the Red Book of Ossory (see "The Maid of the Moor in the *Red Book of Ossory*," *Speculum* 27 [1952], 504–06), he argued that the Bishop of Ossory had composed the Latin hymn in order to replace the "profane" words with a sacred text. Dronke (pp. 195–96) argues that the moor-maiden is a version of German water sprite who sometimes takes human form and mingles with young men at village dances. Speirs argues that we need not know who the maiden is, but he points toward a tradition of well-worship in the Middle Ages and suggests that the maiden might be "the spirit of the well-spring," a fertility symbol (p. 63). For further criticism, see Mahmoud Manzalaoui, "*Maiden in the Mor Lay* and the Apocrypha," *Notes and Queries* 210 (1965), 91–92; Siegfried Wenzel, "The Moor Maiden — a Contemporary View," *Speculum* 49 (1974), 69–74; and Ronald Waldron, "'Maiden in the Mor Lay' and the Religious Imagination," *Unisa English Studies* 29 (1991), 8–12.

1   *mor.* Robertson: "The moor is the wilderness of the world under the Old Law before Christ came" (p. 27).

3   *Sevenyst.* Robertson: "The number seven indicates life on earth, but life in this instance went on at night, or before the Light of the World dawned. The day is this light, or Christ, who said 'I am the day.'" And it appears appropriately after seven nights, or, as it were, on the count of eight, for eight is also a figure of Christ" (p. 27). The *dies octavus* designates Easter and the Resurrection after the time of darkness under the Old Law. See glosses on Matthew 28:1; Mark 16:2; Luke 24:1; and John 20:1 in the *CA.*

8   *was.* MS: *wat.* Robbins' emendation.

10   *primerole.* Robertson: "The primrose is not a Scriptural sign, but a figure of fleshly beauty. We are told three times that the primrose was the food of this maiden, and only after this suspense are we also told that she ate or embodied the violet, which is a Scriptural sign of humility" (p. 27).

14   *violet.* See note to line 10.

15   MS omits *was hire dryng.* As supplied by Robbins.

17   *water.* Robertson: "The maiden drank the cool water of God's grace" (p. 27). The well is a natural symbol of life and rebirth; compare §53, note to line 5.

17–20   Robbins supplies these lines, abbreviated in MS.

22   *bour*. Robertson: "her bower consisted of the roses of martyrdom or charity and the lilies of purity with which late medieval and early Renaissance artists sometimes adorned pictures of the Blessed Virgin Mary, and, indeed, she is the Maiden in the Moor, the maiden who was at once the most beautiful of all women and the divinity whose humility made her the most accessible of all saints" (p. 27).

24–27   Robbins supplies these lines, abbreviated in MS.

§82

Lulley, lulley, lully, lulley (The Corpus Christi Carol). *Index* no. 1132: *He bare hym up, he bare hym down.* MS: Balliol College Oxford 354, fol. 165b (c. 1500?). Editions: Ewald Flügel, "Liedersammlungen," *Anglia* 26 (1903), 175; Ewald Flügel, *Neuenglische Lesebuch* (Halle: Niemeyer, 1895), p. 142; CS, no. 81; R. Dyboski, *Songs, Carols and Other Miscellaneous Poems from Balliol MS. 354,* EETS e.s. 101 (1908; rpt. Millwood, NY: Kraus, 1973), p. 103; John J. Manly, *English Prose and Poetry (1137–1892)* (Boston: Gill, 1907), p. 94; Cook, p. 440; W. W. Greg, *Review of English Studies* 13 (1937), 88; *EEC*, no. 322A; Rickert, p. 193; Charles Williams, ed., *New Book of English Verse* (New York: Macmillan, 1936), p. 112; Niles, *Carol Study Book*, p. 35; Gilchrist (see below), p. 35; Segar, no. 11; Greene, *Medium Aevum* 29 (1960), 10–11; Chambers, p. 11; Mason, p. 146; Greene, *Selection*, no. 67a; Speirs, pp. 76–77; Davies, no. 164; Fowler, p. 58; Oliver, p. 108; Gray, *Themes*, p. 164; Sisam, *Oxford*, p. 524; William Tydeman, *English Poetry 1400–1580* (London: Heinemann Educational, 1970), p. 53; Geoffrey Grigson, *The Faber Book of Popular Verse* (London: Faber and Faber, 1971), p. 308; Manning, pp. 115–16; Stevick, no. 99; Burrow, p. 303. Selected criticism: Greene's survey of interpretations (*EEC*, pp. 423–27) is indispensable. See also Annie G. Gilchrist, *Journal of the Folk-Song Society* 4 (1910), 52–66 [associates the poem with the grail legend]; Greene, "The Meaning of the Corpus Christi Carol," *Medium Aevum* 29 (1960), 10–21 [argues that the poem refers to Catherine of Aragon and Anne Boleyn, whose badge was the falcon]; and Stephen Manning, pp. 115–18 [reads the poem as Marian]. Greene, *Selection,* prints two nineteenth-century versions in which the Marian reading is explicit. On the riddling nature of the poem, see Peck, pp. 466–67.

2   *fawcon*. Some have interpreted the falcon as death, which meaning Greene believes is unlikely; see *EEC*, p. 246.

4   *brown*. Greene notes that "brown" may simply mean "dark," though it could suggest "autumnal" or "dying." *Brown* can mean "shining," however — see MED n.3 and adj.5 in its OE etymology — though usually that sense is restricted to armor and weapons, not orchards.

6   *purpill and pall*. Both designate a rich, perhaps royal, cloth; purple is the color of royalty.

§83

Of on that is so fayr and bright. Index no. 2645. MS: BL Egerton 613, fol. 2a (thirteenth century). Also in Trinity College Cambridge 323 (B.14.39), fol. 24b. Editions of Egerton: Wright and Halliwell, 1:89–90; Mätzner, 1:53; Morris, EETS o.s. 49, pp. 194–95; CS, no. 46; Cook, p. 457; Segar, no. 33; Patterson, no. 32; B13, no. 17b; Kaiser, p. 285; William O. Wehrle, *The Macaronic Hymn Tradition in Medieval English Literature* (Washington: Catholic University of America, 1933), pp. 30–31; *EEC*, no. 191Ba; Bruce Dickins and R. M. Wilson, eds., *Early Middle English Texts* (Cambridge: Bowes and Bowes, 1951), pp. 125–26; Davies, no. 5; Stevick, no. 11; James J. Wilhelm, *Medieval Song* (New York: Dutton, 1971), p. 349; Karl Reichl, *Religiöse Dichtung im Englischen Hochmittelalter* (Munich: Wilhelm Fink, 1973), p. 293; Gray, *Selection*, no. 7; Bennett and Smithers, *Early Middle English Verse and Prose*, pp. 129 ff.; Sisam, *Oxford*, no. 13; Wilhelm, *Lyrics*, no. 272. Edition of Trinity: B13, no. 17a.

The stanzas are printed according to Greene's reading of margin instructions, which matches the order given in the Trinity MS. For a fifteenth-century version of this carol, see *EEC*, no. 191A.

5   Trinity: *I crie be grace of the.*

10   *flour*. Trinity: *best.*

10–18   This is stanza 4 in the Egerton MS, marked to move to the present location.

18   *Es effecta*. "You are the effect" (i.e., the best ever made, the ultimate creation, through which God Himself would be born).

19–27   This is stanza 2 in the Egerton MS, marked to move to the present location.

20   *Felix fecundata.* Stevick suggests an allusion to Elizabeth's greeting of the pregnant Mary to gloss: "i.e., blessed is the fruit of thy womb" (p. 15), though there is no direct verbal connection: *Benedicta ta inter mulieres, et benedictus fructus ventris tui* (Luke 1:42).

21   *Of.* Trinity: *To.*

23   *Bisek.* Trinity: *Bihold.*

29   *Eva.* Trinity: *Thoru Eva.*

30   Trinity: *To forn that Jhesu was iborn.*

32   *With.* Trinity: *Thorou.*

34   *Salutis.* "Of Salvation," from *salus, salut/are, -arium,* but with a possible pun in the fifteenth century on "greeting" or "salutation," the effect being that with *Ave* (line 32), dark night goes away and *Salutis* ("Voilà" or "Hello"), the day comes; in which case *The welle* in line 35 is a "well of light" as well as a spring of virtue (*Virtutis,* line 36); likewise, in line 37, a possible pun on son/sun along with connotations of light in *blis / Superni* (lines 42–43), and of darkness in *Inferni* (line 45).

37   *he.* Trinity: *thou.*

41   Trinity: *So god and so milde.*

42   *He havet brout ous.* Trinity: *He bringet us alle.*

§84

Adam lay ibowndyn. Index no. 117. MS: BL Sloane 2593, fol. 11a (c. 1450). Editions: Wright, *Songs* (Warton Club), p. 32; Wülcker, 2:8; Fehr, *Archiv* 109, p. 51; CS, no. 50; B15, no. 83; Davies, no. 71; Stevick, no. 53; LH, no. 164; Rickert, p. 163; Manning, p. 6; Cecil, p. 18; Charles Williams, *The New Book of English Verse* (1936; rpt. Miami: Granger Books, 1978), p. 23; Auden and Pearson, 1:27; Chambers, p. 91; Kaiser, p. 290; Silverstein, no. 70; Burrow, p. 300. Selected criticism: Speirs, pp. 65–66; Manning, pp. 6–7; Woolf, pp. 290–91; Reiss, pp. 139–42.

1   *Adam*. The Hebrew name means "man"; Adam's bondage to sin symbolizes that of all humankind.

2   *Fowre thowsand wynter*. Gray: "A traditional estimate. In *Paradiso* xxvi Adam tells Dante that he spent 4,302 years in Limbo; in the York play of the *Harrowing of Hell* (lines 39–40) he says that he has been there for 4,600 years. According to F. Vigouroux, *Dictionnaire de la Bible*, s.v. 'Chronologie Biblique', there are some two hundred early attempts to date the creation of Adam from the chronological indications in the Hebrew and Septuagint versions of the Old Testament" (*Selection*, p. 98). See also C. A. Patrides, "Renaissance Estimates of the Year of Creation," *Huntington Library Quarterly* 26 (1963), 315–22.

3   Gray calls attention to the first stanza of a carol found in MS Sloane 2593:

> Adam our fader was in blis
> And for an appil of lytil prys
> He loste the blysse of Paradys
>   *Pro sua superbia.*   *For his pride*
>   (*EEC*, no. 68)

5–8   The *felix culpa* ("happy Fall") idea expressed here echoes these lines from the *Praeconium*, a hymn for Easter Eve: *O certe necessarium Adae peccatum: quod Christi morte deletum est. / O felix culpa: quae talem ac tantum meruit habere redemptorem.* ["O truly necessary sin of Adam, which was blotted out by the death of Christ. / O happy guilt, which was meet to have such and so great a redeemer"] (Frederick Brittain, ed. *The Penguin Book of Latin Verse* [Baltimore: Penguin, 1962], p. 94). On the background of the concept, see Arthur O. Lovejoy, "Milton and the Paradox of the Fortunate Fall," *ELH* 4 (1937), 161–79. In this poem, the cause for celebration is not humankind's redemption, but Mary's queenship; the contrast is between Adam and Mary rather than Adam and Jesus.

§85

Swete and benygne moder and may. By William Huchen. *Index* no. 3228. MS: New College Oxford 320, fol. 44b (c. 1460). Editions: Furnivall, EETS o.s. 15, pp. 291–92; Patterson, no. 69; Paul Sauerstein, *Charles d'Orléans und die Englische Bersetzung seiner Dichtungen*, (Halle: E. Karras, 1899), p. 47.

Notes

2   *Turtill trew.* Patterson writes, "This epithet is not found in the English liturgy, nor in English religious lyric poetry before Chaucer. The expression was extremely popular, however, in French poetry" (p. 196). The figure may originate in Canticles (Song of Solomon), where the bride is referred to through dove metaphors.

20   *Empres of helle.* See note to §56, line 10.

22–23   *Stormys . . . do assayle.* Patterson calls attention to St. Bernard's second homily on the Virgin Mary: "O you, whoever you are, who feel that in the tidal wave of this world you are nearer to being tossed about among the squalls and gales than treading on dry land, if you do not want to founder in the tempest, do not avert your eyes from the brightness of this star [Mary, the 'sea star']. When the wind of temptation blows up within you, when you strike upon the rock of tribulation, gaze up at this star, call out to Mary" (*Homilies*, p. 30).

§86

O hie emperice and quene celestiall. Possibly by William Dunbar, but ascribed to Chaucer in this MS. (It is written in an eight-line stanza form that resembles that of The Monk's Tale.) *Index* no. 2461. MS: Bodl. 3354 (Arch. Selden B.24), fols. 137b–38a (late fifteenth century). Also in National Library of Scotland 16500 (Asloan), fol. 292a (first five stanzas, c. 1515); transcript of Asloan, Edinburgh University 521. Edition of Arch. Selden: B15 no 13. Edition of Asloan: Craigie, pp. 245–46; Laing, Supplement, p. 305.

6   *floure.* Asloan: *barne.*

7   *spue.* Asloan: *spyce.*

8   *clerare than cristall.* See note to §50, line 13.

14   *path.* Asloan: *pace.*

17   *fillit.* Asloan: *fulfillit.*

28   *Anournyt.* Asloan: *Adorned.*

33   *Leviathan.* For a description of this creature, see Job 40:20–41:25 (RSV 41:1–34). See also Isaias 27:1: "In that day the Lord with his hard, and great, and strong sword

shall visit leviathan the bar serpent, and leviathan the crooked serpent, and shall slay the whale that is in the sea."

33   *serpent.* MS: *spent.* Brown's emendation.

34   *parenes.* Asloan: *paran.*

        prothoplaust. OED *protoplast*[1] cites another use of this form in Giles Du Wes' 1532 introduction to the French language: "Comyng from God to the firste father or prothoplauste . . . ."

36–37   The penalty for Adam and Eve's sin was death; see Genesis 3:19.

§87

Glade us, maiden, moder milde. Index no. 912. MS: Trinity College Cambridge 323 (B.14.39) fols. 28b–29a (c. 1250). Edition: B13 no. 22.

This is a literal rendering of the Latin hymn *Gaude virgo, mater Christi.* In the MS the Middle English text alternates stanza by stanza with the Latin. The Latin hymn reads:

Gaude virgo, mater Christi,   Gaude, quae post Christum scandis
quae per aurem concepisti   et est honor tibi grandis
    Gabriele nuntio: in coeli palatio,
gaude, quia deo plena   ubi fructus ventris tui
peperisti sine poena   per te detur nobis frui
    cum pudoris lilio.   in perenni gaudio.

Gaude, quia tui nati,
quem dolebas mortem pati,
    fulget resurrectio:
gaude Christo ascendente
in coelum, qui te vidente
    motu fertur proprio.

F. J. Mone, p. 162, provides a transcription of the Latin; he emends the order of *detur nobis* in line 17 to *nobis detu*, and notes that the second stanza in Trinity 323 is a conflation of the last three lines of the second stanza and the first three lines of the third stanza of what appears as the first four stanzas of the Latin hymn he transcribes. The Middle English translation follows the rhyme scheme of the Latin. The hymn in three stanzas appears as Prosa i in *Die Martis: Ad Magnificat* in Dreves and Blume, 24.57. Dreves and Blume's source reads: *Gaude, quod post ipsum scandis* in line 13, and, line 11, *Et in soelum*; otherwise the hymn is identical to that found in Trinity 323. The opening three lines of the hymn occur in about a dozen other Latin hymns, with some running to eleven or twelve stanzas (see the *Index* to Guido Maria Dreves and Clemens Blume, *Analecta hymnica medii aevi*, ed. Max Lütolf *et al* [Bern: Francke, 1978]). Brown notes that another English lyric based on this Latin poem appears in Sloane MS 2593, fol. 10a. See §5, above, for comparisons.

1   *Glade us.* The poem enumerates the five joys of Mary, recalling her gladness at the Annunciation, Nativity, Resurrection, Ascension, and Assumption.

2   *herre.* The Holy Spirit approaches in a beam of light as Gabriel speaks to the Virgin. That she receives the divine insemination through the ear suggests that she is meditating upon the Word, which is as painless as having a bright idea (see lines 5 and 15). For a discussion of Mary's conception through her ear, see *DBT*, p. 43. Warner mentions this specific poem as her example of the aural divine conception (p. 37).

3   *Gabriel he seide it thee.* See the first five poems in this volume and Chaucer's *ABC*, lines 114–15, for further instances in which the Holy Spirit works in conjunction with Gabriel as Mary conceives at the Annunciation.

4   *ful of gode thine.* The *deo plena*, like the *gratia plena* of the *Ave*, here becomes "full of you [Mary's] goodness/God" The trope of fullness implies that Mary is God's chosen vessel, like the *vas electonis* St. Paul describes of himself when God fills him with the Holy Spirit in Acts 9:15.

5   *thu bere buten pine.* See note to §15, line 3.

6   *lilie of chasteté.* On the lily as sign of chastity, see Ferguson, pp. 33–34.

9–10   *up aros* refers to the Resurrection; *up stey* alludes to the Ascension.

12   *clos.* MED cites this line for its gloss on *clos* n. 3 as a designation for a dwelling place or apartment; or, with regard to God, the mansion of heaven (Christ's abode).

15   *in thi paleis.* The poet imagines Mary watching, as Queen of Heaven, from her palace on high, over all who are under her aegis.

17   *fonden*. This word is rich with resonances germane to its context — the sense being "to encounter"; "to become acquainted with, or involved with"; "to discover or to learn through experience"; "to procure, support, or maintain"; "to ascertain" — all of which heighten the sense of Mary as mediatrix between mankind's ignorance and the endless joy in Christ.

§88

Marye, mayde mylde and fre. Index no. 2107. MS: BL Addit. 17376, fols. 204b–05b (mid-fourteenth century). The poem appears among a group of poems ascribed to William of Shoreham, but a note following this poem suggests that it is a translation of a piece by Robert Grosseteste (see Konrath [below], p. xiii). Editions: Thomas Wright, *Poems of William de Shoreham*, Percy Society 28 (London: T. Richards, 1851), pp. 131–34; M. Konrath, *The Poems of William of Shoreham*, EETS e.s. 86 (London: Kegan Paul, 1902), pp. 127–29; B14, no. 32; Davies, no. 34; LH, no. 195.

2   *Chambre*. See Psalm 19:5 (the sun like a bridegroom leaving his chamber) and compare §56, line 2, and §57, line 5.

5   *fet onclene*. MS: *fet un onclene*, with *un* marked for deletion.

5–6   The *Fasciculus morum* relates one version of a relevant popular legend: "There is a story about a cleric who was lustful and yet very devout in the worship of God and the Blessed Virgin. The Blessed Virgin appeared to him, carrying a sweet drink in a dirty dish, and offered it to him to drink. As he said that he could not do so because of the stench of the dish, the Blessed Virgin replied: 'Just so do your prayers not please me nor my son as long as the vessel from which they come is tainted'" (p. 35). For other versions of this story, occurring in collections of Miracles of the Virgin, see H. L. D. Ward, *Catalogue of Romances in the Department of Manuscripts in the British Museum* (London: Trustees of the British Museum, 1893), 2:651, 665, 669, 672.

10   *Wythoute . . . sore*. See note to line 19.

13   *colvere of Noe*. See Genesis 8:11.

19   *bosche of Synay*. See Exodus 3:2 ff. Mary is often figured as the burning bush in which God appeared to Moses, e.g., Chaucer's The Pardoner's Tale (*CT* VIII.467) and the *Biblia Pauperum* Nativity leaf (Plate A), which juxtaposes Moses and the burning

Notes

bush (left) and Aaron's flowering rod (right), mentioned in lines 27–28. The *Biblia Pauperum* Nativity plate also cites Exodus 3:2 and Numbers 17:8, and adds a verse at the bottom of the plate which reads "*Absque dolore paris Virgo Maria maris*" (Labriola and Smeltz translate: "You gave birth, O Virgin, without pain"); compare line 10 of this poem.

20   *rytte Sarray.* Abraham's true wife; see Genesis 16 for the story of Sarai and her handmaid Agar, who gives birth to Abraham's son.

22   *calenge.* Konrath rejects the OED definition, "accusation, charge, reproach, objection," preferring "claim": "after the lapse of Adam, the Devil laid his claim upon sinful mankind, from which Mary released us by giving birth to our redeemer" (p. 236).

24   *of Davyes kende.* On Mary's presumed kinship with David, see note to §1, line 7, and compare §8, lines 41–42.

25   *slinge . . . ston.* See 1 Kings (RSV 1 Samuel) 17:49.

27–28   *yerd . . . spryngynde.* See Numbers 17:8.

28   *Me dreye isegh spryngynde.* I read *Me* as a dative of agency (as in "methinks"). Luria and Hoffman gloss the line "Which though dry was seen bringing forth a shoot."

31   *temple Salomon.* See 3 Kings (RSV 1 Kings) 5:1–6:38.

32   Mary is often compared to Gideon's fleece wet with dew; see note to §8, line 26.

33–36   See Luke 2:22–35.

41   *lef.* Konrath emends to *luf.*

42   *wylle.* Perhaps *well.* Konrath argues that *come* must rhyme with *bynome* in line 40, and must therefore be the verb. It follows that *wylle* is a noun, "well," or fountain (pp. 236–37). He connects this well to the story of Judith (compare line 37), in which Holofernes cuts off the water supply in Bethulia and prevents access to the wells, and Judith opens the wells and saves the city by beheading Holofernes.

43   *Hester*. Jeffrey writes: "St. Anthony had built on the story of Esther and Assuere a complex of prefiguration for the relationship between Christ and Mary (and between Christ and the Church) in which Esther's finding favor with Assuere (Esther 5:2) foreshadows the way in which God shows favor to Mary. Christ is the Assuere who crowns Esther in Esther 2:15–17, the Blessed Virgin" (*DBT*, p. 237).

45   *Thee*. MS: *they*. Brown's emendation.

46   *he*. Konrath: "read *the*?"

49–52   See Ezekiel 44:2. This passage is picked up as a sign of the Virgin Mary in the Annunciation plate of the *Biblia Pauperum*, where the scroll reads "This gate shall be shut, and it shall not be opened."

52   *yschet fram manne*. I.e., perpetually a virgin. The verse on the scroll at the bottom of the *Biblia Pauperum* Annunciation leaf reads *"Virgo salutatur innupta manens gravidatur"* (Labriola and Smeltz translate: "the Virgin is saluted; she is impregnated remaining a virgin").

55–56   See Daniel 2:34–35, 45.

57   *Emaus*. The road outside Jerusalem on which Jesus appeared to two of his followers after his Resurrection. See Luke 24:13–35.

60   *wan yspeketh*. MS: *wany speketh*. So emended by Konrath and Brown. See Isaias 7:14.

63–66   The unicorn is a symbol often affiliated with the Virgin Mary, interpreted as an allegory of the Annunciation and Christ's incarnation. According to legend, the unicorn could not be captured by force, but would come willingly to lay its head in the lap of a virgin.

65   *ytamed*. MS: *ytamend*, with *n* marked for deletion.

67–70   *Ine the Apocalyps*. . . . See Apocalypse 12:1. This image is often depicted in Books of Hours; see, for example, Plate B in this volume, "The Assumption of the Virgin — Compline" from *The Hours of Catherine of Cleves*.

69   *mone*. MS: *mowe*. Brown's emendation. Konrath emends to *mow[n]e*.

71   *Swyl.* Konrath emends to *Swych.*

        nas nevere non. Compare §13, "I syng of a myden," line 18.

73 ff. On the metaphor of sunlight through glass, see note to §17, lines 18–20.

§89

Ros Mary, most of vertewe virginall. Attributed to William Dunbar. *Index* no. 2831.8. MS: National Library of Scotland 16500 (Asloan), fol. 301a (c. 1515). Other MSS: Edinburgh University Library 205 (Laing III 149, the Makculloch MS), fol. 183b (early sixteenth century); BL Harley 1703, fol. 79b (late sixteenth century) with eight stanzas (printed by Mackenzie) and several additional stanzas by William Forrest. Lines 1–40 appear inside a bifolium of the binding of Advocates 18.5.14 (a late fifteenth-century MS of Boethius' *Consolation of Philosophy*). Editions of Asloan: Laing, Supplement, pp. 283–84; John Small, *The Poems of William Dunbar,* STS 4 (Edinburgh: William Blackwood and Sons, 1884), pp. 272–73; Schipper, *Poems,* pp. 372–74; Schipper, *Denkschriften,* 69–72; H. B. Baildon, *The Poems of William Dunbar* (Cambridge: Cambridge University Press, 1907), pp. 197–98; Craigie, pp. 271–72. Edition of Makculloch: George Stevenson, *Pieces from the Makculloch and the Gray MSS. Together with The Chepman and Myllar Prints,* STS 65 (1918), pp. 24–25. Editions of Harley: MacCracken, "New Stanzas by Dunbar," *Modern Language Notes* 24 (1909), 110–11; Mackenzie, pp. 175–77. Edition of Advocates: Ian C. Cunningham, "Two Poems on the Virgin (National Library of Scotland, Adv. MS 18.5.14)," *Edinburgh Bibliographical Society Transactions* 5 (1988), 36–38.

4   *for.* MS: *wes.* Emended from Makculloch.

5   *refute.* Harley: *truyt.*

        of. Advocates: *and.*

        of mercy spring and well. A common fifteenth-century image of Mary, the well symbolizes new life. See note to §53, line 5.

6   *chois.* Harley: *cheeif.*

7   *of paradys. Of* omitted in Advocates and Harley.

10   *circulyne.* Advocates: *cristallyn.* Harley and Makculloch: *chrystallyne.*

12   *angell ordouris nyne.* See note to §51, line 2.

13   *Haile.* Other MSS: *O.*

18   *but curis criminale.* If *but* is a conjunction, the meaning is "but heals criminals." But compare the syntax in §91, lines 22 and 31, where *but* means "without."

      curis. Harley and Makculloch: *crymes.*

20   *Tartar.* The devil is here compared to Genghis Khan and his successors. Harley: *terrour.*

22   *wicht.* Omitted in Advocates.

      Sampson. See Judges 13:2–16:31. Sampson prefigures Christ; he is shown on the *Biblia Pauperum* Resurrection leaf (·i·) "having unhinged the gates of Gaza, one of which he carries across his left shoulder; the other gate is under his right arm" (Labriola and Smeltz, p. 172).

22–23 In Harley, these lines read: "Illustrat lyllye, to thee Ladye I saye, / Withe infynyte Aveis, Hayle, floure of women all!"

23   *Beliale.* Another name for the devil.

25–31 An allusion to the harrowing of hell, a story found in the fourth-century apocryphal Gospel of Nicodemus and based on suggestions in Matthew 27:52–53, Luke 23:43, and 1 Peter 3:18–20 that Jesus descended into hell between his death and his resurrection.

26   *in to stowr.* Advocates: *schoir.* Makculloch: *stowr.*

30   *Syne.* Advocates, Makculloch: *he.*

31   *all.* Omitted in Advocates.

34   *moder myld.* Advocates: *myld moder.*

37   *bled his blude apon a tre.* Advocates: *lyis bludy bled on ye tre.*

§90

All haile, lady, mother, and virgyn immaculate. Index no. 181. MS: BL Addit. 20059, fol. 98b (this poem is a fifteenth-century addition to an earlier MS). Edition: B15, no. 12.

3   *clarified cristall.* See note to §50, line 13.

5   *yssue.* The word is difficult to gloss. It clearly refers to birth, or to giving birth, but according to Christian theology, Mary does not give birth to the Holy Spirit, nor does the Holy Spirit give birth to Jesus. This line is nevertheless an allusion to Matthew 1:18 ("she was found to be with child by the Holy Spirit") and Luke 1:35 ("The Holy Spirit shall come upon thee").

9   *hye.* Added above line.

12   *solempnysaunte.* See MED *solempnisen* (v.) and *solempnising* (ger.); the word suggests an occasion of ceremonial dignity and celebration, and the sense here is that the nativity (Mary's rather than Christ's, here — the Feast of the Nativity of Mary is September 8 in the Sanctorale) is an important and joyful Church feast.

14   *verum solem.* Multiple readings are possible: "the true sun"; "the one truth"; or "the truth alone."

16   I.e., the Annunciation signaled and foretold our redemption.

§91

Hale, sterne superne. By William Dunbar. *Index* no. 1082.5. MS: National Library of Scotland 16500 (Asloan), fols. 303a–04b (c. 1515). Editions: Laing, 1:239–42; John Small, *The Poems of William Dunbar*, STS 4, pp. 269–71; J. Schipper, *The Poems of William Dunbar* (Vienna: Kaiserliche Akademie der Wissenschaften, 1891), pp. 369–71; Schipper, *Denkschriften*, pp. 67–69; G. Gregory Smith, *Specimens of Middle Scots* (Edinburgh: William Blackwood and Sons, 1902), pp. 14–17; Baildon, *The Poems of William Dunbar* (Cambridge: Cambridge

University Press, 1907), pp. 195–97; Craigie, pp. 275–78; Mackenzie, pp. 160–62; James Kinsley, *The Poems of William Dunbar* (Oxford: Clarendon Press, 1958), pp. 8–9 (three stanzas); Davies, no. 144 (three stanzas).

11   *Yerne us guberne.* The syntax is not clear here. Laing glosses "Move us, govern"; Schipper glosses "Earnestly govern us"; and Smith suggests the present reading.

14   *Alphais.* See Apocalypse 1:8: "'I am the Alpha and the Omega, the beginning and the end,' says the Lord God, 'who is and who was and who is coming, the Almighty.'"

15   *dyng.* A form of *digne,* "worthy."

31   *plicht but sicht. Plicht* suggests a pledge or guarantee; *but sicht*, "without sight" or "without visible evidence."

34   *nychttingale.* The Latin Bestiary identifies the nightingale as *Lucina*, suggesting that she "takes this name because she is accustomed to herald the dawn of a new day with her song, as a lamp does (*Lucerna*)." She is ever watchful, tempering the "sleepless labour of her long night's work by the sweetness of her song," cherishing her brood "not less by her sweet tones than by the heat of her body" (T. H. White, *The Book of Beasts, Being a Translation from a Latin Bestiary of the Twelfth Century* [London: Jonathan Cape, 1954], pp. 139–40). As a light in darkness and harbinger of day and as a hard-working mother careful of the spiritual and physical welfare of her brood, she is an apt emblem of Mary, who tirelessly sustains and guides weary mankind (lines 35–36).

41   *Haile, clene bedene ay till conteyne.* Schipper glosses: "Hail to thee quickly, thou pure one, and to continue forever." Or perhaps *conteyne* suggests a vessel, as in Acts 9:15, where Saul is described as God's *vas electionis*; this reading implies that Mary is God's chosen instrument, perpetually in service but perpetually clean, proclaimed (*bedene*) ever to enclose. See MED *conteinen*, v.1.a: "c 1390 *Psalt. Mariae* (1) 1210: Whos wombe is maad wiþ mylde steuene, Conteyning þat is content [L continens contentum]."

43   *grene daseyne.* Mackenzie writes: "'Green' probably represents a Latin adjective, such as *florens.* 'Daisy' as 'The emperice and floure of floures all' (Chaucer, *Legend of Good Women,* l. 184)" (p. 277).

Notes

50   *swetar be sic sevyne.* In biblical imagery, the number seven often suggests perfection or completion.

56   *oddis eveyne.* See note to line 58. If we are like odd numbers, seven and eleven, our lot is a gamble; but if Mary makes all even, then we are secure.

58   *ellevyn.* Schipper traces the word to *élever*, "extolled," but Mackenzie argues that the number eleven is arbitrary, "apparently to serve the rhyme" (p. 277). If it is "eleven," the resonance perhaps derives from the odd/even figure in line 56, and is idiomatic like "seven come eleven." The key to reading the passage is *lowde.* If it is disyllabic, then Schipper's interpretation pertains; if monosyllabic, then the numerological reading seems inevitable. If rhyme affects sense, the idea of resounding Mary's name forever (line 60) is perhaps best enhanced by *ellevyn* with *Ave Maria* loudly extolled.

72   *grayne.* I.e., Christ. See note to §8, lines 25 ff. Citing John Jamieson, Schipper notes that *grayne* may refer to "the branch of a tree, the stem of a plant"; such a reading would evoke the "rod of Jesse" image (see note to §8, line 17).

73   *Imperiall wall.* Mary is a bulwark, a palatial haven. Compare Canticles 8:9–10, where the bride is described as a wall, and Chaucer's The Second Nun's Tale, which describes Mary's "cloistre blisful of thy sydis" (*CT* VIII[G]43). The architecture here is in terms of the first estate rather than Chaucer's second.

80   *Fulfillit of angell fude.* According to the apocryphal legend recorded in the Book of James 8:1, the child Mary lives in the Temple and receives her food from angels (Schneemelcher, p. 429). The line might also imply that in pregnancy Mary is full of the food (Christ/the Eucharist) for Angels and humankind.

Appendices: Chaucer's Marian Lyrics

Appendix A: An ABC[1]

Incipit carmen secundum ordinem litterarum alphabeti.

Almighty and al merciable queene,
To whom that al this world fleeth for socour,
To have relees of sinne, of sorwe, and teene,
Glorous virgine, of alle floures flour,
5   To thee I flee, confounded in errour.
Help and releeve, thou mighti debonayre,
Have mercy on my perilous langour.
Venquisshed me hath my cruel adversaire.

Bountee so fix hath in thin herte his tente
10   That wel I wot thou wolt my socour bee;
Thou canst not warne him that with good entente
Axeth thin helpe, thin herte is ay so free.
Thou art largesse of pleyn felicitee,
Haven of refut, of quiete, and of reste.
15   Loo, how that theeves sevene chasen mee.
Help, lady bright, er that my ship tobreste.

Comfort is noon but in yow, ladi deere;
For loo, my sinne and my confusioun,
Which oughten not in thi presence appeere,
20   Han take on me a greevous accioun
Of verrey right and desperacioun;
And as bi right thei mighten wel susteene

---

[1] Ed. R. T. Lenaghan. Rpt. With permission from Larry D. Benson (editor), *The Riverside Chaucer*, third ed. © 1987 by Houghton Mifflin Company.

That I were wurthi my dampnacioun,
Nere merci of you, blisful hevene queene.

25   Dowte is ther noon, thou queen of misericorde,
      That thou n'art cause of grace and merci heere;
      God vouched sauf thurgh thee with us to accorde.
      For certes, Crystes blisful mooder deere,
      Were now the bowe bent in swich maneere
30   As it was first of justice and of ire,
      The rightful God nolde of no mercy heere;
      But thurgh thee han we grace as we desire.

      Evere hath myn hope of refut been in thee,
      For heer-biforn ful ofte in many a wyse
35   Hast thou to misericorde receyved me.
      But merci, ladi, at the grete assyse
      Whan we shule come bifore the hye justyse.
      So litel fruit shal thanne in me be founde
      That, but thou er that day correcte [vice],
40   Of verrey right my werk wol me confounde.

      Fleeinge, I flee for socour to thi tente
      Me for to hide from tempeste ful of dreede,
      Biseeching yow that ye you not absente
      Thouh I be wikke. O, help yit at this neede!
45   Al have I ben a beste in wil and deede,
      Yit, ladi, thou me clothe with thi grace.
      Thin enemy and myn — ladi, tak heede —
      Unto my deth in poynt is me to chace!

      Glorious mayde and mooder, which that nevere
50   Were bitter, neither in erthe nor in see,
      But ful of swetnesse and of merci evere,
      Help that my Fader be not wroth with me.
      Spek thou, for I ne dar not him ysee,
      So have I doon in erthe, allas the while,
55   That certes, but if thou my socour bee,
      To stink eterne he wole my gost exile.

He vouched sauf, tel him, as was his wille,
Bicome a man, to have oure alliaunce,
And with his precious blood he wrot the bille
60 Upon the crois as general acquitaunce
To every penitent in ful creaunce;
And therfore, ladi bright, thou for us praye.
Thanne shalt thou bothe stinte al his grevaunce,
And make oure foo to failen of his praye.

65 I wot it wel, thou wolt ben oure socour,
Thou art so ful of bowntee, in certeyn,
For whan a soule falleth in errour
Thi pitee goth and haleth him ayein.
Thanne makest thou his pees with his sovereyn
70 And bringest him out of the crooked strete.
Whoso thee loveth, he shal not love in veyn,
That shal he fynde as he the lyf shal lete.

Kalenderes enlumyned ben thei
That in this world ben lighted with thi name,
75 And whoso goth to yow the righte wey,
Him thar not drede in soule to be lame.
Now, queen of comfort, sith thou art that same
To whom I seeche for my medicyne,
Lat not my foo no more my wounde entame;
80 Myn hele into thin hand al I resygne.

Ladi, thi sorwe kan I not portreye
Under the cros, ne his greevous penaunce;
But for youre bothes peynes I yow preye,
Lat not oure alder foo make his bobaunce
85 That he hath in his lystes of mischaunce
Convict that ye bothe have bought so deere.
As I seide erst, thou ground of oure substaunce,
Continue on us thi pitous eyen cleere!

Moises, that saugh the bush with flawmes rede
90 Brenninge, of which ther never a stikke brende,

287

Was signe of thin unwemmed maidenhede.
Thou art the bush on which ther gan descende
The Holi Gost, the which that Moyses wende
Had ben a-fyr, and this was in figure.
95   Now, ladi, from the fyr thou us defende
Which that in helle eternalli shal dure.

Noble princesse, that nevere haddest peere,
Certes if any comfort in us bee,
That cometh of thee, thou Cristes mooder deere.
100   We han noon oother melodye or glee
Us to rejoyse in oure adversitee,
Ne advocat noon that wole and dar so preye
For us, and that for litel hire as yee
That helpen for an Ave-Marie or tweye.

105   O verrey light of eyen that ben blynde,
O verrey lust of labour and distresse,
O tresoreere of bountee to mankynde,
Thee whom God ches to mooder for humblesse!
From his ancille he made the maistresse
110   Of hevene and erthe, oure bille up for to beede.
This world awaiteth evere on thi goodnesse
For thou ne failest nevere wight at neede.

Purpos I have sum time for to enquere
Wherfore and whi the Holi Gost thee soughte
115   Whan Gabrielles vois cam to thin ere.
He not to werre us swich a wonder wroughte,
But for to save us that he sithen boughte.
Thanne needeth us no wepen us for to save,
But oonly ther we dide not, as us oughte,
120   Doo penitence, and merci axe and have.

Queen of comfort, yit whan I me bithinke
That I agilt have bothe him and thee,
And that my soule is worthi for to sinke,
Allas, I caityf, whider may I flee?

288

125 Who shal unto thi Sone my mene bee?
Who, but thiself, that art of pitee welle?
Thou has more reuthe on oure adversitee
Than in this world might any tonge telle.

Redresse me, mooder, and me chastise,
130 For certeynly my Faderes chastisinge,
That dar I nouht abiden in no wise,
So hidous is his rightful rekenynge.
Mooder, of whom oure merci gan to springe,
Beth ye my juge and eek my soules leche;
135 For evere in you is pitee haboundinge
To ech that wole of pitee you biseeche.

Soth is that God ne granteth no pitee
Withoute thee; for God of his goodnesse
Foryiveth noon, but it like unto thee.
140 He hath the maked vicaire and maistresse
Of al this world, and eek governouresse
Of hevene, and he represseth his justise
After thi wil; and therfore in witnesse
He hath the corowned in so rial wise.

145 Temple devout, ther God hath his woninge,
For which these misbileeved deprived been,
To you my soule penitent I bringe.
Receyve me — I can no ferther fleen.
With thornes venymous, O hevene queen,
150 For which the eerthe acursed was ful yore,
I am so wounded, as ye may wel seen,
That I am lost almost, it smert so sore.

Virgine, that art so noble of apparaile,
And ledest us into the hye tour
155 Of Paradys, thou me wisse and counsaile
How I may have thi grace and thi socour,
All have I ben in filthe and in errour.
Ladi, unto that court thou me ajourne

That cleped is thi bench, O freshe flour,
160   Ther as that merci evere shal sojourne.

Xristus, thi sone, that in this world alighte
Upon the cros to suffre his passioun,
And eek that Longius his herte pighte
And made his herte blood to renne adoun,
165   And al was this for my salvacioun;
And I to him am fals and eek unkynde,
And yit he wole not my dampnacioun —
This thanke I yow, socour of al mankynde!

Ysaac was figure of his deth, certeyn,
170   That so fer forth his fader wolde obeye
That him ne roughte nothing to be slayn;
Right soo thi Sone list as a lamb to deye.
Now, ladi ful of merci, I yow preye,
Sith he his merci mesured so large,
175   Be ye not skant, for alle we singe and seye
That ye ben from vengeaunce ay oure targe.

Zacharie yow clepeth the open welle
To wasshe sinful soule out of his gilt.
Therfore this lessoun oughte I wel to telle,
180   That, nere thi tender herte, we were spilt.
Now, ladi bryghte, sith thou canst and wilt
Ben to the seed of Adam merciable,
Bring us to that palais that is bilt
To penitentes that ben to merci able. Amen.

Explicit carmen.

Appendix B: The Proheme of The Prioresse Tale[1]

Hengwrt MS, fols. 209b–10a

Domine dominus noster

O Lord, oure Lord, thy name how merveilous
Is in this large world ysprad, quod she,
For noght oonly thy laude precious
Parfourned is by men of dignytee,
5   But by the mouth of children thy bountee
Parfourned is, for on the brest soukynge
Somtyme shewen they thyn heryynge.

Wherfore in laude, as I best kan or may,
Of thee and of the white lilye flour
10   Which that thee bar, and is a mayde alway,
To telle a storie I wol do my labour:
Nat that I may encressen hir honour,
For she hirself is honour and the roote
Of bountee, next hir sone, and soules boote.

15   O mooder mayde, O mayde moder free,
O bussh unbrent, brennyng in Moyses sighte,
That ravyshedest doun fro the Deitee,
Thurgh thyn humblesse, the Goost that in th'alighte,
Of whos vertu, whan he thyn herte lighte,
20   Conceyved was, the Fadres sapience,
Help me to telle it in thy reverence.

Lady, thy bountee, thy magnificence,
Thy vertu, and thy grete humylitee
Ther may no tonge expresse in no science,
25   For som tyme, Lady, er men praye to thee,

---

[1] This selection and the next are based on the Hengwrt MS (National Library of Wales, Aberystwyth, MS Peniarth 392) and are edited according to the procedures of this volume.

Thow goost biforn of thy benyngnytee,
And getest us the lyght, of thy preyere,
To gyden us unto thy sone so deere.

My konnyng is so wayk, O blisful queene,
30   For to declare thy grete worthynesse
That I ne may the weighte nat sustene;
But as a child of twelve month old, or lesse,
That kan unnethe any word expresse,
Right so fare I, and therfore I yow preye,
35   Gideth my song that I shal of yow seye.

Appendix C: *Invocacio ad Mariam*, from The Second Nun's Prologue

Hengwrt MS, fols. 165b–66b

And thow that flour of virgines art alle,
Of whom that Bernard list so wel to write,
To thee at my bigynnyng I first calle;
Thow confort of us wrecches, do m'endite
5   Thy maydens deeth, that wan thurgh hire merite
The eternal lyf and of the feend victorie,
As man may after reden in hir storie.

Thow mayde and mooder, doghter of thy sone,
Thow welle of mercy, synful soules cure,
10   In whom that God for bountee chees to wone,
Thow humble and heigh over every creature,
Thow nobledest so ferforth oure nature,
That no desdaign the Makere hadde of kynde
His Sone in blood and flessh to clothe and wynde.

15   Withinne the cloistre blisful of thy sydis
Took mannes shape the eternal love and pees,
That of the tryne compas lord and gyde is,
Whom erthe and see and hevene out of relees

292

Ay heryen, and thou, virgyne wemmelees,
20   Bar of thy body, and dweltest mayden pure,
The Creatour of every creature.

Assembled is in thee magnificence
With mercy, goodnesse, and swich pitee
That thow that art the sonne of excellence
25   Nat oonly helpest hem that prayen thee,
But often tyme of thy benygnytee
Ful frely, er that men thyn help biseche,
Thow goost biforn and art hir lyves leche.

Now help, thow meke and blisful faire mayde,
30   Me, flemed wrecche, in this desert of galle;
Thynk on the womman Cananee, that sayde
That whelpes eten somme of the crommes alle
That from hir lordes table been yfalle.
And thogh that I, unworthy sone of Eve,
35   Be synful, yet accepte my bileve.

And, for that feith is deed withouten werkis,
So for to werken yif me wit and space,
That I be quyt fro thennes that most derk is.
O thow that art so fair and ful of grace,
40   Be myn advocate in that heighe place
Ther as withouten ende is songe *Osanne*,
Thow Cristes moder, doghter deere of Anne.

And of thy light my soule in prison lighte,
That troubled is by the contagioun
45   Of my body, and also by the wighte
Of erthely lust and fals affeccioun;
O havene, O refut, O savacioun
Of hem that been in sorwe and in distresse,
Now help, for to my werk I wol me dresse.

Index of First Lines

Index of First Lines

Index of First Lines

Index of First Lines